Routledge Revivals

Instinct, Intelligence and Character

First published in 1924, *Instinct, Intelligence and Character* provides a lucid and forcible account of the currents of thought in educational psychology, from intelligence tests to psychoanalysis, from character training to the laws of learning. It brings themes such as talk on instincts and habits; laws of heredity; nature of satisfaction and dissatisfaction; the learning process; interests and prejudices; individual differences in intellect; general and special abilities; differences in will and temperament; and the wings of thought. This historical reference work is useful for teachers and students of educational psychology.

Instinct, Intelligence and Character
An Educational Psychology

Godfrey H. Thomson

First published in 1924
by George Allen & Unwin Ltd.

This edition first published in 2024 by Routledge
4 Park Square, Milton Park, Abingdon, Oxon, OX14 4RN

and by Routledge
605 Third Avenue, New York, NY 10017

Routledge is an imprint of the Taylor & Francis Group, an informa business

© Godfrey H. Thomson, 1924

All rights reserved. No part of this book may be reprinted or reproduced or utilised in any form or by any electronic, mechanical, or other means, now known or hereafter invented, including photocopying and recording, or in any information storage or retrieval system, without permission in writing from the publishers.

Publisher's Note
The publisher has gone to great lengths to ensure the quality of this reprint but points out that some imperfections in the original copies may be apparent.

Disclaimer
The publisher has made every effort to trace copyright holders and welcomes correspondence from those they have been unable to contact.

A Library of Congress record exists under LCCN: 25007847

ISBN: 978-1-032-94546-0 (hbk)
ISBN: 978-1-003-57135-3 (ebk)
ISBN: 978-1-032-94547-7 (pbk)

Book DOI 10.4324/9781003571353

Instinct, Intelligence and Character :

An Educational Psychology

By

Godfrey H. Thomson, D.C.L., Ph.D., D.Sc.

Professor of Education and Head of the Teachers Training Department, Armstrong College, Newcastle-upon-Tyne; sometime Pemberton Fellow of the University of Durham ; and visiting Professor of Education, Columbia University, New York, 1923-24

LONDON : GEORGE ALLEN & UNWIN LTD.
RUSKIN HOUSE, 40 MUSEUM STREET, W.C.1

First published in 1924
Reprinted 1925
Reprinted 1927
Reprinted 1946
Reprinted 1949

(*All rights reserved*)

Printed in Great Britain by
Billing and Sons Ltd., Guildford and Esher

PREFACE

THE leisure and incentive to prepare for the press the lectures which form this book I owe to an invitation from Dean Russell of Teachers' College, Columbia University, New York City, to spend the session 1923-24 there as Visiting Professor of Education. To him, and to Dr. E. L. Thorndike, at whose suggestion the invitation was extended to me, I owe a debt which I am glad to acknowledge ; and no less to Sir Theodore Morison and the Council of Armstrong College in Newcastle for acquiescence in the necessary leave of absence, made possible by the great kindness of my predecessor and old friend, Mark R. Wright, in emerging from his retirement to take up for another year his former duties.

The lectures were three times delivered, in the winter, spring, and summer semesters, and are here printed substantially as given on the last occasion. Any merits they may have they owe to my audiences, for from a class ranging in age from nineteen to fifty-five years, possessed of teaching experience of every conceivable sort, and gathered not only from every State of the Union, but from every continent, the teacher could not fail to learn, whatever they may have learned from him. And to them, to " 251 C," I dedicate the present volume.

CONTENTS

		PAGE
PREFACE	. . . .	7

CHAPTER		
I.	A PRELIMINARY TALK ON INSTINCTS AND HABITS .	11
II.	THE LAWS OF HEREDITY	19
III.	INSTINCTS IN MAN	27
IV.	PLAY	33
V.	THE LEARNING PROCESS	39
VI.	THE NERVOUS SYSTEM	48
VII.	MAZE EXPERIMENTS	57
VIII.	THE NATURE OF SATISFACTION AND DISSATISFACTION .	65
IX.	THE ASCENT FROM INSTINCT TO INTELLIGENCE:	
	(a) IMAGERY	79
X.	VARIOUS USES OF VISUAL IMAGERY	90
XI.	BRAIN LOCALIZATION	101
XII.	THE ASCENT FROM INSTINCT TO INTELLIGENCE:	
	(b) THE USE OF WORDS IN THOUGHT. . . .	111
XIII.	MATHEMATICAL AND OTHER SYMBOLS	124
XIV.	THE TRANSFER OF TRAINING	134
XV.	INTERESTS AND PREJUDICES	149
XVI.	REPRESSION AND SUBLIMATION	157

INSTINCT, INTELLIGENCE AND CHARACTER

CHAPTER		PAGE
XVII.	INDIVIDUAL DIFFERENCES IN INTELLECT	170
XVIII.	INTELLIGENCE TESTS	180
XIX.	ACHIEVEMENT TESTS	193
XX.	GENERAL AND SPECIAL ABILITIES	204
XXI.	THE INFLUENCE OF SCHOOLING ON INTELLIGENCE AND THE LIMIT OF ITS GROWTH	216
XXII.	DIFFERENCES IN WILL AND TEMPERAMENT	227
XXIII.	PYGMALION OR PROCRUSTES ?	238
XXIV.	BACK TO THE LEARNING PROCESS. THE BEST METHODS OF MEMORIZING AND OF ACQUIRING SKILL	247
XXV.	THE WINGS OF THOUGHT	257
XXVI.	REVIEW	273
	INDEX	279

Instinct, Intelligence and Character

CHAPTER I

A PRELIMINARY TALK ON INSTINCTS AND HABITS

THIS book does not concern itself, except indirectly, with the aims of education, though no attempt will be made to keep the writer's own views completely out of sight. The purpose is primarily to set out what appear to be the facts of mental life which are most important, clearly, and with illustrations drawn as far as possible from teaching practice. Among the questions to which a thoughtful educator wants answers are such matters as the following :—Are there any laws which describe the best way of acquiring skill, such as skill in writing or in handling tools, or of acquiring knowledge such as the multiplication table or the formulæ for solving triangles ? Can a teacher make *any* ordinary boy into a great scholar if he can only teach him well enough and persuade him to work hard enough, or are there inborn limits in each child beyond which he cannot go ? And if so, how early can we find out, with reasonable certainty, what these limits are ? How ought we to deal with children of different temperaments, the sullen, the flippant, the stodgy and the cocksure ? Does chemistry give as good an education as the classics ? Were all successful business men the despair of their schoolmasters, or is there something about the atmosphere of Speech Day which leads them untruthfully to say so ? Do children fall into types, the bookish, the mechanical, the abstract thinker, the linguist, the mathematician, the artist ? Or is the clever boy usually clever all round ? At what age should specialization begin ? What about the Dalton Plan, the heuristic method, the evils of competition, self-government, intelligence tests, psycho-analysis, and the Boy Scouts ? Are there general laws by means of which we can judge new fads, or must we essay them one by one and learn by trial and error of the crudest kind ?

To these and a host of similar questions a common-sense psychology can give at any rate partial answers. True, the great majority are ready with answers themselves. But in many cases, the answers are conflicting, and yes and no are urged with equal force and on the same grounds. In such a case it is necessary to take stock of the whole situation, to discover what is common to the apparently opposed views, to expose experimental error or invalid reasoning where it can be seen, to plan and suggest crucial experiments, to bring to the inquiry the resources of the sciences of heredity, of statistics, and of comparative psychology. No one is fully qualified to act this part of judge ; but by placing on record his own views, his own experiences, and his own solutions, everyone can serve on the jury.

Man is an animal, and no part of his body exists but can be paralleled in less developed or in otherwise developed forms found among the animals. Yet there is a tremendous gap between man and even the highest anthropoids. It will be part of our duty to study particularly those mental points in which man is most superior and by which he has won his commanding position in the world, to ask how he appears to have acquired these advantages, and whether education can modify them and raise him higher in the scale towards an ideal being.

A PRELIMINARY TALK

But this we cannot do without also studying what man has in common with the animals, his instincts and the physical laws of his body.

INSTINCTS.

The purely reflex actions themselves hardly call for much notice from the educator. They are uneducable, or very nearly so, and only disappear in serious illness or when submitted to very unnatural treatment, as when the apprentice sword-swallower "tires out" his vomiting reflex. Some are quite unconsciously performed (as the dilation and contraction of the pupil of the eye) and are quite uncontrollable. Others are not quite so completely below the conscious level and are subject to a certain amount of control. Stand inside a large plate-glass window while someone violently and suddenly throws a pailful of water against the outside. It is nearly impossible not to wink and flinch. Sneezing is a little more controllable. A large part of the training of a little baby consists in teaching him to acquire control over actions which at first are reflex, and to learn habits of cleanliness. Instincts range all the way from responses which are practically reflex actions, made irresistibly to certain narrowly defined stimuli, on the one hand, to rather vague instinctive tendencies to act in more or less such and such a kind of way in response to a wide class of stimuli, on the other. Fairly near to the lower end of the scale is, for example, the little child's tendency to put a new toy into its mouth. Near the other end is the "collecting instinct" which arises in very varied situations, and which leads to the collecting of all kinds of things, from cigarette cards to birds' eggs, from postage stamps to the titles of scientific articles on the applications of Mendelism to human eugenics. Near the lower end there is little doubt about the innate nature of the instinct, for it is usually very widespread, is often shared with the higher animals, and has often been

INSTINCT, INTELLIGENCE AND CHARACTER

seen to arise spontaneously in situations where it could not well have been learned from others. Near the upper end there is usually considerable doubt about the inborn nature of the response and much controversy, for the response differs significantly in different individuals, and arises often or always in circumstances where it might well have been learned from others. Boys, for example, usually collect stamps because other boys do so, and acquire their interest and their skill from their school friends. Is the wish to collect (something or other) also acquired, or is the influence of the environment limited to directing an inborn instinct to the particular object, "stamps"?

In popular language, the words instinct and instinctive are very often misused. They are often applied to actions which are not instinctive at all, but habitual. "Seeing the child run across the street," writes the newspaper reporter, "the tramcar driver instinctively applied his brakes." This is a well-fixed habit in the driver, not an instinct. The child's action in starting back and shrieking when it saw a large tramcar bearing down upon it was on the other hand instinctive, and so was its mother's action in rushing forward to its help. The best examples of pure instinct are seen in lower animals, for example in the spiders, of which Fabre has written so vividly. The banded Epeira cannot be taught by her mother to make her wonderful nest, for her mother died when the first cold of last winter came. Yet at the proper time she will make her silk bag, ovoid in shape, crowned with a scalloped rim, composed of compact white satin and of reddish brown wadding, covered with patterns of spindle shape in fanciful meridian waves; a nest quite different from that of the silky Epeira, her relative. Of course, saying that the spider builds the nest by instinct is not an *explanation*, it is merely a short way of saying that she does so without being taught, without learning.

Few actions of the higher animals are so purely instinctive as this. In man, shortly after birth, sucking is instinctive.

A PRELIMINARY TALK

Later, walking is probably, almost certainly, instinctive; though the child hardly ever is allowed to begin to walk without being taught. If left quite to himself in this respect, however, the baby will, somewhere between ten months and sixteen months, stand up and walk rather suddenly, though the walking is not at all perfect on the first occasion. Most of man's actions are a mixture of instinct and learning. The human child is always being taught, not only in an impersonal neutral way by the environment, but actively and of set purpose by his parents, his brothers and sisters, older children, aunts and uncles, and teachers. It is small wonder, therefore, if we hardly know just what things he would, under other circumstances, do instinctively. He does not learn English, or French, or German, instinctively, for an English baby transferred to a French home acquires French as his mother tongue. Nor would he speak any language at all if he could be brought up without human companionship, or by dumb mutes. But the babbling sounds he takes a delight in making from about the sixth month, the repetitions of ma-ma-ma, and ga-ga-gu, these are made instinctively, and form the foundation upon which the mother tongue is built up. The truth about the instinctive nature of man is probably this, that he has a large number of instincts, but that these instincts are very indefinite compared with those of animals, especially lower animals. They would not in themselves enable man to survive, but are capable of being directed and diverted to a surprising extent, and they form the basis of education, which consists in building on these instincts those habits which the civilization and culture of the period demand from the adult. It is just because man's instincts are only vaguely directed that he is far the most highly educable animal, excelling in this respect to an incredible extent. Not only what are commonly called habits and customs, but also all forms of dexterity and muscular skill, and even all forms of artistic appreciation and intellectual performance, thought and reasoning itself, are all probably possible in man just because he has indefinite instinctive tendencies rather than specific and narrow instincts, and can learn. To a preliminary talk on habit and the laws of learning we may next turn our attention.

Habit and Learning.

A habit is distinguished from an instinct by being acquired, not inborn. In an instinct, there are ready-made nerve connections which ensure that such and such a response will occur in a certain situation. In a habit, the nerve connections have to be made by exercise and satisfaction. The water-chick which dives for the first time in its life when frightened by a barking puppy, and which has never seen another water-hen, having been brought up in an incubator, nevertheless gives the characteristic water-hen dive.[1] This is instinctive, and the nerve connections which run from eye and ear to spinal cord and brain, and thence to the diving muscles, must be set ready to produce this particular act by the hand of Nature through the mechanism of heredity. But a boy does not dive instinctively. He has to learn to dive, and the nerve connections which ultimately co-ordinate his muscles when as a practised diver he plunges into the water have been brought to this state of readiness by long practice, by dissatisfaction at failures, and satisfaction at successes. Diving in the case of the boy is habitual, not instinctive. It is an acquired skill.

The word habit in ordinary conversation is most frequently applied to moral or immoral actions, as early rising or drunkenness. But even in ordinary speech it is extended to cases of skill, as when we say that Jones dives badly, or writes badly, because he got into bad habits of diving or of writing when he was first learning. We shall not in the present section speak much, or at all, about good or bad

[1] Lloyd Morgan, "The Natural History of Experience," *Brit. Journ. of Psychology*, 1909, iii, 11.

A PRELIMINARY TALK

habits, but rather of the way in which all habits, whether good or bad, are learned.

An animal which possesses quite fixed, definite, strong reactions in connection with a certain situation cannot well form any habits in response to that situation. A moth flies to a light in a way which has become proverbial, and it would be impossible, or at any rate tremendously difficult, to form habits in a moth as regards its behaviour to a lighted candle. But if an animal does not always respond in quite the same way to a situation, then education is possible and habits can be formed quite different from the responses due to instinct, out of which they are developed. The differences in response may be due to the failure of those first tried, as when a dog attempts in vain to jump over a fence and then tries to squeeze under it. It could be trained always to do the latter by associating some "reward" with this response and "punishment" with the jumping response. Or the differences may be due to the attitude of the animal at the moment, to being more hungry, or more tired, or the like. If there is variability, there is the possibility of learning.

Popular psychology about habits of skill sums itself up in the saying "Practice makes perfect." Everyone knows that repetition makes an act easier, more certain. What is not explained by this popular psychology is how it is that we get better in any action, such as serving at tennis, when as a matter of fact we practise the wrong actions much more often than the right ones in the early stages of our practice, and indeed for months or years. Clearly another law of skill is needed to explain this, in addition to "practice makes perfect." What that law is we shall in a moment see.

The "practice" law, "law of use," or "law of exercise," as Thorndike calls it,[1] can be expressed in terms of nerve action by saying that nerve connections are the more easily made the more often they have been made before,

[1] *Educational Psychol. Briefer Course*, New York, 1914, p. 70.

and the more recently : and that the longer time we allow to elapse without making such and such a nerve connection, the less likely it is to be made, other things being equal. On the whole, this general statement is borne out by common experience, by laboratory experiment, and by schoolroom observation. But there must be something more, or errors made so frequently in the early stages of practice would be perpetuated. That other law is this, that satisfaction, the glow of pleasure, which follows a successful movement, somehow stamps in the nerve connections which have just been made, and causes them to be a little more readily made again than would have been the case had dissatisfaction ensued. How this is we do not understand ; but that it is so, in practice, we know. It follows at once that practice will have the more rapid effect, the more certainly the pupil can know when he has, by chance or forethought, made a more than usually successful try, and the more pleased he is at his success. So that teachers should make known clearly to their pupils when they have done even slightly better than usual, and should do whatever is likely to increase the pupil's satisfaction at this improvement. The most effective means of doing this is to ensure that improvement in the habit shall tend to satisfy some powerful instinct, so that here again we see how habits depend upon instincts. They arise out of instincts, and are developed often in the satisfaction of instincts. They are so similar in their certainty and quickness of response that it is with difficulty we distinguish between them. Habits, let us repeat, are acquired ; instincts are inborn, inherited. And as an aid to their study and understanding, we must give some attention to the laws of heredity, to which we turn in our next chapter.

CHAPTER II

THE LAWS OF HEREDITY

PERHAPS the greatest event in the nineteenth century was the publication of Darwin's *Origin of Species*, in which he propounded the doctrine that different species and genera of animals, including man himself, have been formed by the influence of the environment in weeding out the "unfit," that is, those unsuited to the environment. It is true that Darwinism in its original form is no longer entirely accepted by biologists, but the notion of the "survival of the fittest," the idea of "natural selection," is so fundamental to all thinking to-day that it is essential that we should first grasp it. Consider, say, a country in which there lived lions and antelopes, the former preying on the latter. Then if an individual antelope is a slow runner, it will fall an early prey to the lions and will leave few or no progeny. If, on the other hand, an antelope is a very good runner, then it will live long and have many children. The antelopes of the next generation will, therefore, be descended from the faster runners of the previous generation, and will be, if there is anything in heredity, a faster set of runners than was that generation. And so on and so on. The lions keep speeding the antelopes up. Note that it is not by practice in running that the antelopes get faster, but by selection, the bad runners being killed off and the good runners allowed to breed. This is exactly what cattle breeders do, or dog fanciers, when they wish to alter or to improve a strain.

At the same time the antelopes are speeding up the lions, for a lion will starve if it cannot sprint or jump. And the process will go on until some limit set by other factors is reached. Instead of speed, the quality selected may be matching the background, or lying perfectly still, or going for long periods without water, or hibernating, or anything which has "survival value" in any animal. So the lions and antelopes may come in many thousands of years to be very different from what they were. And so, indeed, all animal species have come to exist. Such is a crude account of Darwin's famous theory.

This theory clearly assumes that children are, on the whole, like their parents, and this is of course supported by common experience. It is desirable, however, to have some more exact way of stating this fact, for it is also common knowledge that a child may be unlike either parent. A convenient way of stating the facts quantitatively is the following. For clearness, take a definite and easily measurable quality such as height, and let us confine ourselves to males. If we obtain the heights of, say, 1,000 English fathers selected at random, each of them having an adult son whose height is also measured, we have material for ascertaining what is called the "correlation" between height of father and height of son. If each son always and invariably grew to just the same height as his father we should say that the correlation was perfect; and in that case we could, of course, predict a boy's ultimate height with certainty. The facts, however, are not so: yet there is a *tendency* for the sons of tall fathers to be tall, and of short fathers to be short. That tendency we wish to measure by the coefficient of correlation.

Let the average height of Englishmen be 5 feet 7 inches, and let us choose from our data the set of fathers who are each and all four inches above the average, i.e. 5 feet 11 inches tall. These fathers will have sons of varying height, some taller than their fathers, others not so tall, some even below the English average. But the *average* height of these sons will lie *between 5 feet 11 inches and 5 feet 7 inches*. They will not average as tall as their fathers, but they will average

THE LAWS OF HEREDITY

taller than the common man. Instead of being four inches above the racial average, they will be about two inches above it. The ratio of this two inches to that four inches is what is called the correlation coefficient, here equal to $0 \cdot 5$. Had the set of fathers selected been, say, three inches each *below* the racial average, then their sons, though scattered in height, would tend to be short, though not so short as their parents, and would, in fact, average about an inch and a half below the race.

The cause of this "regression" from the parental towards the racial height is presumably the influence of the more remote ancestry, and also the influence of the mother's side. But even if instead of correlating with the father's height we correlate with the average of father and mother, such regression still takes place. If, however, the selection of tall parents for survival continued, all below a certain height being exterminated before they bore any or many children, the regression to the original racial average would, it may be supposed, grow less and less, as more and more of the ancestry became tall, until in time a race of tall men would be arrived at, who would continue tall for very many generations, even should the conditions which exterminate short individuals cease to act.

This, then, is the method by which orthodox Darwinism supposed species, and even genera, to be created. Ever so small a variation might, if it had survival value, become fixed as a permanent feature, provided that the environmental conditions which gave it survival value continued to act for a sufficiently large number of generations.

It is by no means certain that such evolution by the cumulative effect of tiny variations has not taken place. But the convictions held by the scientific world on this question of evolution have been profoundly modified by the progress of Mendelism, the study of the inheritance of certain unitary characters which was begun by the Abbé Gregor Mendel in the garden of the monastery at Brünn or Brno,

INSTINCT, INTELLIGENCE AND CHARACTER

in what is now Czecho-Slovakia, in the year 1865. The general essence of Mendelism is still best explained by an account of one of Mendel's own original experiments, in which he cross-fertilized two different species of peas, one tall and the other dwarf.

The ordinary pea, both tall and dwarf, is self-fertilizing; but in his experiment Mendel took the pollen from a tall plant and dusted it on the ovules of a short plant, or vice versa, and carefully preserved and planted the resulting

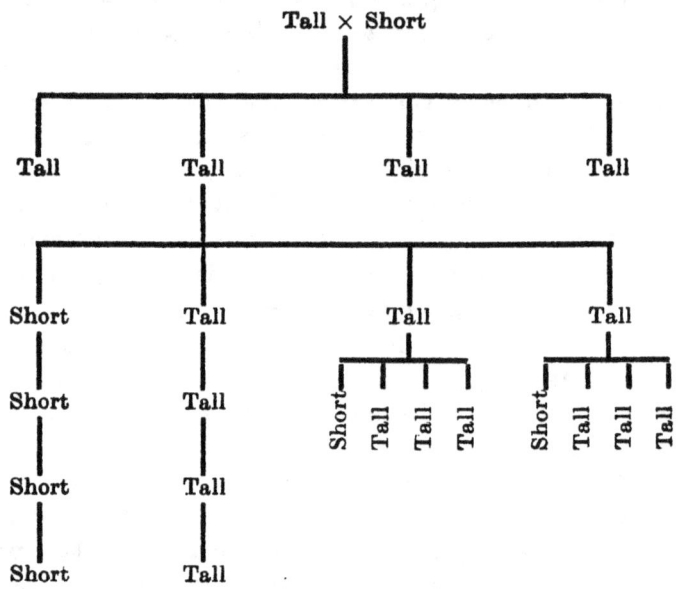

peas. These all grew into tall plants, resembling the tall parent. This is the first filial generation. These resulting tall plants were allowed to mature and to self-fertilize themselves, and the peas planted to grow into the second filial generation. The members of this second filial generation, though all descended from tall parents, were not all tall. One quarter of them were short like the short grandparent, and these short plants proved to be pure in breed, that is, their descendants to many generations were invariably

THE LAWS OF HEREDITY

short. The other three quarters of the second filial generation were tall: but one of these three-quarters proved to be pure tall, giving only tall descendants, whereas the remaining two quarters produced both short and tall offspring, in the proportion of 1 to 3. All this is better seen in the diagram on page 22.

The theory advanced to explain this (at first sight complicated) inheritance was, that the factors for tallness and shortness do not blend, but that the sexual cells contain *either* the one or the other factor (or we may, perhaps, speak of a single factor whose presence causes tallness, and whose absence causes dwarfness).

Tallness is said to be *dominant* and shortness *recessive*, so that when either parent supplies the tall factor, as in the original cross, then the offspring are tall.

But though tall in outward appearance, these plants have only a single dose of the tallness factor, not a double dose as when both parents are tall. Their sexual cells will in half the cases contain the T factor, in half they will lack it. In any single blossom of this first filial generation, therefore, there will be many pollen grains, half the number bearing T and half not, and a number of ovules, half the number bearing T and half not. When the pollen falls on to the ovules, it will be sheer chance whether both pollen and ovule contain the T factor, or both lack it, or one have it and the other lack it.

Exactly the same chance pairing takes place when we throw two pennies. If we mark the two sides of each coin with Tall and Short, and throw them, we may get

$$\begin{array}{c} \text{Tall} \times \text{Tall} \\ \text{Tall} \times \text{Short} \\ \text{Short} \times \text{Tall} \\ \text{Short} \times \text{Short} \end{array}$$

In one quarter of the cases the result will be a pure tall plant, both pollen and ovule containing the T factor. Such a plant will give tall plants in all succeeding generations if

INSTINCT, INTELLIGENCE AND CHARACTER

self-fertilization only is allowed. It is pure bred despite its short grandmother. The plants resulting from pollen and ovules which both lack the tall factor will produce pure short plants, from which only short descendants can arise as long as only self-fertilization is possible—a purebred short plant despite its tall grandfather. The plants resulting from tall-*bearing* pollen and tall-*lacking* ovules will be just like the first filial generation, and so also those from tall-*lacking* pollen and tall-*bearing* ovules.

Since the rediscovery in 1900 of Mendel's work (which had been buried in the archives of a Brünn society) a large number of unit factors like this "tallness" factor has been investigated, in many plants, and also in animals. The theory becomes complex when many factors are involved, but it is essentially the same in principle as in the simple case considered above. Sometimes pairs or groups of factors are found which are partially linked together, so that the group *tends* to act together, and thus further possibilities arise.

It is clear that this changing by definite jumps, by mutations, is a different process from Darwin's progress by small variations. But upon these mutations, as upon any variations, environment can still exercise its selective influence, and the essential idea of Darwinism, the "survival of the fittest," remains in force.

This idea of evolution by selection (whether from small variations or from mutations) explains much of evolution without any appeal to the idea of the environment improving the individual and thereby improving his progeny. In the pure selection theory, the environment eliminates a harmful quality, not by improving, but by killing off, the individuals who possess it. Indeed, though Darwin probably thought otherwise, it has for long been the opinion of most biologists that acquired characteristics are not inherited, that is to say that any quality which an individual acquires by training during his lifetime will not be passed on to his children.

THE LAWS OF HEREDITY

Of course, he may in his turn teach it to his children, but what is here meant is that it will not be inborn in his children.

This is a hypothesis which many students find it hard to grasp, and indeed it does make one wonder where all the numerous qualities now exhibited by all the innumerable species of animals and plants can have come from. If nothing acquired is inherited, then it would seem that all these wonderful qualities, the colours of the humming bird, the homing instinct of the pigeon, the longneckedness of the giraffe, the shortneckedness of the bulldog, the wings of the albatross and the brain of man, all must have been potentially present in the first form of life which appeared on this planet. But great as this difficulty may be, we must not, as scientists, assume the inheritance of acquired characteristics if there is no evidence for it, and if the evolution of species as we see it taking place (without worrying about the first beginnings) can be explained by selection without it.

Occasionally experiments are reported which seem to imply inheritance of acquired characteristics[1]. But since most experiment points against it, confirmation of their results must be awaited.

Meanwhile, if nothing acquired is inherited, education loses importance in one direction and gains it in another. If the educator could know that his work would be perpetuated by inheritance, that the children would start, in intellect and in character, from where the parents left off, or at any rate from a higher starting point than did their parents, then every act of the teacher would be fraught with consequences to untold generations.

---

[1] For example those of Kammerer. And more recently still, since the above was written, a report of a lecture by Professor Ivan P. Pawlow has appeared (*Science*, Nov. 9, 1923, vol. lviii, p. 359–361) in which it is asserted that conditioned reflexes may be inherited. Some white mice were trained to run to the feeding place on the ringing of an electric bell, 300 lessons being required. Succeeding generations required in turn 100, 30, 10, and only 5 lessons. The sixth generation was awaiting Professor Pawlow's return to Russia, and he confidently expected that ultimately the offspring would exhibit the reaction without any training at all. But repetition of these experiments must be awaited.

INSTINCT, INTELLIGENCE AND CHARACTER

But if it is not so, if the work has to be begun again with each generation, then education becomes doubly important. Without it, mankind would *at once*, in one generation, slip back from civilization to savagery. It has to provide a social inheritance, to pass on the acquired mental wealth of the race which biological inheritance refuses to transmit. It has to improve its methods so as to get more and more done in each generation. The torch of learning is passed on, but he who receives it has to begin the race anew. He receives no allowance of so many yards or miles, and he can only go farther if his way be made smoother. It is the business of education to smooth the way.

CHAPTER III

INSTINCTS IN MAN

Just what the instincts are which man inherits from his forefathers is difficult to say, because in man all instinctive reactions are so rapidly and deeply covered by a crust or cake of custom. That is why opinions have been so varied as to what proportion the instinctive basis of human behaviour bears to the whole, and why lists of human instincts have differed so much from one another.

William James was one of the first writers, and was the most forceful, in urging that instinct was at the root of a good deal more of man's behaviour than was commonly admitted: and every teacher should read what he has to say. Since his time, an increasing emphasis in the same direction has been shown by one psychologist after another: but in their classifications of instincts two schools have shown themselves, the one using a few wide classes, the other giving long lists of separate instincts. A classification of the former kind which has been popularized by Tansley's widely read volume, *The New Psychology*, is that into ego-instincts, herd-instincts, and sex-instincts, corresponding to self-preservation (and aggrandizement), tribal preservation, and racial preservation respectively. Most remote from this is Thorndike's classification, which is indeed hardly a classification at all, but rather an enumeration of one specific situation after another, with the specifically instinctive response in each case. Instead, for example, of a general instinct to imitate, Thorndike enumerates the specific things which he sees being imitated in an instinctive manner.

INSTINCT, INTELLIGENCE AND CHARACTER

He cannot see any general tendency towards imitating anything and everything, but he sees a tendency towards "yelling when others yell, laughing when others laugh, smiling when smiled at, looking at what others observe, listening when others listen, running with or after people who are running in the same direction, running from the focus whence others scatter, jabbering when others jabber, and becoming silent as they become silent, crouching when others crouch, chasing, attacking, and rending what others hunt, and seizing whatever object another seizes."

Between these two extremes is a list like that of McDougall, containing about a dozen simple instincts, to each of which is linked a primary emotion: for in McDougall's treatment an emotion becomes almost the "inside" of an instinct, an instinct as it feels when occurring to one. The list is:

Instinct.[1]	*Emotion.*
Flight, Concealment, or Immobility	Fear
Pugnacity	Anger
Repulsion	Disgust
Submission	Subjection
Self-assertion	Elation
Curiosity	Wonder
Parental Instinct	Tender Emotion
Reproductive Instincts	
Acquisition	the emotions corresponding to which are not so definitely named by McDougall
Feeding	
Gregariousness	
Construction	

Tansley makes an attempt to reconcile McDougall's classification with his own, or rather to show how he would further classify McDougall's twelve heads to reduce them to his three. Under the *ego-complex* he places:

Self-assertion (with pugnacity and curiosity).
Feeding, acquisition, and construction.
Submission (with flight, etc., and repulsion).

[1] In his latest book Professor McDougall adds to these two more, *appeal* and *laughter*.

INSTINCTS IN MAN

Under the *sex-instincts* he places :

Parental Instincts and
Reproductive Instincts,

leaving for his *herd-instinct* McDougall's

Gregariousness.

This does not, of course, imply that these subheadings exhaust what in Tansley's opinion is the content of any one of his three heads.

For the actual problems of teaching and education Thorndike's attitude is useful. It is important to the teacher to know just what a child may be expected to imitate, just what kind of situations lead to self-assertion, and so on. In combining and redirecting instincts, in checking some and encouraging others, it is, however, wise to take account of the three centres of attraction to which our instinctive forces converge. The development of proper relations with one's fellows, learning to live with them without losing one's identity, and the skilful guiding of the forces of sex into the right channels, are the three most important tasks of the educator. But the professional knowledge which will enable him to accomplish these tasks is composed of those units which the "situation-response" psychologists enumerate. Among the innumerable situations and responses described with admirable clearness and absence of theoretical bias by Thorndike, the following are perhaps of greater educational value, in nursery and school. His own words are freely used.

To sudden changes and sharp contrasts a universal response is "attentiveness, i.e. such fixating of eyes, head, etc., that the objects showing the change or contrast are brought into clearest observation."

"Any not too large object which" thus, or otherwise, "attracts attention, and does not possess repelling or frightening features, incites to approach, reaching, touching,

INSTINCT, INTELLIGENCE AND CHARACTER

grasping, putting in the mouth, general manipulation." If it is portable, it may be carried home or to some familiar human being, and there contemplated and fingered. If it is alive, there is a tendency to dismemberment or mauling, especially if it has run away, and been hunted. If it runs away and is large, it will be chased and stoned and perhaps thrown down. As Booth Tarkington says, when he tells how Penrod and Sam pursued the old white horse, boys in such a situation are not being bad, they are merely being historic.

Should any person "grab or make off with a recently acquired object" the response will be "anger, a tight clutch on the object, pushing, striking, and screaming at the intruder."

Toward other individuals present in the same room there is an instinctive tendency to be truculent if they do not kow-tow; or at any rate a desire to attract their attention. Approval expressed by other human beings is an instinctive source of great satisfaction, scornful or derisive looks of "discomfort extending to utter wretchedness."

Gorgeous display, acts of daring or skill, victory in competition or combat, produce in the onlooker staring, smiles, ejaculations, encouraging shouts. The presence of others taking part in the same activity as ourselves leads to increased vigour in our own performance, and to great satisfaction at any manifest superiority.

In the presence of a baby, women have a special endowment of instinctive acts, including interested attention, exclamations of pleasure at its gurglings and smiles, instinctive comforting acts when it shows pain or grief. Boys and men have conflicting impulses. For them the small child is sometimes a small animal to be chased and teased as might any other. But Thorndike sees in them instinctive actions when they "offer scraps of food to see it eat, snatch it from peril, and smile approvingly at its vigorous antics."

These paragraphs may give some idea of the attempt to

INSTINCTS IN MAN

set down situation by situation. Such a list might go on for pages, and the contrast with the threefold "ego, herd, sex" classification is very striking. The "new psychologists" are scientific in making some classification out of chaos—provided that their classification is not, in their own words, a mere rationalization. Thorndike is scientific in wishing to avoid the "faculty fallacy" of saying, for example, that there exist general powers of memory, of imitation, and the like, and in wishing to stick close to the facts and to say just what those facts are.

In any case, it seems clear that man's instincts are more difficult to enumerate than are the instincts of the animals: and especially those lower animals which are to the popular mind the embodiment of instinct, such as the ant or the wasp. And the thesis will presently be put forward that it is just exactly the vagueness of instincts in man which has contributed most to his rise to overlordship in the animal kingdom. A typically "instinctive" animal makes automatic and definite responses to certain definite situations. In a "natural" or "suitable" environment these automatic responses are beneficial on the whole and in the majority of instances, but their fixed character precludes any adaptation to a new environment, and precludes any learning. If there is enough variation among the individuals of the species, a fairly large change of environment may still leave the *race* surviving, for the individuals more fitted to the environment will become the parents of the next generation. But this is not learning, it is not adaptation; it is decimation, purification by killing off the unfit. For the *individuals* of a species to be able to learn, to be able to adapt themselves, there must be some freedom from rigidity in the instinctive responses. Variation *within the individual* is the prerequisite of improvability of the individual, just as variability from one individual to another is the prerequisite of improvability in the race. In the latter case there is a selection of individuals, some to survive and some to die. In the former case

INSTINCT, INTELLIGENCE AND CHARACTER

there is just as truly a selection of responses. What the selective agent is, and how it works, will be the subject of discussion in later chapters. The period of life during which this process of selecting and training instinctive responses is carried out is the period of infancy, of dependence on the parents, a period which in man necessarily extends to the age of eight or nine, and commonly is extended to the age of fourteen or even twenty-one years. The most instinctive feature of that period is the activity known as "play," difficult to define, but easy to recognize. In the opinion of the present writer, play is the most important fact of human life, inasmuch as thereby that adaptability to environment is secured which has won for man his superiority to environment. To the study of "play" we turn in Chapter IV.

CHAPTER IV

PLAY

WE all know what we mean by play, though it is difficult to define it so as to distinguish it in every instance from other non-play activities. Children are playing when they are merrily enjoying a game of ball. Two young dogs are playing when they chase one another alternately, pretend to bite, roll one another over, and bark. A kitten plays with a ball of wool. A little boy plays at building castles and moats and systems of canals on the seashore. A little girl plays at houses. Three or four bigger boys play at Indians. A team of high-school girls plays hockey. A schoolmaster plays golf.

In most of these cases, especially those earlier in the list, we have no doubt that the activity is play. There may be some doubt about the hockey match if it is a compulsory game. The schoolmaster may go through his weekly task of obtaining exercise, though he hates it. Does the professional golfer *play* ? Sometimes he assuredly does, just as anyone else might. Sometimes he feels that it is his daily work by which he obtains his daily bread. Do we not on the other hand know men who treat their work as play and would rather play the game of being a chemist, or a lawyer, or a soldier, than do anything else ?

The two dogs are not playing when they begin to fight *really*, as we say ; when bites are given to draw blood and a deeper note comes into the growl. The kitten is not playing —or is it still playing ?—when it chases a mouse instead of a ball of wool. Certainly it is not playing if it is a really hungry, starving kitten.

INSTINCT, INTELLIGENCE AND CHARACTER

It is clear that the dividing line between play and earnest is an uncertain one. Play passes continuously and without break into work, or into real hunting or real fighting. The theory of play which it is the purpose of this section to uphold, the theory mainly associated with the name of Karl Groos, is that *play is a preparation for the earnest activities of life*, and that when nature began to select species for their playfulness she had turned a corner in the great experiment of evolution, and had embarked on the journey which led to the creation of man. If this theory be true, it is play which more and more distinguishes the higher animals as we rise in the scale of ability, and which most of all marks out man. It is "play" that gives man that other great implement of progress, speech, which some have almost believed to be equivalent to thought and intelligence, so great is the advantage enjoyed by its possessor. It is play, if we are right, which is the natural educator and which therefore points the way for the human educator, the teacher.

It is worth while dwelling a little longer on that change in the march of evolution which has just been referred to. Previously, the selection had been for those most fitted, as they stood, to the environment. It was like buying ready-made clothes. If they really do fit, well and good, but the man who buys uncut cloth and employs a tailor is more likely to look well dressed. The lower animals inherit fixed instincts, they must take their "ready-mades" and wear them. The higher animals inherit less well-fixed instincts, better able to be fashioned to fit the life of the times. The trying-on process is the period of play, and the journeyman tailor, the workman carrying out the design of the Master Craftsman, is the teacher. He has not a free hand, he must cut his coat according to his cloth: but his is the power of ensuring assimilation to the civilized society of to-day and of reducing misfits of defect or delinquency to their lowest numbers. He has not the power, that is to say, to write whatever he will on a clean slate. But he has the

PLAY

task of directing, modifying, sublimating the instincts, and if we are right he will do this most readily by utilizing the tendency to play. English schools have long used play as the chief means of training character, and have expressed their ideal as " playing the game " in the real affairs of life. And now "playways" of learning are coming more and more into favour in the provinces of skill and of reasoning as well as in the moral province.

The impulse to play is just the impulse to carry out certain instinctive actions in the absence of the *usual* inner set or trend of the organism. As this is perhaps rather a novel way of looking at play, it may be worth while amplifying the statement and illustrating it. How an animal acts in any situation depends not only upon the outer situation but also upon the inner "set" of the animal,[1] whether it be hungry or replete, fatigued or fresh, in a period of sexual excitement or sexual quiescence.

Now consider, say, the hunting instinct. In the sedate mature animal the urge of hunger makes the animal restless, it wanders observantly about in its usual hunting ground, certain smells and sights presently cause it to pause, flatten, crawl, jump, sprint, pounce upon its prey. The process has been well described by James as a chain of instincts, hunger causing restlessness, restlessness leading to sight of a small escaping animal, this sight leading to pursuit, and so on. But throughout, the inner set of the organism, the drive of hunger, is a part of the total situation and were that drive not present the hunting response would not be carried out. In an animal born with perfected instinctive responses, fitted to enable it at once, or very soon, to lead an independent life, the whole situation is comparatively fixed. But in an

---

[1] A similar doctrine holds good in the cognitive or intellectual realm. What a given sentence makes me think about depends upon what I am already thinking about. In the vacation time, digging in my garden, I respond to the question " What do you think of James ? " by thoughts of little boys, perhaps. In my psychology class I respond by thoughts of the great American psychologist. (I forget whence I borrow the illustration.)

INSTINCT, INTELLIGENCE AND CHARACTER

animal which plays, and has a period of more or less protracted childhood, there are two differences in the combination of situation and response. In the first place, the hunting response can be set off by the sight of the small escaping animal without that inner drive of hunger being needed. And secondly, other small escaping animals only remotely resembling the natural prey may set it off, or even a whirling dead leaf or a bit of stick may do so.

The inner drive which belongs to the mature instinct being absent, the hunting which ensues is not carried out so far as to lead to eating the prey or, in the case of the fighting instinct, to actual wounding or killing of the opponent. Instead of the directed drive of hunger or of anger, there is just the aimless drive of youthful energy easily diverted into any channel. All the instinctive actions of the mature animal may, in fragmentary portions, take a place in the play activity of the young: but they are divorced from the emotions of anger, fear, lust, from the inner states such as hunger, which accompany them later, and instead they are pervaded all alike by a general sense of well-being and light-heartedness.

The picture thus presented is one showing, in the young animal, imperfectly developed instincts, or portions of later instinctive chains, partially divorced from any binding alliance with specific situations, and from association with definite emotional drives. The selection and survival of the fittest which formerly went on among the individuals of a generation now goes on among the responses of that individual to the environment of his childhood. For the specifically equipped animal, the absence from the environment of just its own proper prey would cause death. For the animal that we are discussing, the absence of what had formerly been the usual prey of its parents would only cause the more generally directed hunting instinct to learn to attach itself, during the play of childhood, to the nearest available similar prey. The hunting play would shift its

PLAY

association gradually from bits of fur or leaves to bits of the mother's food, to wounded specimens of prey now hunted by her, to any small suitable animals in the neighbourhood, and accommodation to the environment would (if too violent an alteration were avoided) take place in the individual, instead of whole generations having to be decimated to bring about adaptation. Natural selection by survival of the fittest individuals would, it is true, still go on; but the selection would be of those most fitted to learn by play, not of those fitted to perform perfect specific acts. If the fashions changed (to return to our tailor analogy), there would be no need to buy and scrap hundreds of garments in search for the right cut : attention could be concentrated on getting good cloth, leaving the cut to the tailor.

To take a specific example, and the most important one, consider the difference between an animal born with instinctive cries attached to certain situations such as being alarmed, being alone, courting, etc., and an animal born with just an aimless tendency to make vocal sounds and to enjoy doing so. The former animal cannot learn vocal connections, his small repertory is ready made. The latter animal learns speech. The human child has the connection of the vocal responses to things and events made, during the period when he plays aimlessly at the game of babbling, by the enthusiasm with which some of his efforts are hailed, and imitated, by his nurse and parents, which causes him to repeat them and associate them with objects, while other of his efforts are ignored and sink into disuse. It would be a long course of evolution before beings were evolved who said "milk" when thirsty, if we followed the plan of killing those who didn't. It would no doubt be conceivable under certain circumstances. But nature found it easier to select just those who enjoyed aimless babbling, leaving to another kind of selection the job of attaching the response "milk" to that situation of being thirsty.

And this throws, I think, a light on that non-inheritance

INSTINCT, INTELLIGENCE AND CHARACTER

of acquired characteristics spoken of on page 24. If it be true that selection for plastic response and a period of play was found by Nature to produce races of animals who conquered those who possessed ready-made fixed instincts, would one not expect as a corollary to find that acquired characteristics are not inherited? If they were, would not that be a retrograde step, undoing the step in advance made when play entered the world. To put on the worn garments of the previous generation will be just as bad as to put on ready-mades. A race of beings with fixed inherited habits would be just as unfitted to survive as a race with fixed unalterable instincts, and indeed would be indistinguishable from them. Man has won in the race against animals with more fixed instincts, and can, if he wishes, exterminate any one of them, just because of his childhood period of play. And the adaptability which that play period gives him would be just as much jeopardized by the inheritance of newly fixed habits as of older fixed instincts. Man is *par excellence* an animal that learns. It is far more important to be able to learn than to have learned. Progress in evolution is like finding the centre of a maze. It is better for each generation to re-enter the maze with the power of learning than to start at the point, possibly in a blind alley, at which the previous generation finished. Inheriting acquired characters would involve blind alleys.

CHAPTER V

THE LEARNING PROCESS

MAN is *par excellence* the learning animal. He is not the *only* learning animal; indeed, far down in the scale of animal life there are creatures which can perform simple acts of learning. But man can learn more readily, and can learn more subtle responses, than any other being—far more. Just because of this, however, it is very desirable to begin our study of the learning process with animals, and later see to what extent the laws there found can be applied to man.

There is a little microscopic organism called the stentor which is in shape rather like a trumpet. Its stalk attaches it to some water-plant or bit of debris in the water in which it lives, and it constructs a tube of flocculent matter into which it can withdraw for protection. When protruding from this tube it draws the surrounding water into its "mouth" by means of a fringe of cilia or hairs which move backwards and forwards, quickly in and slowly out. By this means small fragments of edible substance are brought to its digestive apparatus.

Whenever any obnoxious substance is thus swept into its mouth, this animalcula has a reflex response adapted to getting rid of it, for the stentor first bends to one side, and then, if this does not suffice, its cilia change their flickering so as to reverse the current which until then they had been creating. This can be observed when a little cloud of carmine dye is put into the water near at hand.[1] After a

[1] Jennings, H. S., *Amer. Journ. Physiol.* 1902, viii, 23–60.

moment the cilia then resume their previous action, sweeping neighbouring water into the mouth.

If the quantity of dye placed in the water is such that a short reversal of the cilia is not sufficient to clear it away, further reversals will occur. While if three or four such reversals are not successful, the animalcula contracts its stalk, thus retreating into its tube, and waits till the clouds roll by.

Presently, after half a minute or more, it emerges again, and its cilia recommence their wave motion. If dye is very shortly reintroduced into the adjacent water, the former responses will again be made, first the bending, then the cilia reversal, and then, when this proves unsuccessful, the stalk contraction.

So far there is nothing which need, perhaps, be called learning. This animal has two or three responses to the presence of obnoxious matter in the surrounding water. One of them it tries first: and when several efforts with this response have failed, it carries out the other. The situation which causes the first response is just the presence of dye in the water. The situation which causes the other response is different. It is the presence of dye in the water, plus the recency of a number of failures to obtain relief. We must suppose that something of the nature of memory exists in the animalcula, not in the sense that it consciously remembers, but in the sense only that some change in its organism has taken place as a result of these failures to obtain relief from the carmine dye.

If now the experiment be continued, and dye is every time introduced into the neighbourhood as soon as ever the animal emerges, we find that a kind of learning process goes on, inasmuch as on each occasion fewer and fewer efforts are made to sweep the dye away by ciliary movements, more and still more quickly does the creature take refuge in its tube, until finally it does so without any preliminary ciliary reversals at all. After a few more trials a new kind

THE LEARNING PROCESS

of response sets in, a response now to the situation, "presence of dye in the water and a large number of unsuccessful responses of all the earlier kinds." The new response is for the creature to jerk itself away from its anchorage and swim off to seek new quarters.

We must, of course, beware of attributing to the animalcula any of the feelings and thoughts which a human being would have under similar circumstances. We need not postulate any consciousness at all. But to obtain learning it is essential that the organism under study should have more than one response to the same situation, or otherwise there will be nothing from which to select. The most one could then do would be to teach the organism not to respond at all, a form of teaching which is indeed of great importance in character training.

The "same situation" here is the presence of dye in the water, and the four responses possible are bending, ciliary reversal, withdrawal into the tube, and swimming away. True, the situation progressively changes owing to the continued non-success of the first response, in the sense that the inner "set" of the organism changes. But the external situation is the same, and the animal "learns" presently to make not the ciliary response but the withdrawal response.

Multiple response to the same situation is, then, necessary for learning to set in. From these responses one can be selected because it brings some kind of advantage, whereas the others do not. In the case we have been considering the possible responses are arranged in a kind of order already, since we know that an ordinary stentor[1] will try the bending first, the ciliary reversal next, then the withdrawal, and then the swimming away. And it is probable that a very short period of vacation from our "teaching" would make our "pupil" forget what he has "learnt" and return to his ciliary reversal. Permanent learning is probably not in this

[1] In some cases the ciliary reversal comes first, but not usually.

INSTINCT, INTELLIGENCE AND CHARACTER

case possible, and it is doubtful whether it can really be called a case of learning in the sense of the formation of habits of response.

With animals higher in the scale, however, the various responses to the same situation cease to be arranged so definitely in an order. One cannot say with certainty which of the possible responses will be made first. No doubt the actual response is determined by the total situation and the inner set of the organism. But a very slight change in either may change the response. Suppose we shut up a hungry chicken inside an enclosure which is rather confined and small for it, and from which two passageways run, one being a blind alley and the other leading to food and the companionship of other chickens and the mother hen.[1] To this situation the chicken responds by peeping, by rushing about, by attempting to scale the walls of the enclosure in a sort of flying scramble, and by running along the passageways. Just which of these things it will do first cannot be predicted. What can be predicted is that it will do them in rapid succession and apparently aimlessly. It will repeat trials which did no good before, and will, up to a limit, become more and more vigorous in its efforts. Sooner or later it will run far enough along the passage which leads to companionship and food, will rejoin the hen and recommence pecking.

If it is presently placed again in exactly the same outer situation, and in the same inner condition as regards hunger, sleepiness, etc., it will do the same. It will not immediately choose the passage which leads to freedom, but will make a large number of aimless rushes, etc. Yet if the experiment is repeated again and again, the length of time taken by the chicken to escape will *gradually* become less. It will try the correct response earlier and earlier, until finally it has "learnt" to make its way out of the enclosure without delay.

[1] Thorndike, *Educ. Psychol. Briefer Course*, p. 126.

THE LEARNING PROCESS

Now one law of learning which everyone knows is what might be called the Law of Practice, namely that any action which is done frequently becomes on that account easier to do and more likely to be done. But this case of the chicken shows very clearly that the Law of Practice is not the only factor in learning. The chicken practised the correct response only once per trial, for after a correct response the trial ceased, it got out of the enclosure. Incorrect responses, on the other hand, such as jumping up at the wall, may be made, and are made, several times in each trial, indeed, very frequently in the earlier trials. Practice alone, therefore, ought to have fixed the incorrect rather than the correct response. In what way then does the correct response differ from the others? Common sense tells us that it differs because it puts the chicken into a new condition, it relieves it from loneliness and hunger, it satisfies certain inner cravings. We must assume that this satisfaction somehow makes this response more likely to recur when next the situation is reconstituted. Not certain to recur, for then the chicken would on second trial go straight out by the proper passageway, and that is not what we actually find; but more likely to recur, and therefore recurring at an earlier stage at the later trials.

The type of learning thus illustrated may be called Trial and Error learning. It arises when an animal has more than one response to a situation. Confronted by the situation, the animal tries its responses over until one succeeds. Confronted later by the same situation, it again tries its responses over, but the response which was associated with satisfaction somehow has thereby become facilitated a little, and so the improvement goes on till the proper response comes to be made without other trials. It is *Satisfaction* which has selected the response. *Practice* will now stamp it in. For as the trials progress the correct response, which at first got less practice than the incorrect, comes to catch up in this respect. Toward the end, while the correct

INSTINCT, INTELLIGENCE AND CHARACTER

response is always made, each of the various incorrect responses is only made occasionally.[1] Finally only the correct response gets practice. If the situation is left unpractised for a long time, the chicken will partly or wholly forget its trick, and will have to relearn it.

This learning by Trial and Error, by the aid of the laws of Satisfaction and Practice, will occupy us a good deal, for we shall wish to find out whether all learning is of this type, or whether any new laws are needed as we proceed to study learning in higher animals and in man. It will be our duty, if we wish to act in a scientific manner, to avoid making any further hypotheses unless we feel absolutely forced to do so. Of course, the Law of Satisfaction includes the opposite case of punishment or dissatisfaction. If a third passageway had been open, so arranged that when the chicken went along this passageway it received an electric shock, it would have learned to avoid this passageway sooner than it learned to avoid the non-electrified one. Going along the blind alley in any case, however, leads to disappointment, to dissatisfaction; and so we ought perhaps to call our law the Law of Satisfaction and Dissatisfaction.

Now let us contrast with our chicken the behaviour of a

[1] To illustrate the way in which, it is suggested, the reward resulting from the successful movement makes it more likely to occur when the situation is again met with, imagine an experiment with a pack of cards, the fifty-two cards of which represent the random responses made by the imprisoned and hungry animal. Draw a card, which will represent the first response the animal makes. Replace it in the pack, shuffle well, and draw another card, representing the second response made. One response will follow another in random order, and sometimes a card may recur. Sooner or later, however, the card representing the successful response will be drawn, say the six of hearts. Now, to represent the stamping in effect of the satisfaction which success brings, suppose we add another six of hearts to the pack (making fifty-three cards in all). When we now repeat the whole experiment, the six of hearts will be a little more likely to be drawn. It will not, as a rule, be drawn at once. The successful response will not, that is, be made at once as soon as the second trial is begun. But the odds are in favour of its appearance a little earlier than in the first trial. Every time the six of hearts is drawn, let an additional six of hearts be added to the pack. After a while the chances in favour of this card being drawn will be very high, though on any one occasion it may take many draws before it appears. Gradually it will come to be the almost certain event, as the pack comes to contain dozens and even hundreds of this particular card.

THE LEARNING PROCESS

human being in a similar situation. Suppose a man just about dinner time is shut in a room with two doors, one leading to the dining-room and a company of friends, the other leading into a blind alley. His behaviour will, at any rate apparently, differ from the chicken's. He will not rush about in fruitless dashes at the walls. He will at once select a door, open it, and if it is the wrong one he will go to the other and enter the dining-room. If placed in the same situation next day, he will avoid the wrong door; or if he should perhaps fail to remember, he will learn in a very short series of trials. It may be said that the man consciously remembers and acts accordingly, whereas the effect on the chicken is some influence on the nerves which facilitates but does not ensure the correct choice next day, an unconscious influence.

But is the situation into which we have placed the man really comparable with that into which we placed the chicken? Suppose a giant had taken the man and put him into a dungeon, would there not then be the possibility of rushing about and acting vigorously but aimlessly? Or suppose, instead of fluttering his feelings, we simply give the man something harder to do. Give him a mechanical puzzle in which two pieces of bent metal have to be separated without the use of force; which can only be accomplished by getting them into just the correct relative positions, or into a sequence of such positions. When we try such a puzzle, do we not find ourselves making "trial and error" movements? Do we not usually succeed, after a long series of aimless manipulations, without knowing exactly what it was we did to achieve success? Do we not make many fruitless manipulations even after one or two successes, and only come gradually to reduce the time taken?[1] Perhaps there is no essential difference, but only one of degree, between the chicken's learning and the man's learning.

The reader may reply that sooner or later the man "under-

[1] See Ruger, *Archives of Psychology*, 1910, No. 15.

stands" how to solve the puzzle, and after that moment the trials and errors disappear suddenly. Though this is not what is actually found if the puzzle is a difficult one, we must bear the point in mind, and ask ourselves whether there are two kinds of learning, one by trial and error, and the other by insight and understanding. There are certainly some provinces of learning in which man uses mainly trial and error. For instance, consider learning to drive a long and straight ball at golf. There is no doubt very considerable advantage to be gained by having a teacher who gives us a good model, and warns us against faults. But in any case a very considerable amount of trial and error there must be, and good driving can be learnt, and has been learnt, just by driving and driving and driving. Naïve learning of this sort, indeed, is probably best, provided that there is a strong enough incentive to continue, that the dissatisfaction at bad drives does not lead to discontinuance of the game, and that there is occasionally seen a model of what can be achieved. When anyone learns in this way he cannot usually say just what it is that he does differently that causes him to drive better this month than last. When he does say what it is, the chances are that he is mistaken, and that attention given to this analysed point will only check his learning. People drive best when they do not think about it, but just put the ball down and smack it away. Since they do certainly get better with practice even when unconscious of what changes they are making, and since at first they certainly practise the wrong thing oftener than the right thing, we are forced to assume that in man also, satisfaction at a successful movement can somehow cause that movement to be repeated more easily, can select it from among the dissatisfying movements, even when he is not conscious of the exact muscular combinations which formed the successful movement. Some change, some unconscious change, must take place in the nervous system. We turn next to an elementary study of the nervous system to see whether this

THE LEARNING PROCESS

sort of thing is at all possible or conceivable. Our study must be a very elementary study, for only a course of practical work in physiology and anatomy could give a competent basis to it. We shall indeed speak mainly in analogies and similes : and our similes must not be pushed too far.

CHAPTER VI

THE NERVOUS SYSTEM

An animal is like a colony of cells which have each specialized and taken on separate jobs, just as in a human colony some men are farmers, some cartmen, some hunters, and so on. A mere agglomeration of cells would not resemble an animal: it is essential that they be organized into a unit, into a whole, by something which will enable them to co-operate as one being. The cells whose job is to form the left leg must co-operate with each other; the left leg must co-operate with the other legs; the heart must co-operate with the arteries and with the lungs; the cells which secrete gastric juices must co-operate with the stomach muscles, and so on. In the animal body, and in the human body, some cells have specialized in duties which have for their object just this integrative action. Two kinds of such integration exist, which have been likened by Sir Arthur Keith[1] to a postal system and a telegraph system respectively. The telegraph system is formed by the nerves which are our present object of study.

These run away from all the sense organs, including the various sense spots in the skin, into the central nervous system situated in the spinal column and in the skull. The messages they bring in cause other messages to go out to the muscles and glands of the body, and lead to their action in a regular and organized manner. The fact that such and such muscles are moving is itself reported to the central

[1] *The Engines of the Human Body*, Williams & Norgate, London.

THE NERVOUS SYSTEM

office, and the receipt of these messages may cause further orders to be sent out. It is rather like the telegraph and telephone system of a large army in the field. Messages come in from the eyes of the army, from the scouts, the aeroplanes, the observation posts, etc. These messages do not usually go direct to the commander-in-chief and his staff, they are received and considered first by lower officers; and in the case of many of the messages these lower officers issue the orders which lead to the simple movements of troops necessary to deal with the situation. When the situation which the various messages reveals is more complicated, however, the information is relayed on to headquarters, and there is discussed by the heads of staff, who may call each other up repeatedly on their office telephones to consult about it. Finally orders go out from the commander-in-chief which lead to co-ordinated movements of battalions, to speeding up of ammunition supply, to stopping leave and stopping letters, and to an increase in the activity of the medical units in anticipation of the necessary evacuation of the wounded. The battalions concerned will send in reports of their movements during the battle, and further orders issued from headquarters will depend largely upon these reports. The telegraph and telephone system of a modern army is engaged in this integrating work which co-ordinates the army into a unit acting under control from headquarters.

The nerves which form the cables of the human telegraph system are composed of bundles of long thin nerve cells called neurones. A neurone is a cell just like any other cell of the body or just like an independent animal cell such as Amœba. But its form is specialized and its composition is specialized in a way directed entirely towards its duties as a carrier of messages. From its cell body goes out a long, thin projection (often with a tasselled end) called the axone, and it is these axones which, grouped in cables, form the nerves. One of these may be several feet in length, for

INSTINCT, INTELLIGENCE AND CHARACTER

instance an axone reaching from the lower part of the spinal column to the toe. From the cell body, too, there go out in the opposite direction, much-branched thin, hair-like projections called dendrites.[1] The whole, dendrites, cell body, and axone, form a unit along which a "message," a change of chemical composition, can pass. Moreover, the message only goes one way. A different neurone is required to bring back a reply. The disturbance passes from the dendrites to the axone in each neurone.

In the simplest kind of nerve message it is conceivable (though it is highly improbable that anything so simple ever really occurs) that only two neurones are concerned. One of these starts in a sense organ, say in a pain spot in the hand. It runs in to the spinal column where its tassel-like endings are entangled with the dendrites of another neurone, an efferent neurone (those which carry messages *in* are called afferent, *out* efferent). The chemical excitement, or whatever it is, passes from the one neurone-ending to the other, such a a place of crossing being called a synapse, and the message goes out along the efferent neurone to a muscle which jerks the hand away from the pin which has pricked it. Such a unit of response is called a reflex arc, and the action a reflex action. Invariably, no doubt, several or many such reflex arcs are stimulated together, even by the narrowest stimulus and for the simplest response. The action need not be at all conscious : or if we are conscious of it we become so after it has happened. Such actions occur, for example, when we slip and regain our balance, when we dodge a sudden snowball, when we start from a curtain which touches the face in the dark.

If we return to our analogy with the army, we may liken such situations to sudden emergencies of a well-known kind, dealt with at once by the nearest officer. A sentry in Sector D 7 sees an enemy patrol in the darkness. He wakens his

---

[1] In some neurones the dendrites are represented by one very long unbranched projection ; and there are many other varieties.

THE NERVOUS SYSTEM

next superior officer. The officer does not wait to communicate the news to the commander-in-chief and ask what he is to do. On his own initiative he gives orders for rapid fire. He passes on the news later, after he has done this.

We may almost look upon what occurs in the spinal column in a reflex movement, as being analogous with this prompt action on the spot of the non-commissioned officer or second-lieutenant. In another case, however, where consideration was required, or where the counter measures needed orders from a higher rank, the lieutenant in question might have passed on the information before acting in any way. And the reply might not have come through him at all. Indeed, the message might have been relayed back till it reached general headquarters. Not otherwise does it happen in the spinal column. Instead of going out again at once and causing a reflex action, the incoming nerve currents may pass from the nerves which brought them in, to other neurones which carry them higher up the spinal column, or up to the mid brain. And thence, passing over synapses to yet other neurones, they may go to the great brain itself, the cerebral hemispheres, where complicated systems of neurones may carry the excitement hither and thither before finally a downward-carrying set convey currents which at some lower level pass to efferent or motor nerves and cause muscular movement to occur.

The expression "carrying the nerve current" must not be allowed to mislead. The first analogy is with currents of water such as waterpipes carry. That is certainly most unlike what occurs. The second analogy, that suggested by our telegraph system, is with wires which direct an electric current. That, also, however, is in many respects unlike what occurs. In the first place, nerve currents do not travel anything like as fast as electric currents. Then detailed examination shows that, although there are certain electrical manifestations which do take place, the disturbance which

INSTINCT, INTELLIGENCE AND CHARACTER

passes along a neurone is more like the slow explosion or rapid burning which passes along a fuse. Behind the burning point the fuse is dead and incapable of further action. And so indeed is the neurone for a fraction of a second, but it recuperates with extraordinary rapidity. We can ascertain how long the fatigue-period is by sending impulses along a neurone one after the other quicker and quicker till it begins to miss every other one out.

Reflex actions, then, are actions where a number of connections between incoming nerves and outgoing nerves are ready made by Nature. These connections are always there. They need no operator to make them. And they are not accompanied by any consciousness, or at any rate need not be. Some are so unconscious that most people do not know about them. Such is the narrowing of the pupil of the eye which takes place in a bright light.

In a continuous series from the pure reflex actions come the instinctive actions, such as striking back at a man who strikes me, cheering and yelling at a successful feat of strength or skill in which a friend has overcome a stranger, or shutting my eyes at a repulsive sight. Neurone connections exist in us which make these things happen very easily, but not with such certainty as the contraction of the pupil of the eye. It is probable that these are relayed back to a higher level before the return messages start off. They are accompanied, too, by consciousness in an increasing degree. We are aware of them, we have inner feelings called anger, or enthusiasm, or disgust, we are aware of the effort to prevent their expression on some occasions, an effort which frequently succeeds, or succeeds in part.

Finally we come to actions where it is probable that the incoming nerve messages are relayed back right to the cerebral hemispheres themselves, and where a very, very large number of neurones is involved before the nerve currents go out to command the muscles to act. Take the case of a man walking from the station to the town hall in

THE NERVOUS SYSTEM

an unfamiliar city of which, however, he possesses a map. Every turn he takes is the subject of consideration and reflection. He is very conscious of his actions and the reasons for them.

But if he makes the journey daily for some weeks he ceases to ponder over each turn. The choice of a certain route has become habitual. If the habit is practised daily for a longer period, it may become so firmly fixed that when he wishes to go to some other destination than the town hall he may find himself, without thinking, taking the habitual path. What has happened, in terms of neurone connection, in this case? Compare it with the army. The case was at first that the situation was reported right to the general commanding, whose decision was made after some thought. Later the action became habitual. The general-in-chief no longer troubles himself about it. What has happened to the route taken by the messages? Have they been short-circuited, and is the proper response made by some lower officer without waiting for a reply from H.Q.? Or is it that the messages still take the same course, going right up to the general's office, but that their presence attracts no attention there, and ready printed orders are just sent out, with no delay, and by smooth working relays of messengers? In terms of neurone action, we suppose that on first traversing the route the incoming neurone messages describing the situation are sent up to the brain, that large numbers of neurones there flash nerve currents back and forth, and that finally, other neurones carry messages which are relayed on to the muscles. When the action becomes habitual, has the neurone circuit been short-circuited at some lower level, or does the same set of neurones still respond, only without hesitation and without so much consciousness accompanying their activity?

This is a question we cannot with certainty answer. It is probable, however, that there is both some short-circuiting and also some facilitation of the paths through

INSTINCT, INTELLIGENCE AND CHARACTER

the upper brain, through the general's office. Consider the army again. Lieutenant A receives the news of a certain enemy action. He passes it on up the hierarchy of officers to the general. But his duty also requires him to warn his fellow lieutenants B, C, and D. Presently the order comes back for C and D to move, and finds them ready to move, thanks to A's warning. Suppose this identical situation recurs again and again. C and D will get more and more accustomed to receiving orders to move, a little while after receiving A's warning. Some day they may be so ready to move that they do so as soon as the telephone message from headquarters begins, or as soon as the general's messenger is seen approaching. There is both short-circuiting and less attention to A's message at headquarters.

B, C, and D are instinctive or reflex, or earlier habitual actions, and A is a situation a little bit like that which sets off B, a little like that which sets off C, a little like that which sets off D. A sends neurone messages to all of them, but they are not quite the right messages. Not until the further message from the brain comes do C and D act; while B relapses into quiescence. C and D are ready to act, they receive orders to act, and this situation is satisfying. B is ready to act but receives no orders, or no permission, to act. This situation is unsatisfying. B will gradually cease taking any notice of A's warning, while C and D will go off on that warning with little or no further encouragement.

It is at the synapses, where one neurone makes communication with others, that, as we believe, the events take place which decide the path the nerve current will take. It may pass along various paths, and these will have different degrees of resistance. That path which is frequently taken by a nerve current comes to have a less resistance. This lessening of resistance, which is believed to take place at the synapses, may be an actual growing into closer contiguity of the end brushes, or tasselled ends of the neurones,

THE NERVOUS SYSTEM

as two trees might closely interlock their twigs and small branches. Or it may be some change in the chemical composition of the intervening substance.

Whatever it is, the facts as to acquiring skill which we considered in the previous section seem, at least to the present writer, to imply that when an action is successful, as when a drive at golf is successful, the state of body and mind which we call feeling satisfied at the success, pleased at the success, must somehow act on the synapses over which the nerve currents have just passed to direct that successful action, and cause them to acquire a slightly lowered resistance. This does not seem to be physiologically impossible, though as far as I am aware there is no physiological evidence to show that it takes place. Its physiological possibility would depend on the condition of the neurones and synapses remaining slightly differentiated for a long enough period to allow of the afterglow of pleasure somehow influencing them differently from others.

There is no necessity for the psychologist to interpret his facts, or to couch his theories, in physiological terms, and it is as well to emphasize this point here. The observed psychological fact from which we started some pages ago was that improvement in the skilful performance of some action does actually take place, even although the clumsy elements of the action are in the early stages of practice repeated more often than the correct elements. From this the need of something more than the mere law of practice follows : and the required addition, it is suggested, is that satisfaction encourages and dissatisfaction discourages the repetition of certain muscular patterns, even if we are not clearly conscious, or not at all conscious, of what those patterns are. To make this explanation conceivable in terms of what is known of the neurones and their connections is the object of the present section, but the law of satisfaction and dissatisfaction does not stand or fall with the correctness of what is here said, and surmised, about the neurones.

INSTINCT, INTELLIGENCE AND CHARACTER

Only one has a strong desire to make the whole of knowledge hang together, and few students can speak and think of the learning process without forming some picture of what goes on in the brain and nerves. Let us, however, return to the observation of acts of learning once more, and in particular to that form of experiment known as maze-running.

CHAPTER VII
MAZE EXPERIMENTS

MAZE experiments have been carried out by a large number of experimenters, with mice and rats mainly, but also with other animals, including tortoises. They can also be performed with human beings, either with large mazes, or with small drawings, or in the special way to be described later in this section.

The simplest form of maze for experimental purposes is one in which at each choice of paths one path is a cul-de-sac. Such a maze is shown for example in the accompanying figure. The rat is put in at P, and when he reaches the centre H he finds some favourite food. The length of time taken, the number of blind alleys entered, the number of false returns over any alley, are all noted, and a gradual improvement is found in all these respects till the maze is learned and the rat runs unerringly to the food box. Needless to say, care has to be taken that he does not run by following the scent of a former trial.

In such a maze, the law of satisfaction may be conceived of as operating because of the dissatisfaction at having to retrace one's steps out of a blind alley, when a wrong turn is taken, and the satisfaction at being able to penetrate more deeply when a correct turn is taken. On the occasion of the first run this, and the further dissatisfaction of being returned to the maze should the entrance P be reached again, suffice to cause the food box to be reached ultimately. On future runs there is the memory of the food to incite to perseverance. Exploring along alleyways when in a state of hunger is no doubt a native tendency in a rat, and

INSTINCT, INTELLIGENCE AND CHARACTER

provided he keeps moving, and is turned back whenever he tries to come out at P, he will by sheer chance come finally to the middle, even if he did not avoid blind alleys just previously explored.

Let us try an artificial experiment in which we throw a coin at each choice of paths and imagine we turn to the right

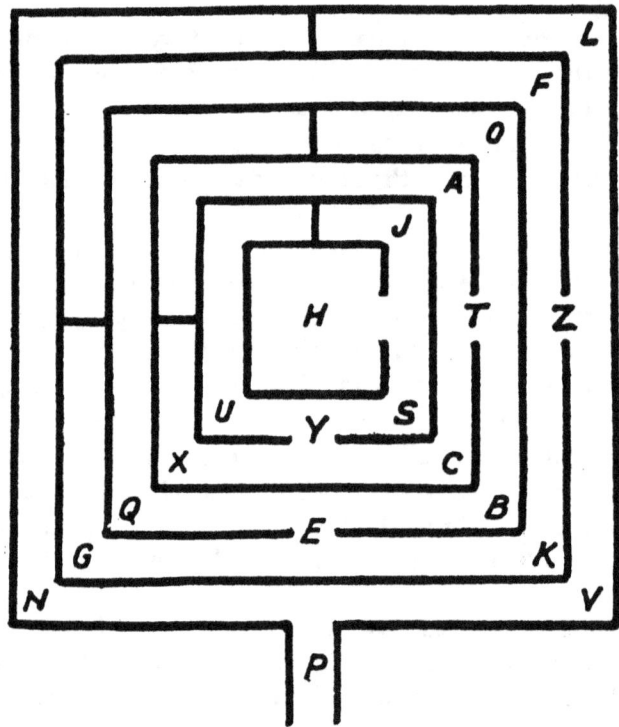

hand for heads, left hand for tails. Here is one such trial, made by actually throwing a coin (the letters show the path according to the letters of the diagram).

P
N or V ? The coin gives a tail, so we take N. Go in to N, discover
         it is a blind alley, come out again, and then ask :
P or V ? The coin gives tail, so take V.
Z or L ? The coin gives head, so take L.

MAZE EXPERIMENTS

On coming out of L we ask :

V or Z ? Coin says V. We reach P and ask :
P or N ? Coin says N.
P or V ? Coin says V,

and so on, the path finally being found to be (including the above moves) as follows :

P N V L V N V L V P V L V N P N V Z F Z V
P N V L V P V Z F Z L Z K E Q B O B Q B
O T A T O T C Y S J S U S J H

This path, if traced out on the diagram, looks quite like a real maze-run ; but really a rat would not keep on taking blind alleys repeatedly, for dissatisfaction at coming to a dead wall would make them less likely to be re-entered. However, assume that, on this first occasion, chance alone has led the rat, as chance alone led our choice of a path with the aid of a tossed penny.

Now suppose the rat is started on a second run of the maze, and let us see what would happen if only the law of use acted. Moreover, suppose that it acts infallibly. On entry at P, will the rat take N or V ? If we examine the record we find that on its previous entries it took N three times and V only twice. It will, therefore,[1] take N, and the law of use alone will never enable it to get rid of entering N. In the same way we can find the whole route which the rat would take on this its second trial. It would be P N V L V P N V L V P N V L V P and so on *ad infinitum*.[2] By the law of use it would never reach the food box. Indeed, we only allowed it to reach the food box at all in the first run

---

[1] V is a more *recent* reaction than N, and if *recency* as well as *frequency* were regarded, this following paragraph would have to be rewritten in its details. If we take *recency* entirely to override *frequency* we get the following : P V Z K E Q B O T C Y S J H. The blind alleys Q, O, J, in this run would never be eliminated by recency or frequency if they alone acted. And *recency* if applied during the first run would effectually prevent any rat which once took a return path from ever getting to the centre, which is not true to the facts.

[2] In other cases it might reach the centre : but some blind alleys would always remain and would never be eliminated.

INSTINCT, INTELLIGENCE AND CHARACTER

by not allowing the law of use to act till the run was over: for otherwise the rat having once returned to P would keep on doing so always.

Clearly then a Law of Satisfaction and Dissatisfaction is essential to explain improvement. Let us say that when a blind alley has been already negotiated in the same run, the chances are only 1 in 4 of the rat entering it, if again confronted with a dilemma of which that particular blind alley is one horn. Start a second rat off on its first trial, turning it to right or left by the head or tail of a penny at each alternative, except that when a " previous " blind alley is reached two successive heads (or two tails) are needed before the rat enters. In an actual trial I obtain the following:

P N V L Z K E B O T C Y U Y C A C X C A C Y S H

This has considerably shortened the run: but if the reader will actually make the experiment for himself he will see that unless we add some device to represent reluctance to return along an alley already traversed (other than the blind alleys, already considered) there is great danger that the rat, once reversed, will run backwards clean out at P just because of his reluctance to enter blind alleys.

If the reader will in imagination put himself in the place of the rat he will see that one difficulty is to recognize whether any present alternative has been negotiated before, and to recall which of the two paths was chosen. To get information about this it is very helpful to try a maze oneself, but without looking at the diagram, for that makes it too easy. Try the following experiment on some friend, and later get him to try it on you after changing all the letters.

Give the following instructions:

I am going to ask you to find your way through a simple maze. You will not be shown the maze, but I will ask you to choose between a pair of letters which I will say to you, in order to see which turn you take. Every time you are offered such a choice, one of the letters offered will stand for a blind alley from which, if you enter

MAZE EXPERIMENTS

it, you must emerge by the same way as you go in. The other letter stands for the proper route. I shall sometimes give the blind alley first of the two, and sometimes second, so pay no attention to the order of the pair of letters. Each alley has its own letter by which it is always called, just as streets have names: and the letters have been distributed to the alleys quite at random. Now, after entering, do you choose N or V ?[1]

Now offer at each question that pair of letters to which the subject's wanderings in the maze have brought you, and record all his answers. When he reaches H say "That is the goal," but do not emphasize the letter. Give your subject as many "runs" as his good nature will stand:[2] and get him to give the maze or a similar one, to you, first altering the letters. You will find, as with rats, that your performance on the whole improves, whether measured by time taken or number of errors made, though not without relapses into former errors. You will recognize that you have been in a blind alley by the fact of the recurrence of letters already passed by. You may formulate a certain rule (can you state it ?) about your proper action in case the same letter occurs in consecutive pairs presented to you. You may find a blind adherence to this rule, if you should carelessly get "reversed," leading you clean out of the maze again. You will certainly have more poignant feelings as to the laws of use and of satisfaction in maze-running than you would have otherwise experienced.

An actual experiment on these lines, in which the run was shortened by making T the goal, gave the following "runs":

1. P N V L Z K G E Q B T   = 11 moves
2. P V Z F Z L Z F Z L Z F Z L Z K E B T = 19 „
3. P V Z F Z L Z F Z V N V L Z F Z V
   N V Z F Z V N P V Z F Z L Z F Z L Z
   K G E B T   = 40 „
4. P N P N V L Z F K E B T   = 12 „
5. P N P V Z F K E B T   = 10 „

[1] Modified from Peterson, *Journ. Exp. Psychol.*, 1920, iii, 257–280.
[2] It is probably best, unless he has very great patience, to shorten the maze by finishing the run at some earlier point, as in the example below.

INSTINCT, INTELLIGENCE AND CHARACTER

6. P V L Z K E B T	=	8 moves
7. P V L Z K E B T	=	8 ,,
8. P V Z K E B T	=	7 ,,
9. P V Z K E B T	=	7 ,,

This is typical in that blind alleys near the goal are rapidly eliminated. Note how soon the final run home of K E B T is acquired. It seems to show also the persistence of a bad habit (a reluctance to go into K), and there is a strong suggestion that after the third run a sudden "insight" occurred, after which learning was rapid.

In this experiment the subject has the advantage that each alley was uniquely designated by its letter: and therefore a good memory could enable him to say whether a certain situation had been experienced before. But when the rat runs its maze the alleys are all alike. It may observe minute differences: but this is unlikely, for all efforts to reduce any such fail to check its powers of learning. Suppose you try a mental maze again, being asked only "right or left" at each alternative, and being told whenever you enter a blind alley. This makes your knowledge that you have gone wrong at any point more immediate and definite. On the other hand you will be able on a second "run" to recognize where you have got to in the maze only by the sequence of previous right and left turns. You will indeed learn the maze as a pattern of right and left turns following one another. You may form rational rules, such as that if you get into a blind alley by a left turn, you had better make another left turn when you emerge. If you blunder once and get reversed, you will find such a rule leading you back steadily to the entrance, and you will have no letters to warn you that you are traversing familiar streets. However, it may occur to you that an *infallible* obedience to such a rule, which one might call a "general sense of progress," would do instead of a Law of Satisfaction and Dissatisfaction. Let us try another coin

MAZE EXPERIMENTS

experiment, only making the correct turn always on coming out of a blind alley. In an example with the same maze figured on page 58 I get:

P N V Z F K E Q B O T C X Y U S J H

Avoiding all return runs makes the success of the run assured in a fairly short time. But consideration will show that on the second run the Law of Use (whether frequency or recency be taken as most important) will simply cause a repetition of the identical run with all its blind alleys as on the first trial. A Law of Satisfaction and Dissatisfaction is still required to explain improvement.

The actual facts of maze learning by rats and other animals show that:

1. Learning takes place gradually as a rule, but cases are quoted where sudden improvements occur.
2. At first returns are just as frequent as forward movements, but they are rapidly eliminated, much more rapidly than the entering of blind alleys.
3. Blind alleys near the food box are eliminated more quickly than those near the entrance.[1]
4. Returns also persist longer near the entrance.
5. The distance penetrated into blind alleys decreases before the alley is eliminated.
6. Short blind alleys are more rapidly eliminated than are long.

As teachers we can learn that mere repetition is useless, there must be pleasure at success; that such satisfaction must not be too long delayed; that a single bad habit may hold up a whole learning process; and that there must be a general sense of progress.

The general conclusion which we seem able at this point

[1] This has been questioned and is not always found. See for example Warden, *Journ. Exp. Psychol.*, 1923, vi, 192-210. But in Warden's maze the blind alleys were different in other respects; and he does not seem to have answered Peterson's 1920 paper, which indeed he does not, I think, refer to.

INSTINCT, INTELLIGENCE AND CHARACTER

to draw from all this is, that the Laws of Frequency and Recency do not appear to explain learning in the sense of acquiring a concatenation of responses (for they would perpetuate errors) and that some selective influence must be at work. That selective influence appears to be the satisfaction or dissatisfaction felt at this or that result of a response. What then, we may well ask, is this satisfaction or dissatisfaction which thus plays the part of the fates, or of the god of progress ? Selection in the racial group of individuals was made by the environment. What is this which makes a selection among the responses of an individual ?

FOOTNOTE, 1931.—Professor C. J. Warden, who is an authority on maze experiments and is referred to on the preceding page, has, in an interesting exchange of letters, expressed disagreement with this chapter. He considers that in most experiments the different blind alleys are widely different in difficulty, even in mazes which seem to be constructed along highly homogeneous lines, and that these differences in difficulty have so complicated the issue as to make most experiments inconclusive. From his own work he inclines to the belief that the primacy-recency order of elimination of blind-alleys holds (see Warden, *Journ. Exp. Psychol.*, 1924, an article which had not appeared when this book went to press). The interested reader should follow the controversy by turning up in the *Psychol. Bulletin* the articles reviewing maze experiments, as e.g. in August 1927, xxiv (8), 453, and then consulting the more important original papers.

CHAPTER VIII

THE NATURE OF SATISFACTION AND DISSATISFACTION

THE obvious first step in endeavouring to answer such a question is to go over in one's mind situations which bring satisfaction or dissatisfaction, and it will then be agreed, I think, by everyone, that these situations are such as permit expression of some response which is either instinctive or habitual: and if the latter, then it can usually be seen that the habit has grown out of an instinct, by its sublimation, diversion, or perversion. The rat in the maze was in a state of hunger. The acts of eating are the natural response; and the food box, by giving them possibility of expression, brought satisfaction. The state of hunger causes various changes in neurones and hormones[1] which make a state of readiness for food. Or if you like, the state of hunger *is* that state of readiness. The actual translation into fact of these responses which are so ready to happen brings satisfaction.

This is, more or less, Thorndike's Law of Readiness. The feeling of satisfaction itself, however, is a state of consciousness, *sui generis*, which occurs when the organism is given opportunity to carry out responses which it is ready to carry out: dissatisfaction, one which occurs when such responses are prevented, or when unready responses are compulsorily performed.

Satisfaction and dissatisfaction, then, are the result of the interaction between the situation and response on the

[1] See below.

one hand, and the inner set or attitude on the other. These inner attitudes are, in the naïve animal, of instinctive origin: hunger, thirst, lust for the opposite sex, desire to be with other members of the species, anger at opposition, desire for recognition and homage, fear. The inner drives which have been commonly used in psychological experiments on animals have been hunger, desire to be with others of the same species, and pain. It may be presumed that other inner desires would give results of a similar kind, but this has not been widely put to the test. With humans more complex motives have been employed.

It may be pointed out in passing that to call this hypothesis—that satisfaction and dissatisfaction select among our responses—the " pleasure-pain " theory is hardly correct: for dissatisfaction may be produced by a situation of which pain in the proper sense forms no part, while pain may be present in a satisfying situation.

Those things are satisfying, then, which, in another psychological language, permit instincts or habits, once aroused, to run their course. Both instincts and habits fall into chains of situations, the response to one situation forming the incitement to the next response. One thing leads on to another, as we say. And it is satisfying to follow on, dissatisfying to check when in full cry.

Thorndike's way of looking at this is, that a situation not only causes certain neurones to act, but puts other neurones in readiness to act. It is perhaps pedantic, but it is not absurd to ask just how neurones are put in readiness to act. Does some message flash along the neurones telling them that they are presently going to be asked to transmit a message? That would be to assume that there are two kinds of messages which can pass along neurones, one a " get ready " signal, the other an " action " signal. The difficulty, it will be seen, is to know how the communication system can communicate ahead of its own reactions: and especially this is a difficulty if one accepts the doctrine,

SATISFACTION AND DISSATISFACTION

for which there is a considerable amount of experimental evidence, that the reaction of a neurone is an " all-or-none " reaction, so that it either goes off for all it is worth, or not at all.

But this difficulty, which is perhaps of my own making and possibly would not have occurred to my reader, is not necessarily insurmountable, though I think it is serious. It arises mainly from thinking of the neurones which act in a chain-instinct, or in a chain-habit, as lying end to end, like the different sections of the telegraph wire from London to Edinburgh. Then, indeed, it would be difficult to see how, a message being started at London, any instructions to get ready for it could get ahead of the message itself. But if we think of a complex of neurones, instead of a linear chain, then it becomes easier. We might, for example, think of action to be taken by persons in different towns in succession. The individuals in Norwich might well be warned and assembled in their proper places ready for action, and the telegraph operators concerned with communication between London and Norwich might be warned to be in their places, ready for the completion of some action at Plymouth which was to give the cue to Norwich. In such a way are revolutions, or campaigns, or business operations planned, without any need to use any quicker method of communication than the telegraph itself.

But can, then, a neurone carry different messages, as a telegraph wire can ? No, almost certainly not. The analogy with a telegraph or telephone system breaks down at this point. Instead of the different messages which one telegraph wire can carry, we have in the neurone system different combinations of neurones acting together. It is as though each subscriber to the telephone exchange could ring up but couldn't speak. When the subscriber owning a telephone rings up, the telephone girl at the central exchange sees a little lamp glow at his number on the switchboard, asks him what number he wants, and connects him accordingly. Instead of that, however, imagine that the telephone girl did not ask each subscriber with what number he wished to be connected, but instead looked at the whole switchboard, saw the pattern which the innumerable little lamps formed, and let this decide her as to what connections should then be made. *The whole pattern* of incoming nerve currents decides whither the excitement shall be diverted.

A naive reader again may not ask, but some other reader is sure to ask, who is the switchboard operator who makes the connections ? To her there is nothing equivalent in the neurone system, whatever there may be in a psychical account of the consciousness which accompanies the neurone action. Somehow the pattern of incoming nerve currents settles the " whither " itself. The end brushes of a neurone, and the synapses where these end brushes are entangled with those of other neurones, somehow not only are stimulated by a message having come along their own neurone, but are differently stimulated according to the pattern of surrounding stimulation in others. That is not really surprising when one considers the very extensive ramifications and complexities of many end brushes. The whole system is so very complex as to be beyond comparison with any mechanical means of communication, mechanical in the sense of man-made, artificial.

We are, let us remind ourselves, discussing the nature of satisfaction and dissatisfaction ; we have contemplated Thorndike's view that these consist in a consummation of neurone connections which are ready for action, or a denial of that consummation ; we have thought over some of the difficulties in the way of making a neurone picture corresponding to this idea ; and we return now to the possibility of the readiness for action, whether of the neurones or of the muscles and organs, being somehow otherwise controlled. On page 48 a hint was dropped that there exists in our own bodies not only a telephone or telegraph

SATISFACTION AND DISSATISFACTION

system, but also a postal system. That postal system is one which makes use of the blood circulation to carry round the body various drug-like chemicals which are produced by glands, and which exercise an important influence on the action, and on the readiness for action, of the different muscles, organs, and neurones themselves.

It is well known to everyone that what we eat and drink can have a considerable effect on what we want to do, and on how we do it. I am tired and depressed, and don't want to study. After a cup of coffee I feel quite different, and turn with interest to my work. I am nervous and worried about that after-dinner speech, but the dinner puts me all right. Indeed, if I have a glass of champagne I may become quite confident and want to speak several times. Drugs, whether taken as medicines or as bad habits, have an effect on our bodies and on our moods. We want to do different things when drugged, whether by bromide or cocaine or champagne or coffee or roast beef, from what we want when we are not drugged. We want to do different things at different times even if we do not take drugs : and the suggestion lies very near that, somehow, we are being drugged then, even although we do not take anything into the system from without. And so indeed it is. We are constantly being drugged by the products of our own glands, and the difference between a man who is depressed and one who is elated is not very dissimilar to the difference before and after taking a stimulating drug, say alcohol. "Intoxicated with delight" is rather more than a mere phrase.

The glands of the body, which produce the "drugs" of which we speak, are of two main kinds. The first are those which deliver their secretions along tubes or ducts to just the places where they are wanted. They are mostly connected with the alimentary canal, and serve the processes of digestion and assimilation. Such are the salivary glands of the mouth, the glands of the stomach, and the

INSTINCT, INTELLIGENCE AND CHARACTER

pancreas, which pours its juices into the small intestine, as does also the liver. All these glands, perhaps, and certainly the liver, have functions wider than that of merely supplying digestive juices, but this wider function can best be described and studied in the other class of glands, those which have no ducts, but whose products simply pass directly through cell walls into the blood circulation. Among these are, for example, the thyroid and the parathyroid glands on the sides of the neck, the supra-renal glands just above the kidneys, the pituitary gland, and the pineal gland. Each of these is secreting its special product and turning it into the blood-stream. The rate of production of each secretion varies from time to time, so that now there is more of this, now more of that. These changes may be gradual, and take place over long years, as when the sex glands gradually come to maturity, or they may be quicker, even very sudden. When something startles us and gives us a really fundamental fright, these glands change in their action, some speeding up, others ceasing to function. Different changes occur when we are angry, or when we see someone whom we love. The different composition of the blood is felt in all kinds of organs all over the body : it so affects them that there are changes in their readiness for action. Some arteries are dilated—in anger those going to the muscles of the limbs—some are contracted—in the same case, those feeding the organs of digestion. An excess of one *hormone* (as these secretions are called) will make the whole nervous system excitable and easily irritated. Another soothes and composes. What we want to do is in some way dependent upon these hormones. What will give us satisfaction depends on them in some way.

This method of communicating throughout the body by means of the blood-stream may perhaps be illustrated by an addition to our analogy of the telephone system. Suppose, instead of calling up all the other subscribers in

SATISFACTION AND DISSATISFACTION

order to incite them to a certain action, one subscriber just telephoned to the waterworks and had a drug put in the water. It would reach all the subscribers, and when they drank from their water supply the drug would do the necessary inciting—or it might be, soothing.

You will notice that the subscriber who originated the action did use the telephone system a little. And so it also is in the human body. The eye sees an armed enemy. The nervous system carries messages to the adrenal glands, they pour adrenin into the blood, and it courses round the body, producing certain effects. The analogy with the water supply would be closer if in that case some of the townspeople were influenced in one way by the drug, others in another way, and a third section were unaffected: as might be, supposing the drug were, say, whisky. The teetotallers would act in one way, bibulous people in another. Adrenin, for example, as a larger amount than usual courses round the blood, has the effect of stimulating those parts of our organism which are likely to have heavy demands made upon them in vigorous muscular action (such as a fight with another man), and of putting comparatively out of action those parts which are for the moment useless in a fight, such as the digestive organs.

We see, then, that the whole man is "integrated," is caused to act as one unit, by this interlocking of the glandular system with the nervous system on one hand and with a large number of organs on the other. Hardly ever, or perhaps never, can any isolated stimulus influence just one isolated part of the body. By means of the nervous system and its ally, the gland system, a response is called forth in practically every part, though in the case of the simple reflexes and the best established simple motor habits the localization of the effect may be fairly complete.

On the whole, then, that readiness for action which undoubtedly occurs in our neurones, when the first of a chain of situations is encountered, may at least in part be due to

INSTINCT, INTELLIGENCE AND CHARACTER

hormonic action. For the rest, especially in chains of purely motor responses, accompanied by little or no feeling, we may perhaps picture the state of chemical tension at certain synapses being changed by the particular pattern of neurone activity which has just recently occupied neighbouring synapses, or indeed some of the same synapses, just as railway points may be imagined to be set in a certain way because trains in such and such a direction had recently passed. Indeed, we know that in complicated systems of points at large crossings there are interlocking devices which determine within limits what levers the signalman must next operate. Something or other, anyhow, causes a readiness for action, to "satisfy" which is "satisfactory."

As we advance in life, the situations which bring us satisfaction or dissatisfaction change. Children are bored by a grown-up party, grown-ups are irritated by childish amusements—unless they are in childish mood or are the parents of the children. Boys talk of their patrol and the week-end camp; young men, of girls and games; men, of politics or business. Partly, these changing satisfactions are due to ripening instincts, as the sex instinct. Partly, perhaps, they may be due to other instincts waning and losing strength. But also they are due to the steady growth of habits, to increase in knowledge, and to the building up of sentiments. These different points must each in its place engage our attention.

In part, at least, the changes in what we like or dislike as we grow older arise from instinctive sources. The great changes in the instincts occur at the period of adolescence, and are indubitable. But before then, many have thought to see different instinctive likings emerging at different ages, and have endeavoured so to arrange school education as to fit in with these observations.

One fairly clear case of such emergence of instinctive desires seems to me to be the tendency which appears in boys at six or seven to form gangs and play fighting games.

SATISFACTION AND DISSATISFACTION

It is most often, perhaps, later than seven, but it is almost always seen by nine. The boy of this age adores Indians and pirates, he is a keen Wolf Cub and, later, Boy Scout. The Boy Scout Movement, indeed, seems almost to make concrete the set of instincts of which I am speaking. They seem to mark the change from infancy to boyhood. The gang spirit passes over into the team spirit which makes the playing of *team* games, like football, a potent appeal at about twelve.

Whether with girls there is anything similar to this it is difficult to say. But from the success of the Girl Guide Movement it seems probable that there is.

It would undoubtedly be a very great aid to the teacher if other activities could be assigned even approximate dates of appearance, but in truth this is a very difficult task. And in so far as it can be attempted, one feels strongly that in many cases it is the ripening of intelligence rather than the ripening of instincts which is the reason of the order of appearance of these activities. Babbling precedes scribbling, drawing precedes writing; playing with scooters, skating on roller-skates, riding a bicycle, riding a motor-bicycle, come in that order, perhaps (but not always); collecting things does seem to set in at about eight to ten; a liking for historical stories is certainly earlier than a liking for mathematics, even for mathematics of simple puzzles forming playthings; and so on. How much of this is really due to the ripening of instincts and how much to the fashion of the suburb or school in which the child finds himself, it is difficult to say, nor does it really matter a great deal to the teacher. What does matter is that the teacher should carefully observe what things in point of fact do most interest her class, and each one of her class, at the present moment, and should modify what she requires of them accordingly, using these things as incentives, and teaching those matters which best fit in with the present desires and interests of the pupil. For these interests will in any case

INSTINCT, INTELLIGENCE AND CHARACTER

change, whether James is right or wrong in his theory of the transitoriness of instincts, will change if not for that reason, then for some reason connected with the growth of habits or the attraction of novelty or what not.

This law of the transitoriness of instincts to which we have just referred is that instincts arise, last for a short or a long time (more or less fixed for each instinct), and then wane and disappear unless, during their period of strength, they have been given opportunity to transmute themselves into habits. The famous instance is the "following" instinct of the chicken which causes it to follow its mother hen and to develop a habit of doing so which outlasts the instinct as instinct; a habit which persists, indeed, when the "following" instinct is replaced by a "fleeing" instinct which makes the chick run away from every animal except those to which it has formed the "following" habit. The proof is that in the absence of a hen the chick of the proper age will learn to follow a dog or a man, at a slightly later age will run in alarm from its own mother. Or if kept from all companionship of whatever sort for a suitable time, it will *never* develop the "following" habit, but will flee from anyone and everything.

By analogy we are warned to strike while the iron is hot in the case of our human pupils. And whether the analogy with the chicken's instincts be correct or not, there can be no harm in piling on the drawing practice, or the roller-skating, or the arithmetic, during the months or periods when the pupil is most in the mood for them, though that does not absolve the teacher from the duty of trying to direct those moods and interests, to invent ways of associating desirable acquirements with the main interest of the moment, and the like.

A theory of education which has been based upon the supposed fixity of sequence in the appearance of the instincts is that known as the Recapitulation Theory. This theory assumes that the order in which the instincts appear in the

SATISFACTION AND DISSATISFACTION

child is the same as the order in which they appear in the race. The child is supposed to climb up his own ancestral tree during his infancy and to pass in succession through a series of phases, each of which was once the end or stopping place and constituted, in some past epoch, the adult form. In each of these stages different things bring satisfaction or dissatisfaction.

The theory is formed by analogy with a similar hypothesis in the province of anatomy and physiology. A common animal in which this hypothesis appears to find a striking verification is the frog, which, living quite apart from its parents and independent of them, passes through the stages of a unicellular animal, a multicellular animal, a fish (tadpole) breathing in the water by means of external gills, a different kind of fish possessing internal gills, and finally the air-breathing frog with lungs. Many other bodily changes, such as the absorption of the tail, accompany this metamorphosis, and it is very easy to imagine the animal stopping at any one of these stages in an earlier epoch, and in that stage developing sex organs and reproducing itself. This imagination is rendered easier and more concrete by the knowledge that other amphibious animals, somewhat resembling frogs, do to-day sometimes, or even normally, stop their development in a tadpole stage and become in that stage sexually mature. Such an animal can sometimes be accelerated in its progress, as in the case of a Mexican example[1] which only rarely proceeds to the air-breathing stage, but can be induced to do so by being fed with thyroid preparation.

This climbing up the ancestral tree, which can almost be said to be directly observable in the case of the frog, also occurs in a hidden manner in mammals. During the prenatal period, while still within the mother's body, the human child, for instance, shows certain slits in the region of the

---

[1] Axolotl. See Huxley and Hogben, *Proc. Roy. Soc. Lond.*, 1922, xciii B, 36, and Jensen, Laufberger, Marie von Chauvin, etc.

INSTINCT, INTELLIGENCE AND CHARACTER

neck which are taken to represent gills : and the short time during which this phenomenon lasts is taken to represent the long ages in which, æons ago, our ancestors were fish-like and breathed under water.[1]

It is by an intuitive leap that this not improbable hypothesis is extended into regions where its probability is much less. In man, the stages representing animal ancestry are all passed through before birth. The young baby is already a human being. The assumption is made, however, that he is passing through a stage representing a very early type of man, and that as he grows older he passes through stages corresponding with more and more modern and civilized periods in man's history. Consequently, the things which will bring him satisfaction at each stage will be those things which brought satisfaction to some type of primitive or savage man. He will be at one time a hunter and a nomad, leading (in his play) an independent existence in gangs or small packs like wolves (hence Baden Powell's Wolf Cubs—though presumably that name comes from Mowgli). The type of mental pabulum suitable to his mental development will therefore most readily be found by bringing him along the story of the ages, giving him the literature and history first of the very earliest known times, beginning with myths and passing through sagas to historical periods. As an educational practice, this plan or a modified form of it has justified itself by experience and needs no support

---

[1] From the writings of Mr. Julian Huxley I gather that often the organs which belong to one period or stage, and which disappear in the following stages (as the gills in the frog), do not disappear entirely and utterly but are cunningly utilized for new functions in the new animal. Thus, the gill slits of the human embryo become the para-thyroid glands of the adult man. If the Recapitulation Theory is also in any measure a correct account of the facts in the mental sphere, as it undoubtedly appears to be to some extent in the physical, then no doubt the natural way would be, not to repress the instincts and interests of one stage when another stage is formed, but to modify and redirect them to fulfil a new purpose. As the para-thyroids (essential to man) grow out of the now useless gills, so out of the gang spirit, the tribal urge, in boys may grow a larger patriotism and a feeling of identity not merely with a little gang but with humanity. Out of the excessive sex instincts of the adolescent may grow knighthood, poetry, art, religion.

SATISFACTION AND DISSATISFACTION

from a recapitulation theory. But its success may be taken as some support of that theory.

There seems to be no doubt that boys do have the Boy Scout instincts strongly developed. And that is about all that direct observation shows in favour of the Recapitulation Theory. On the other hand, it seems probable enough from analogy, indeed once the facts of anatomical recapitulation become realized, the mind almost inevitably passes on to a similar assumption in the province of the instincts. It has been urged against recapitulation, by Thorndike, that the sex impulses, which must have come very early in the race, come very late in the individual. This is, perhaps, hardly a fair objection. The sex impulses occupy a rather special position in the theory, for the steps of development all lead up to the sexually mature form. It is as though indeed the whole matter were a postponement of sex to a later and later stage, as though sex development stopped the cycle.[1] And so the present late stage of sex development is quite in accord with previous phases. Possibly, too, the Freudian conception of sex having its roots away back in infancy is not without some bearing on this.

A more serious objection could, I think, be based on what was discussed under the heading of play. According to the suggestions there advanced, the higher animals differ from those lower in the scale by reason of their less fixed instincts, in place of which they have vaguer instinctive tendencies which are moulded during an educative period whose natural method is the method of play. In their development out of lower animals, therefore, these higher animals have not simply added new instincts to a previous list, they have totally recast those previous instincts; what they have added is not merely additive, it is revolutionary, and so, however tempting it may be, the Recapitulation Theory, in its crude form, must be rejected. There can be nothing

[1] If Axolotl (see page 75) becomes sexually mature in the water-breathing form, the time necessary to produce metamorphosis to the land form (by feeding with thyroid) is increased by 25 to 50 per cent.

INSTINCT, INTELLIGENCE AND CHARACTER

but good in observing and employing any instinctive likes which emerge, at the right time ; but the important thing about childhood is that it is a period when these vague instincts, much more indefinite than a recapitulation theory would suggest, are modified by the action of the learning process.

CHAPTER IX

THE ASCENT FROM INSTINCT TO INTELLIGENCE

(a) IMAGERY.

An animal which has only one response to a given situation, and inevitably makes this response, is not said to be intelligent, but to be a creature of blind instinct. It survives because this response is, in the majority of instances, the suitable response. It sees only the one point in the situation, neglecting all minor shades of difference, and so it is very inadaptable. Moreover, its own inner life is very simple, for it always has the same attitude or set, or if it has different attitudes, the changes are of a crude kind such as hunger, or the mating instinct, can produce. Such an animal on any occasion would try the same response again and again in spite of failure.

An animal with many responses to a given situation would seem more intelligent. It would try a and fail; then b and fail; then c and d and finally succeed. More accurately, it responds to the *new* situation caused by the failure of a, the failure of b, and so on. Or we may put it that its inner set is readily modified by its recent experiences. It might return to a and try it again later, or even quite soon. Very slight differences in the environment or in the set of the organism might alter the order in which different individuals tried their repertory of responses. We should call such conduct "trial and error," and deny to it any *high* degree of intelligence. It is, however, clearly a step higher than the conduct of the animal with one unvarying and inevitable response. That animal did not learn by experience at all.

It seemed to have no memory. This animal does profit by experience, it " remembers " its failure long enough to avoid making the same response a few seconds later. Moreover, if this situation is presented repeatedly to the animal, it comes to omit the responses a, b, and c, and to make the response d without any trials. From its repertory, satisfaction or the reward of success has selected that which succeeds. It is capable of learning. The action of such an animal can be conceivably explained entirely by a comparatively brief persistence of the dissatisfaction of failure, causing it to respond by b when a has failed, and by a comparatively mild stamping-in effect of satisfaction; comparatively mild, for it learns but slowly. Such an animal—a chicken for instance—has to learn each separate simple task separately. It can learn a number of different mazes, or how to escape from confinement in a number of different boxes, now by walking up an incline, now by fluttering over a partition wall and going through a tunnel; but it learns each of these slowly and separately. The most it will do in the way of any improvement is that it may begin to attend, more carefully than would a naïve animal, to certain parts of the gross situation; as Thorndike's cats, which had learned to escape from a number of problem boxes by turning buttons, tweaking pieces of wood, or pulling strings, became more attentive to such little bits of the cage when placed in a new problem box, exhibiting what Thorndike calls the law of piecemeal activity, or the enhanced potency of certain bits of the situation. It is the beginning of analysis.

Let us, however, go a step farther. We have considered the animal which had but one response to a situation, the automaton. Next we pictured the animal with a multiplicity of responses which it tries in aimless sequence until success occurs, showing the typical picture of animal trial and error. An animal, however, which had some means of anticipating the success or failure of each response without completely

THE ASCENT: IMAGERY

carrying it out, would save a lot of time and would do its trial and error by proxy, as it were. The most obvious source of such anticipation is in imagery of various kinds. Instead of carrying out the response, the animal has an image of itself doing so, and of the accompanying success or failure. Probably at first such images can replace only part of the response, the later part of the chain. It is by the failure of a chain of events to follow the accustomed order, indeed, that images first probably occur, as Dr. James Ward has urged. A baby, for example, has come to welcome a chain of events which culminate in some satisfaction, as the sound of an approaching footstep, the opening and closing of the nursery door, the sound of its mother's voice, the embrace which follows, and the culminating pleasure of being nursed and fed. As it begins this chain of experiences, anticipatory excitements occur in the neurones which are to be concerned in the later links of the chain. They are very ready to explode, and if, on one occasion, the familiar chain of situations is broken (say the mother is called away just as she approaches) then some of the "ready" neurones may go off, enough of them to arouse an "image" of the mother's voice or her appearance; much as we take two pulls to a rifle and may take the second even when the expected target fails to appear.

If images can thus arise and carry out chains of response even when the external stimuli cease, then such imaging may take the place of actual response in future situations where various responses are possible. I want to build a picnic fire. I do not really build it here, there, and everywhere until I find a place which is sheltered, yet with enough air, suitable for sitting round, etc., etc. I do so only in imagination; and, practically without trial, I reject a large number of possible (or rather impossible) places. I picture, however, my fire built in the remaining more practicable positions. I imagine that stone placed across the corner of these walls. But I foresee, in imagination, that it will be uncomfortable sitting among these nettles. Not everything is imagination. I stoop down to the stone, I walk towards a second possible place, I move my head from side to side seeking and trying other places. There is plenty of trial and rejection. There may even be fires actually begun and rejected only after failure. But much of the trial is trial in imagination only, image-experimenting. This form of experimenting is undoubtedly rare among animals, and unknown among lower animals. But imagery, which makes it possible, is almost certainly found in some monkeys, in some raccoons, and probably in other animals. In man, imagery is rich and abundant, at any rate in children and in untutored minds. In minds more accustomed to what is called abstract thinking, the imagery is less obvious, but is probably in great measure still present, though now it has become imagery of words and symbols. For the present, however, let us make a short study of concrete imagery, of images which are like the real things, though, being less vivid and unaccompanied by certain expected concomitants, they are not mistaken for the real things.

Images can be experienced in terms of each of the senses ; we can not only see with the mind's eye, we can hear, feel, smell, taste, etc., in an inner way equally well—at least equally well is true of some people. Read through the following passage in a quiet room, closing the eyes from time to time to assist in visualizing, and keeping on the alert for any actual images of smell or taste or motion :

> The scene, as I remember it, had a magical charm. On the left, by the side of the lane, rose a crazy footpath of boards and posts with a wooden handrail, and a sluice or two below. Beyond, the deep millpool slept, dark and still, all fringed with trees. On the right the stream flowed off among the meadows, disappearing into an arch of greenery. On the bank stood the shuttered, humming mill, the water wheel splashing and thundering, like a prisoned giant, in a pent house of its own. It was a fearful joy to look in and see it rise dripping, huge and black, with the fresh smell of the river water all about it (BENSON, *The House of Quiet*).

THE ASCENT: IMAGERY

With what degree of clearness can you picture this scene ? Is it as vivid as a painting ? Has it colour, do you see the arch of greenery *green* ? Have you an image of the fresh smell of the river water ? Does any image, or as some would say, any reproduction, of the emotion of fearful joy arise in you ? Can you hear the humming mill and the splashing wheel, and how do those auditory images compare with your visual images for vividness ? Some people, at any rate when grown up, have only the one kind of imagery and lack the other, or think they do. Such a one would Hilaire Belloc appear to be, who wrote this next extract :

> As I thought this kind of thing and still drank up that port, the woods that overhang the reaches of my river came back to me so clearly that for the sake of them, and to enjoy their beauty, I put my hand in front of my eyes, and I saw with every delicate appeal that one's own woods can offer, the steep bank over Stoke, the valley, the high ridge which hides a man from Arundel, and Arun turning and hurrying below. I smelt the tide.
>
> Not ever, in a better time, when I had seen it of reality and before my own eyes living, had that good picture stood so plain ; and even the colours of it were more vivid than they commonly are in our English air ; but because it was a vision there was no sound, nor could I even hear the rustling of the leaves, though I saw the breeze gusty on the water-meadow banks, and ruffling up a force against the stream (*The Four Men : a Walk through Sussex*).

Now I have no greater difficulty in hearing the rustling of the leaves than in smelling the tide. But no doubt Mr. Belloc is correct when he describes the absence of such auditory imagery in his own case. Here is another paragraph in which the reader will have opportunity of detecting in himself several kinds of imagery, including kinæsthetic imagery, or imagery of muscle movement ; such as you may perhaps have if you think of a company of soldiers marching along, or of waltzing, or playing the piano, or walking upstairs—especially if you think of the occasion in the dark when you step on to a non-existent top step. Does the memory of that jar not consist partly in a recon-

INSTINCT, INTELLIGENCE AND CHARACTER

stitution of the feel of muscular jerk ? Here is the paragraph in question :

> In the early morning the sky was grey and the atmosphere oppressive. But both lightened towards noon, and we were reassured. The tent could be pitched, and tea be served outside upon the lawn, and we could listen, with indolent enjoyment, to the remarks made by the drake in his deep *sotto voce* bass to an intrusive woodpigeon sharing uninvited his meal. In the meadow at the far end of the garden men were cutting the grass ; the ear is not gladdened in this rapid age by the soft sound of scythes sweeping through the stalks, and the ring of blades on the hone ; but the whirr of the machine that has displaced the rhythmically swaying mower is not unmusical, and patient horses still hold this field of labour against petrol-driven engines. So the beautiful fragrance of new-mown grass was borne untainted down the garden, and lent a new fragrance to the heaped dish of raspberries and currants just gathered (*The Lowly Estate*, by CRANSTOUN METCALFE).

In this quotation visual, auditory, olfactory, gustatory, and kinæsthetic imagery are all possible—sight, hearing, smell, taste, and the muscles. To me, at least, the thought of the rhythmically swaying mower is, in part, a kinæsthetic image of swaying as though I were mowing, and especially I feel my left foot take the short stamping step forward at the end of the swing. If it be correct that the left foot moves just in that way at that point, then my muscles have remembered it, it has been stored up in the neurone pattern which actuates them, for it returned as a kinæsthetic image before I was aware of it in any other way.

One can also have images of touch—think of the feel of velvet, or of emery paper, or of soap—and of the senses of warmth and cold. The suggestion which led us to this examination of imagery was that an animal, whose progress from crude animal reactions up to the rational actions of human beings we are considering, takes a step forward when he begins to make his trials and errors in terms of imagery instead of actual physical response. The thought naturally occurs to one, To what extent do animals differ from human beings in their possession of imagery ?

THE ASCENT: IMAGERY

Any answer to this question runs the grave risk of being an argument in a circle. For we cannot, of course, have any actual experience of animal imagery, or, for that matter, of human imagery other than our own. And so we have to conclude from animals' behaviour whether they possess imagery, and then we are going to explain their behaviour by means of imagery, a dangerous circle. Yet it may be worth while to record one or two instances where psychologists of repute have believed that imagery was involved.

Dr. R. M. Yerkes, for example, found such evidence, to his mind, in the behaviour of the monkey, Skirrl, which he used in some of his Californian experiments. In these, the animal had the choice of more than one door. If the correct choice was made, Skirrl was rewarded by a banana after passing through a short passage. If the wrong one, then on entering the passageway the monkey found doors at both ends closed, and was confined for a short time before the door behind him was opened and he was free to choose again. On one occasion Skirrl made a tremendous racket in the passage in which he was confined, and showed so much excitement and disturbance that the experiments had to be discontinued for some days: and it was found that projecting nails had been left in the floor of that passage, one of which had doubtless hurt Skirrl. Many days later, when again in the full swing of experimenting, it happened that the locks of the door closing behind Skirrl grated rather noisily. He acted as he had when hurt, and when released rushed out, *sat down, and examined his foot*. As I said, Dr. Yerkes thought this behaviour strong evidence of imagery.

Dr. W. S. Hunter's experiments[1] on rats, dogs, raccoons and children are suggestive in this connection. In each case—though the dimensions and arrangements of the apparatus differed—the subject had the choice of three doors, one of which led to food. (For the children the plan was to have three bell-pushes, one of which sounded a

[1] Behavior Monographs, 1913.

INSTINCT, INTELLIGENCE AND CHARACTER

buzzer and resulted in "candy.") Above each door was an electric bulb, and the bulb above the correct door was turned on. The animals soon learned to go to whichever door was lighted. Then, in later experiments, the light was turned off before they got to the door, and, ultimately, was extinguished before the glass partition which restrained them was raised. The object was to see how many seconds could be allowed to elapse between showing the light and releasing the animals, without reducing the accuracy of their response. There was considerable individual variation, but the best performances were approximately: rat 10 seconds, dog 5 minutes, raccoon 25 seconds, child of 6 years 35 minutes. The rats and the dogs, however, were only able to make the correct response by facing the light when it was turned on and remaining in that position during the absence of the light until released. They failed if they moved. In their case, therefore, there is in these experiments no evidence of images being retained and recalled to guide delayed action: The raccoons, however (for a few seconds up to 25), and the children (for several minutes) were able to respond accurately without any such device of remaining in a constant attitude. In their case, Dr. Hunter had no doubt of the operation of some intra-organic factor which represented the absent light, in the sense of guiding the delayed response. It is true that Dr. Hunter does not think that this representative was necessarily an image; he develops a theory of "sensory thought" which is not easy to explain or understand. But the more obvious explanation lies in imagery.

Again, imagery is not proved, but is strongly suggested by Dr. L. W. Sackett's Canada porcupine which, opening a problem box by depressing a lever, failed on one occasion to find its usual food on emerging from the box, whereupon it re-entered the box and gave the lever a second push down.[1] But this ought probably to be considered in con-

[1] Behavior Monographs, No. 2.

THE ASCENT: IMAGERY

nection with the readiness of animals which have learned problem boxes to enter them voluntarily. Dr. Sackett does not, I think, profess that imagery played a part.

The oft-quoted case of Dr. Washburn's cat, however, is one in which the psychologist on the spot diagnosed imagery.[1] It started to run upstairs to its nest of kittens, but stopped half-way, and turning went to the new position in the cellar to which it had transferred them on the previous day.

We may perhaps then suppose that animals have the beginnings of imagery, and that this is a first step in the direction of that kind of behaviour which in man we call reasoning. The anticipatory readiness of the next-to-act neurones is increased to such a pitch that their incongruity with the external situation is realized. The incoming train has automatically set the points ahead at a number of crossings, and what it would do if it were diverted this way or that can already be seen.

It is of great interest to see the way in which imagery gradually comes into the human solving of problems as we make them more and more like problems in reasoning. Take first a maze drawn on paper such as that on page 58. If an adult is asked to draw a pencil mark from the entrance by the shortest path through the alleyways to the food box, he does not make excursions with his pencil into any blind alleys unless he is either careless or unintelligent. He makes the entrance into the blind alleys by proxy, in this case by actual eye movements. There is trial and error, but it is trial by proxy, though imagery hardly yet plays much part.

Ask an adult to mark the left-hand figure in the diagram, on page 88, so as to show how it should be cut to give the pieces on the right (I.E.R. Tests, Teachers College, Columbia

---

[1] *The Animal Mind*, New York, 1908. "Idea" is the word used by Dr. Washburn, but from the title of the chapter and from the context I take it that imagery is implied. And she adds, "Errors of interpretation are possible at every turn."

INSTINCT, INTELLIGENCE AND CHARACTER

University, New York). There is here undoubtedly trial and error by imagery. There is also a strong temptation to make actual trials: but the more intelligent refrain from these until imaged trials have been made. Do you consider that there is anything else present beyond such trials? Suppose someone says; "But it can't be done, there are only three corners," is that any other kind of reasoning, or has such a person an image of the three angles put together, and the fourth angle missing? Such an image would be an incorrect image, but images can be incorrect and yet be images and trials. That only shows the importance of actual experiments to check the imaginary experiments. Then suppose anyone who has made the above remark goes on in this

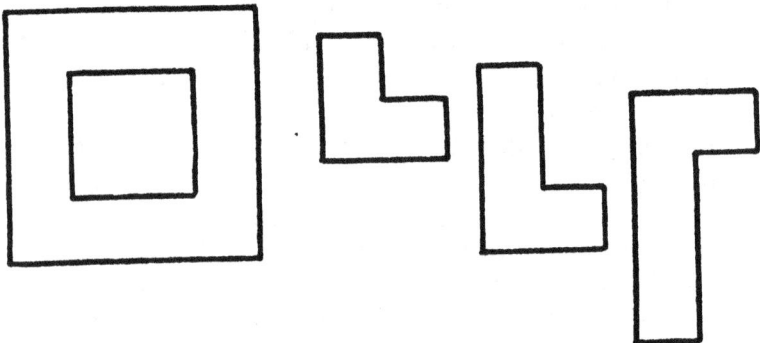

fashion, saying, "Well, the fourth corner must be one of the butt ends." Is this something new? Or an image of a special kind of cut across the hollow square just near a corner? We are getting perilously near a still higher type of thought, in which symbols are used, to which we shall come later.

Try finally this really difficult feat. Imagine a cube, which is going to be cut in two by a straight saw cut. The saw-cut section, the raw face of the cut, can clearly be of various shapes, as square, or triangular (if a corner were cut off). How would you cut the cube so that the section

THE ASCENT : IMAGERY

may be a perfect plane hexagon ? Here is certainly trial and error by images. You must not draw anything, nor look at cubical or nearly cubical objects while thinking it out. Most of those who succeed in this test agree that visual imagery trials are not all that they do. Not everything is plain "trial and error." They "reason" that as they want a six-sided figure they must cut all six faces of the cube. A kind of principle of symmetry teaches them that the edge of the section must lie similarly in each face. And so they come to the correct conclusion that each square face of the cube must be cut along a line joining obliquely the mid-points of adjacent sides. They may come to this conclusion without being able to *see* the resulting cut. This sort of "reasoning" is common in the mathematics, and my own opinion is that despite its new appearance it is really still trial and error by proxy. But in it, use is made to a great extent of symbols, and higher habits of mind are employed which have long ceased to be active thought, and have become habitual responses. Yet there are grave difficulties in the way of such explanation, which we must leave for the present, to return to them later. Meanwhile, we may turn for relief to other aspects of the study of imagery, in teaching, in the use of language, and even in parlour tricks.

CHAPTER X

VARIOUS USES OF VISUAL IMAGERY

PERHAPS the chief importance of imagery in human thinking is that emphasized in the previous chapter, of raising behaviour in the face of a problem above the level of animal trial and error. But once that is granted, other points of view may be used. There are higher levels yet of reasoning, to which we shall come in due course, where imagery either is not used at all (as some aver) or is imagery of a symbolic kind. Imagery of the kind to be considered in the present section, that is imagery of real warm-coloured life as it actually occurs, is of great value as a check upon this more abstract thinking, just as actual concrete experiment is essential as a check upon imagery. And imagery, " a gift as great as can be possessed by a disembodied spirit," brings a wealth of pleasure with it. Let us turn first to the pleasure which a habit of imaging brings into the words of our everyday vocabulary. Nearly every word we use imprisons a picture, which imagery can release. It is indeed curious how we can come to disregard the picture even when it is not in any way concealed : as in words like cupboard, or forecastle, or waistcoat, or holiday, or clerestory—in which last case, however, the spelling, for those who only know the word by sight, is of course a hindrance. In our English language, where so many of the roots come from Latin and Greek and do not, therefore, carry a homely meaning with them, a great deal of loose usage can occur, and vividness of speech and of comprehension can be largely lost, if we do not at times let our minds dwell on the original picture which the words convey. *Consideration*, a consulting of the stars ; *disaster*, when the stars in their courses fight against us ;

VARIOUS USES OF VISUAL IMAGERY

mercurial, jovial, saturnine, martial; all these words can call up pictures of the astrologer practising his art, or the worshippers of the heavens adoring and fearing the mystery of the spheres. *Starboard* brings me a picture of a viking ship with Witta and his heathens, Witta at the *steerboard*, the right-hand gunwale near the stern, threddling the longship through the seas. *Companion* is the better word if it brings up a picture of two breaking *bread together*, sitting perchance on some high pass and looking down into the lowlands, as one looks from Carter Bar into Scotland. A *squatter* entering into *possession* of his land by *sitting down* upon it; a *bursar* equipped with his *purse*; a *pocket* as a little *poke*; a *candidate* standing at the altar dressed in *white*; these are pictures which add to the appeal of the words, and often lead to an association very much to the point. There is no great fear that an over-cultivation of such imagery would lead to a narrowness of usage—not many are so able to see the pictures their words paint as to be hindered in their thought. Most of us only too soon come to use the words as counters without concrete imagery, a tendency which brings to some the power of generalizing and abstract thinking, but which brings to a greater number only verbosity and parrot-pattering fluency.

Another occasion on which the habit of visualizing can be advantageous is when we have to read aloud. Thus the best advice I have ever known, to assist one in holding one's audience, is this which I read long ago, in a most useful booklet on clear speaking and good reading.[1] "*See the scenes as you read the words. Look at them intently in your own mental vision, and pause at each completed picture.*" I recall the illustration used in the book, a very telling one— one of the parables. "The seed . . . is the word of God, . . . Those by the wayside . . . are they that hear; . . .

---

[1] I was unable, as I wrote this, to recall the name of the author, and spent a few minutes in putting down what passed through my mind in the attempt to do so. See page 164 ahead, where the reason why I still refrain giving the name will become clear—it would betray to some the real names there disguised.

INSTINCT, INTELLIGENCE AND CHARACTER

then cometh the devil . . . and taketh away the word out of their hearts."

Children, too, love to close their eyes during a lesson and see pictures. They like to try to draw scenes described from a pupil's imagery, and the pupil has his descriptive powers much improved by the practice, and by the contrasts between his imagery and the drawings which, he has to admit, fit his inaccurate words. And his fellow-pupils criticize looseness in his telling.[1]

Visualizing is a great help in studying a foreign language. " We have a clearer notion of *surplomber* when we reflect that it comes from *sur* = over and *plomb* = lead, and when *des rochers qui surplombent* call up the picture of crags overhanging so much that a *leadline* dropped over the topmost ledge would fall clear of the sides."

" If what is described in the French is really *visualized*, words will rarely fail the translator to express in English the mental picture thus clearly formed . . . Anyone who reads translations written by examination candidates soon perceives that the chief source of weakness is the habit of mentally registering one English word against each French word learned "—instead of visualizing the things, that is, "A single example will illustrate the point. In a passage recently set for translation, there occurred the phrase ' dans la petite maison du garde-chasse.' It was quite an exception to find in the translations offered the natural rendering, namely ' in the gamekeeper's cottage.' Most candidates wrote ' in the gamekeeper's little house,' some even ' in the little house of the gamekeeper.' Yet it is improbable that any one of these candidates would have spoken of a ' little house ' in an English essay in which the same idea had to be expressed." [2] Improbable that they would have said " little house " had they *seen* it, either actually or in the mind's eye.

[1] *The Child Vision.* Dorothy T. Owen, Longmans, Green.
[2] *Translation from French*, Ritchie and Moore, Camb. Univ. Press, 1919.

VARIOUS USES OF VISUAL IMAGERY

Or, for an example of how the power of visualizing can light up a lesson in the classics, turn to Chapter VII of Benson's *House of Quiet*, and read his memory of the vision which came to him "in a dusty classroom, the gas flaring, the lesson proceeding slowly and wearily, with a thin trickle of exposition from the desk," a vision of that scene where Æneas comes on Andromache at her orisons in "a clearing in a wood of beeches"; who ends her burst of passionate grief with the question "Hector ubi est ?" A scene "so intensely real, so glowing, that I could see the pale-stemmed beeches; and below through a gap, low fantastic hills and a wan river winding in the plain. I could see the white set face of Æneas, the dark-eyed glance of the queen, the frightened silence of the worshippers."

Or turn to science. Nowhere perhaps is the use of visualization more obvious. It is true that Sir Francis Galton in a classical inquiry found that famous fellows of the Royal Society of London appeared to be lacking in, or to have lost, the power of visualizing, and relied more on abstract, symbolic, possibly quite imageless thought. But they had, even supposing there was not some error of misunderstanding between them and Sir Francis, arrived at that goal by paths denied to most; and it hardly is to be doubted that, could they have attained their power of abstraction without losing the faculty of vivid visualization, they would have been still greater than they were. Lord Kelvin at least is reported to have said that he could not understand a theory unless he could make a model of it. And Sir J. J. Thomson, himself a President of the Royal Society, writes in his preface to *Recent Researches in Electricity and Magnetism*: "The first chapter of this work contains an account of a method of regarding the electric field which is geometrical and physical rather than analytical. I have been induced to dwell on this point because I have found that students, especially those who commence the subject after a long course of mathematical studies, have a great tendency to regard the whole of Maxwell's theory as a matter of the solution of certain equations, and to dispense with any attempt to form for themselves a mental picture of the physical processes which accompany the phenomena they are investigating. . . . The physical method has all the advantages in vividness which arise from the use of concrete quantities instead of abstract symbols to represent the state of the electric field." And he devotes considerable time to the portrayal of Faraday's method of "tubes of force," which can readily be imagined in mental pictures, and which in Faraday's hands served to interpret all the laws of electrostatics.

Those who are strong in visualizing are not necessarily weak in other forms of imagery. But they have, it must be admitted, a trick of using visual imagery to tide them over difficult links in the chain of memory. Seeing the pictures, as a poem calls them up, is to me a great help in remembering the poem, and I find that the deliberate creation of some picture, even if it be irrelevant and grotesque, often serves to carry me over at that difficult passage from the end of one verse to the beginning of the next, where we are all rather more liable to miss the connection. For example, I taught myself at school Tennyson's ode to Vergil, which was given at length in the introduction to one of my school books.

> Roman Vergil, thou that singest
> Ilion's lofty temples clothed in fire,
> Ilion falling, Rome arising,
> Wars, and filial faith, and Dido's pyre.

Now how does the second verse commence ? Well, I see a good deal of imagery during the first verse, including not only pictures of Ilion aflame, but also a map of the Mediterranean, focused at Carthage : and at that last line I see Dido's pyre. It is in a courtyard of a castle, but I am aware, through the openings of the courtyard, of a wooded countryside, probably exceedingly unlike that which Dido

VARIOUS USES OF VISUAL IMAGERY

knew. And the picture of that landscape lets me know somehow that the next verse begins with the word Landscape.

> Landscape-lover, lord of language
> More than he that sang the Works and Days,
> All the chosen coin of fancy
> Flashing forth[1] from many a golden phrase.

And here it is the word "golden" which brings up a picture of a field of golden wheat.

> Thou that singest wheat and woodland,

and so on. The pictures carry me along, not infallibly, but better than anything else I know. And so I have formed the prejudice that associations in terms of visual images are more easily recalled than are others. No doubt, however, this is quite wrong for some, who recall by auditory images best, or by feeling the shape of the words in the mouth (kinæsthetic imagery). The important thing for a student of psychology is to become interested in his own imagery (or in its absence).

A last example of visual imagery will, however, I think, convince a large number, if they will try the experiment, that such imagery forms very easily recalled associations. The experiment in question is a "parlour trick" of the children's entertainment variety and is really very effective. The audience in turn say words to the experimenter, up to a total of one hundred even, and then on request the experimenter, who has memorized the words by this one repetition, gives any word asked for, as number 27, or number 43, and so on. This sounds startling, but is easily within the power of a majority of those who read this. I saw the device explained in an article by D. S. Hill in the *Psychological Bulletin* of 1918, and it forms one of the best illustrations I know of the kind of manœuvring of psychological powers

---

[1] So I remember it, but the only edition accessible to me says *out*.

INSTINCT, INTELLIGENCE AND CHARACTER

which enables experts of the music-hall stage to perform almost incredible feats of memory, or sometimes apparently of thought-reading.

The key to the situation is that the experimenter, as each word is pronounced, fits it into a mental picture which he has trained himself to use for the number in question. These mental pictures are remembered by the trick of using words which begin and end with certain letters.

For example, instead of 15, the experimenter sees a visual image of an ape, this being chosen because

A P E

begins with the first and ends with the fifth letter of the alphabet. When the experimenter says "No. 15," let us suppose the person in the audience says "bicycle" (it is as well for a beginner to confine the audience to common nouns, names of real things). The experimenter promptly puts his ape on a bicycle, sees this mental picture intently for a moment, and then dismisses it from his mind, calling for No. 16. He can be perfectly confident that when he is later asked for No. 15 he will remember "ape," that the ape was on a "bicycle," and that the required word is therefore bicycle. The essential thing is to see the picture clearly. Here is a list of key words, and anyone wishing to try the experiment should form a definite and concrete picture in connection with each one.

1. Air	11. Acacia	21. Boa
2. Bar	12. Arab	22. Bab
3. Car	13. Alcoholic	23. Boracic
4. Dagger	14. Almond	24. Bed
5. Ear	15. Ape	25. Bee
6. Fur	16. Aloof	26. Beef
7. Garter	17. Aching	27. Bog
8. Hunger	18. Arch	28. Bunch
9. Indicator	19. Alkali	29. Biloxi [1]
10. Acorn	20. Bun	30. Can

[1] For which I see a map of the Gulf of Mexico.

VARIOUS USES OF VISUAL IMAGERY

These are Mr. Hill's words, modified in one instance. The reader may be left the task of completing the list up to 50 or 100 if required.

It will be noticed that n is used for zero, nothing; as in " Bun " meaning twenty: and that all the single figure numbers 1 to 9 have words ending in r. In several instances it may prove desirable, in order to get a good picture, to alter these words to suit personal idiosyncrasies. A final explanation of its working, in case of any confusion in the above: Yesterday at a children's party, when doing this trick as part of the amusement, I was asked for number 7. The key word is Garter, and I immediately saw the scene I had pictured, an alligator with a garter round its body. The word was *alligator*. Asked for 29, I saw a map of the Gulf of Mexico (Biloxi is a town there) with a radiator standing on it. The word was *radiator*. Asked for 22, I saw a baby in a perambulator or baby-carriage (Bab is the key word, and I always see this picture) being run over by a steam-roller. The word was *steam-roller*. Take the above printed list of key words and get some one to try you.

This is, of course, fooling. But it is a piece of fooling which may lead someone who would not otherwise have done so to perform what is really a psychological experiment, an introspective inquiry.

Another province in which one has opportunity of observing visual imagery, and at the same time other forms of imagery, is in instrumental music, or indeed vocal music; but the case I have most in mind is that of playing the piano. One may distinguish between the stage during which one is learning to play a certain piece of music by heart, and the later stage when one is able to sit down and go through the performance without hesitation and without error. I have at various times asked a considerable number of students and teachers of music how they carried out this performance of learning and reproducing from memory.

In the great majority of cases it would seem that the final

INSTINCT, INTELLIGENCE AND CHARACTER

memory is, as it were, "in the fingers." This seems to mean that when the piece of music is once started, the actions of the muscles of the fingers and arms in playing each bar or phrase act as the stimulus to that pattern of neurone excitation which causes the muscles to play the next bar or phrase. The piece is played without any special consciousness of how it is remembered, the imagery present is not concerned with remembering the piece, but with the shades of interpretation and emotion to be brought out on this particular occasion. The whole has become automatic, a "chain habit," each link forging its successor. Some individuals see the printed music while playing from memory and a smaller number claim to be able to read from the imaged page : but in most cases the vision is too hazy for this, although there may be a clear recognition of where the pages have to be turned and on which part of the page each phrase is printed. Auditory imagery does not appear to be employed a great deal in remembering, it is rather released from that task so that it can preside over the whole performance and direct its emotional rather than its mechanical side.

More instructive, however, is the rôle of imagery during the process of memorizing, and during the process of playing a new piece of music from the score. The primary outer stimulus in this last case is visual, is the set of black marks called notes arranged in such and such a way on the printed lines. The performer sees a certain pattern of these, and his fingers play a corresponding sequence of notes and chords on the keyboard. What has passed through his mind in the meantime ? That depends on his degree of familiarity with the art of reading at sight, and with the personal idiosyncrasies which are his because of his inborn nature, because of his previous instruction in music, and because of his previous experience in other provinces of life and education.

In the case of playing the piano, there need be no auditory image at all, the finger response may be made to the visual

VARIOUS USES OF VISUAL IMAGERY

sign just as it might be made by a man stone-deaf from birth. This is hardly likely to be the case when singing, instead of playing the piano, is in question. It is still conceivable that a certain muscular set of reactions in the vocal and breathing organs should be made in response to the notes, without the intervention of an auditory image as a go-between: but it is much *less* conceivable, is indeed hardly admissible, as a practical proposition. For we are much less conscious of just what we do when we sing and articulate. No one, I imagine, has ever tried to teach a stone-deaf child to play the piano from notes, though it could probably be done with fair success. But we have a lot of experience of the difficulty of teaching a stone-deaf child to speak; and the difficulties are very great indeed. Moreover, the contrast between such a stone-deaf child and one who has a trace of hearing left, or one who once heard, is so great as to leave no doubt in my mind as to the immense importance of auditory imagery in controlling the voice organs, even though one could explain this case by the fact of hearing controlling the learning even without imagery. In singing from notes, therefore, I believe the notes call up an auditory image which assists, together with the direct action of the visual stimulus, in determining the proper vocal response. In playing this need not be so, and in many cases does not seem to be so. The sense of hearing checks what is being played, without any auditory image having preceded that playing.

One can in the last resort only relate what one finds in one's own mind in such matters, and the reader should do a little introspection at the piano. In my own case (I possess only very moderate powers of reading at sight) I am conscious of a very definite image of the rhythm of a piece of new music, an image which sits mainly in the arm muscles, with vestigial taps of the foot, swayings of the body, and pattering of the vocal mechanism (without any of these coming to actual expression). I am much less conscious of any auditory imagery. Indeed, when I just look at a strange score, I find it impossible to image the harmonies, though I could play them, and can sometimes feel their emotional significance merely from the score. What I do image with great visual clearness is the piano keyboard, and I see my hands playing. If I am sitting actually at the piano reading, I look, of course, a good deal at the keyboard and at my hands, but mostly at the score, finding my way about the piano by a combined imagery of sight and arm-position.

If I now want to play the piece from memory I cannot do so, even though I have played it hundreds of times with the music, which I hardly feel the need to attend to. Yet remove it, and I must stop. Nor can I, by giving much thought, see any image of the score good enough to replace the actual score. If I want to learn to play by heart, I have to learn to start the action with the keyboard image. I look at my hands more and deliberately. I fix landmarks in the piece according to their keyboard position, and leave the flights between them to the muscle memory of my fingers. There is a distinct strain about the process, as great as, though different in quality from, the strain of first reading.

It seems clear that the attention of learners at the piano might with profit be directed to the question of forming visual images of the keyboard, and to the question of forming auditory images from the unplayed score, and this, I understand, is now done in the practice of the best teachers following the best methods, as that of Mrs. Curwen.

The whole question of the interconnection of these forms of imagery and the way in which visual, auditory, and kinæsthetic percepts and images act as cues to one another, can be more readily followed after one has some knowledge of the way in which some of these mental activities are connected with certain areas of the brain. And we may take the opportunity of making a short study of the brain's topography, and some of its functions.

CHAPTER XI

BRAIN LOCALIZATION

ONLY the most elementary knowledge of the structure of the brain is possible without actual dissections, or at least study of models. It is composed of neurones or nerve cells just as are the nerves and the spinal column. These neurones have cell bodies, mainly situated in the outer layer of the brain, the "grey matter" of the rind or cortex, and have also most extraordinarily complicated interconnections by brush-like dendrites and by longer axone-processes, which latter form a kind of close-packed cable system in the inner part of the brain, the so-called white matter.

The change in the brain which occurs, as the ascent is made up the scale of intelligence from an animal such as a frog to man, is not chiefly in the introduction of anything new, but in a great increase of size of the brain in comparison with the rest of the body, and a great increase in size and complexity of the cerebral hemispheres in comparison with the rest of the brain. A very striking museum exhibit is a comparison of the skeleton of a three-year-old child with the skeleton of a monkey of the same height, where by far the most noticeable difference is in the size of the skull which encloses the brain. In man the cerebral hemispheres, which are only a small part of the brain of a lower animal such as a frog, have developed to such an extent that they cover up most of the rest of the brain. They are very convoluted, like a walnut inside its shell, and like the walnut they are almost completely divided into a right and a left hemisphere, by a deep fissure just underneath the centre-line of the skull, from the root of the nose straight over the top of the head through the crown. But below this fissure, and forming its floor, are closely packed bands of nerves joining the two halves. The right and left cerebral hemispheres form the most unique part of the human nervous system, and it is here that the nervous phenomena take place which always accompany thought. Injury to the cerebral hemispheres invariably is accompanied by some mental deficiency or other. But many forms of mental deficiency or aberration can and do exist without any detectable trouble in the cerebral hemispheres, though we believe, many of us, that this is only because we are not able to see and interpret the finer structure of the hemispheres. We know more about the mind than we do about the brain : but what we know about the brain is more definite, and scientists are more in agreement about it than they are about the mind. The innumerable fissures or clefts between the convolutions of the cerebral hemispheres form a pattern which is much the same in all brains, and yet is individualistic in each brain, as our faces are similar yet different, or as maps of England drawn by hand might all show the same rivers, which yet would have differences in form. Experts know all these fissures ; we must content ourselves with knowing the approximate positions of the fissure of Sylvius, the fissure of Roland, and the Parieto-occipital fissure, which mark the boundaries between the four lobes into which it is usual to divide each hemisphere, viz. the Frontal, the Temporal, the Parietal, and the Occipital. Imagine a man wearing one of those listening-in headphones used with radio sets, where a band of metal joining the two ear-pieces runs over the top of the head. Then the two (right and left) Frontal lobes are approximately the part of the brain in front of this band of metal and behind the forehead. The fissure of Roland is approximately underneath the metal band, and separates the Frontal lobe from the Parietal lobe behind it. Right at the back of the skull lie the Occipital

BRAIN LOCALIZATION

lobes, separated from the Parietal by the Parieto-occipital fissures.

The Sylvian fissure on each side runs roughly parallel with the legs of a pair of spectacles, but about an inch higher, and rising as it goes backward. Below the Sylvian fissures lie the Temporal lobes, behind the temples or flat portions on either side of the head above the cheekbones.

From two classes of experiments we gain knowledge of the particular functions of certain parts of the hemispheres. When *post-mortem* examinations of the brain are possible, in the case of various forms of derangement (such as paralysis of certain limbs, defects of speech, and the like) it can be ascertained in what part of the hemispheres injuries are present. And from experiments on monkeys and dogs, in which the brain of the living animal is exposed and given a mild electric stimulation in various regions, we can plot those parts of the hemisphere whose stimulation results in the movements of different parts of the body. From experiments of this second kind, it is known that such electric stimulation of the convolution just in front of the fissure of Roland results in movements of different sorts, and this part of the cortex, known topographically as the precentral gyrus, is therefore called the motor region. Generally speaking, the upper parts (nearer the top of the head) cause, when stimulated, movements of the lower limbs ; and as we pass down the area, the muscles affected are higher up in the body. Near the point where the fissure of Roland approaches the fissure of Sylvius there are centres which have a connection with, and appear to control, the hands and fingers, and the vocal organs. These two centres are not far apart.[1]

These facts are confirmed by the *post-mortem* examinations. Where a "stroke" paralyses an arm, or a leg, then a clot of blood or other injury is found in the corresponding part of

---

[1] The response from any one cortical point, however, is not entirely constant (Head, *Brain*, 1923, xlvi). It depends on the character of the events by which it has been preceded.

the motor region. If the paralysis is confined to one side of the body, then the brain injury is found in the hemisphere of the *opposite side*; for all connections between body and brain cross over somewhere or other, either in the brain or at some level of the spinal column. A paralysis of the *right* hand, therefore, means probably a lesion or injury in the *left* hemisphere.

The vocal organs are centrally situated in our bodies, not like the limbs one on each side, and they have nerve connections with both hemispheres. But as a result of experiments and observations similar to the above it has been found that invariably there is a specialization of duties. Both hemispheres control the vocal organs (tongue, throat, etc.) in so far as it is merely a question of making noises, executing swallowing movements, and similar crude motions. But when it comes to language and speech, one side of the brain does all the higher work, usually (indeed I believe invariably) the same side as is in control of the more "dexterous" hand: that is to say, the left side of the brain in the case of right-handed workers, and the right side in the case of those who are more skilled with their left hands.

Stimulation of other parts of the brain does not result in any muscular responses. But we know that certain other regions are intimately connected with the senses, and they are therefore called sensorial regions. For example, a part of the Occipital lobe, near the back of the skull, is thus associated with vision, and a lesion here can cause blindness, though the eyes be perfect.

There is a disease to which sheep are subject which illustrates this. Sheep suffering from it become partially blind, and walk in circular or curved paths in consequence. Now the crossing over of nerves from the brain to the body is rather peculiar in the case of the eyes. It is not that the left retina is connected with the right brain, and the right retina with the left. But the right-hand *halves* are connected with the right brain, and the left-hand halves with the left brain An injury to the proper region of the right brain will therefore cut off the right-hand half of each retina; and (as rays of light cross in passing through the lens of the eye) this means that the left half of the field of vision is darkened.

The brain injury is due to a polyp which grows between the sheep's skull and his brain and by pressing on the latter keeps away the blood supply. An old Northumbrian farmer whom I knew was accustomed to operate on the sheep (and no doubt the operation is well known among farmers) by boring into the skull at a place chosen partly by observing the sheep's manner of walking, partly by feeling the skull with the thumbs; whereupon the polyp protruded and was withdrawn, and the wound closed with a tarred bandage.

The auditory region is just below the Sylvian fissure. The regions similarly connected with taste, smell, etc., are on the inner surface between the two hemispheres. Running along the front border of the parietal lobe, and just across the river, as it were—that is, across the fissure of Roland—from the motor region, is a region which is necessary to the sense of touch over the surface of the body and perhaps to the other skin senses; for injuries here result in loss of sensation somewhere on the body. This and the motor region run approximately across the top of the head, and down towards the ears under the headpiece of a radio set when one is "listening-in," separated from one another by the Rolandic fissure.

The other areas of the cortex, though they are not, like those described, intimately connected with groups of muscles or with sense organs, are nevertheless highly important. Called sometimes the silent areas, or association areas, they are essential in even the simplest perception, for we have reason to think that mere excitation of, say, the visual region, would give only a meaningless sensation instead of an understood and significant percept. The words percept and perception have not been used or defined in this book previously, but their meaning can be sufficiently grasped when it is said that looking at an orange and knowing what it is constitutes perception, whereas just seeing a patch of yellowish-red colour is not perception, is mere sensation. An adult, or even a child, hardly ever has mere sensations : he not only *hears* a certain sound but perceives a motor-horn (the words perceive, percept, and perception being used technically for all the senses, not only for sight). The percept may be erroneous, the sensations may call up the wrong percept, as when we are deceived by a painting, or by a figure in a looking-glass, or think the sails of a windmill are revolving the wrong way. And even when we do not recognize a sensation-situation, our condition is seldom one of complete bewilderment, but rather of rapid oscillation between attempted percepts which do not quite fit. This crude account must suffice for explanation of the difference between sensation and perception : and to return to our brain-regions, there is some reason for saying that the regions we have labelled as visual or as auditory are concerned with the mere sensations as such, whereas the translation into perception requires the co-operation of large parts of the " silent " areas.

Part of the evidence which points in this direction, evidence about which there is a great deal of controversy, and which we can only consider as onlookers, consists of the records of cases of aphasia and allied defects, in which a patient loses, for example, the understanding of spoken words, though he may still understand written words ; or is unable to speak sensibly or coherently, though he may be able to write what he wants to say ; or a number of other conditions. As a matter of fact, one gathers from the literature that such cases are rarely or never limited to one particular defect as is suggested above, but are nearly always more complex, and show different symptoms at different stages of the disease. In my own small experience of aphasia patients, as a lay visitor to a local hospital, that has certainly been the case. But approximations to different types appear, nevertheless, to exist. They are explicable on the following lines.

Suppose, for instance, that the auditory region were, through some brain lesion, cut off to a considerable extent from the rest of the cortex. Then, although the sensations produced by spoken words would be heard, there would be no perception of their meaning, since that involves the co-operation of large parts of the "silent" areas. Yet, since the visual region is still in communication with these areas, the printed word may be comprehended. If the communication between the visual centre and the motor centre which regulates speech is intact, it may even be that the patient may read aloud correctly. These cases have in the past been usually classed as cases of (1) motor *aphasia*, or inability to speak ; (2) word-deafness, or inability to understand spoken language ; (3) word-blindness, or inability to understand printed or written language ; and (4) *agraphia*, or inability to write ; though, as we shall presently see, there is every reason to think that these conditions are seldom found as distinct from one another as these names would suggest. As Broca first, in a famous paper published in 1861, was able to show, in motor aphasia there is a lesion of the convolution adjoining the motor region. If this motor region itself is injured, there is partial actual paralysis of the vocal organs. But the corresponding region on the other side of the head can control the grosser movements of tongue, etc. The following case is quoted by Sir James Purves Stewart : [1]

Case 1. W. M., aged 55. "He suddenly became speechless and his face became asymmetrical. His intelligence was unimpaired. He was able to understand and execute all sorts of verbal commands, *to put out his tongue*, to place his hand on any part of his face or head, to move the right or left thumb by bending it half-way or straightening it out,

[1] *Brain*, 1920, xliii, 424–5.

as requested. But he was *unable to utter any word whatever*."
"At the autopsy . . . the brain, after hardening, showed a small area in the lower third of the left precentral gyrus, in which there was a dark marbled appearance, due to embolic blocking of a small cortical arteriole." If Broca's convolution alone is injured, the vocal organs can still be used for making sounds, but not for making words.

It was Wernicke who found the position of lesions, in the case of word-deafness, to be near, but not in, the auditory centre. And similarly lesions which are closely related to the hand centre or to the visual centre, but do not actually encroach on those centres, can cause inability to write or to read, though the hand is not paralysed nor the eyes blinded.

Actual reports of clinical cases are the best illustration: and they will show how confused, compared with this classification, such cases really are—though no doubt from time to time fairly pure cases turn up.

On a table in front of one of Head's patients[1] lay six common objects. The patient was able to point to any one of these when a duplicate was shown him, or was placed (out of sight) in his hand. He could still hesitatingly do so if the object was named by the examiner, or if its name was shown him in print. When asked to name an object indicated, however, he was not always successful. True, he always gave the correct name for the *penny*, and he did pretty well with the *knife*, though he *wrote* " panin " and " Kerrert," and other wrong forms. When the *key* was pointed to, he on one occasion said, " That's mer, may," and on two other trials he took his keys out of his pocket, saying " Mat, latch " and " No, I cannot tell you that." Nor could he write the word. Presumably, under the old nomenclature, he would have been described as a case of motor aphasia and agraphia: but his inability to use words (spoken or written) was only partial. Moreover, though he could point to the object named or printed, he did so in a

[1] *Brain*, 1920, xliii, 95.

BRAIN LOCALIZATION

hovering and hesitating way, and said, "I can't remember what they are unless I think. If it wasn't here on the table I couldn't tell you."

Influenced by a number of cases in which this mixture of the symptoms occurs, Head has asserted that "disorders in the use of language, due to a (left) unilateral lesion of the brain, cannot be classified under the categories of speaking, reading, and writing," and that they are "not due," or need not be due, "to destruction of images." "The patient succeeds in reading or writing under certain conditions although he fails completely if the task is presented to him in a different manner." The function which is disturbed by such lesions he calls "symbolic thinking and expression," while admitting that "every manifestation of this aspect of psychical activity is not . . . of necessity disturbed in any one case." "The more acute and severe the lesion, the graver and more extensive will be the disorder it produces." "At first the whole of symbolic thinking and expression may be rendered impossible, but gradually certain forms return, whilst the recovery of others may be indefinitely retarded. When a man has received a severe injury to his foot, at first he may not be able to walk at all; but after a while he is found to be walking in a peculiar manner according to whether the wound affects his toe or his heel. The gait he assumes is not an elementary component of his normal method of walking; it is due to the fact that he cannot place some one part of his foot on the ground. Provided we bear these principles strictly in mind, we are justified in recognizing the existence of various forms of aphasia."[1]

Head has suggested, in place of the older terms such as agraphia, alexia, etc. (which he rejects because they suggest special centres for writing, reading, etc.) the terms verbal, syntactical, nominal, and semantic disorders of symbolic formulation and expression. The verbal form is seen in a patient who cannot readily pronounce his words, though

[1] Henry Head, *Brain*, 1920, *passim*.

he uses them correctly if he can, or uses their misformed representatives correctly. The injury here lies mainly within or beneath the central convolutions bordering the Rolandic fissure.[1] The syntactical patient talks jargon. He hurries on in the hope of something being understood. He can understand what he reads provided he does not attempt to formulate it in words. The lesion here is in the temporal lobe. Lesions in the parietal lobe seem to lead either to the nominal or to the semantic form of interference with symbolic formulation and expression, the lesion tending to be somewhat farther back in the case of nominal aphasia. In semantic aphasia the patient may to casual observation appear to be normal : but he has difficulty in following or retaining the general drift of an argument. In nominal aphasia his difficulty is in naming, and he often talks round some idea which he is unable to name.

"The processes which underlie the act of speech," says Head, "run through the nervous system like a prairie fire from bush to bush ; remove all inflammable material at any one point and the fire stops. So, when a break occurs in the functional chain, orderly speech becomes impossible, because the basic physiological processes which subserve it have been disturbed. The site of such a breach of continuity is not a 'centre for speech,' but solely a place where it can be interrupted or changed."

[1] *Brain*, 1923, *passim*.

CHAPTER XII

THE ASCENT FROM INSTINCT TO INTELLIGENCE

(b) THE USE OF WORDS IN THOUGHT.

CASES of aphasia such as those noted in the last chapter bring forcibly before one's mind the question of the independence, or the interdependence, of language and thought. Opinions on this question have covered a very wide range, from Max Müller's blunt assertion that speech is thought and thought is speech, to Sir Francis Galton's equally definite statement, in a letter to Max Müller, that he thought absolutely without the use of any mental words.

Words can come before the mind in several different forms. They may be seen, or heard, or inwardly spoken. If the reader will close his eyes and enter upon some train of thought, such as, say, what the consequences of free railway travel would be in a nation, he will be conscious (in addition to a lot of concrete imagery of railway stations, holiday resorts, express trains, and the like) of words arising in his mind, in the case certainly of a majority of those who try this experiment. Things he himself could do, or ways in which business would be facilitated, will at least in fragmentary ways be expressed in words. The thought "What a tremendous increase in the traffic there would be" is, in my case, composed of a jumbled vision of crowds and a porter stooping, a sight of the word "whew!" combined with a puckering of unreal lips to whistle, an actual raising of my eyebrows, and the words "tremendous increase in traffic, anyway" in inner speech, as to which I can never quite determine whether I hear or speak more plainly—

but I do not see more than "tr" and "incr," i.e. one or two beginnings of words.

But as soon as it becomes necessary really to drive the argument through and to determine just what one thinks about the problem, one finds himself (in the majority of cases, as I believe) putting it more definitely into words, even saying words and sentences aloud, and putting them down in notes. Whatever one may believe about the "growing point" of thought, there can be little doubt about the tendency to turn the thought into words as soon as possible. The words form definite foci for thoughts which would otherwise be vague. They are almost essential for communicating our thoughts to others, and mighty convenient for communicating our thoughts to our own selves, e.g. for use in a long train of reasoning. They appear to be the more necessary, the more abstract the thought. "We do not progress far with our thoughts," says H. G. Wells in *Mankind in the Making*, "unless we throw them out into objective existence by means of words, diagrams, models, trial essays. Even if we do not talk to others we must, silently or vocally or visibly, talk to ourselves at least to get on. To acquire the means of intercourse *is* to learn to think, so far as learning goes in the matter."

And in his *Men like Gods* the same writer puts this truth in a still more striking way. For the inhabitants of that Utopian land into which a group of terrestrials had involuntarily penetrated as a result of an experiment in the rotation of matter in the fourth dimension, had given up the use of speech and used among themselves only direct communication of thought (except in moments of emotion and when æsthetic considerations intervened). Now the interesting thing is that the terrestrials *heard* these thought-projecting Utopians speaking—and each hearer heard his own language, French or English or the chauffeur's cockney slang. They were being made the recipients of thoughts, but they "listened in" in terms of language. Moreover, they each

THE ASCENT: THE USE OF WORDS

and all of them found silent patches in the speeches, when they could not understand. How many teachers realize that the thoughts they send out can only be "listened in" to by their pupils in terms of the pupils' own vocabulary and phrasing. And how good if they seemed to be silent when they were abstruse.

Various ways (in addition to the observation of aphasics) suggest themselves for the study of the use of words in thinking. There is introspection, final as regards an individual's own thought, but not to be made the excuse for generalizations including all others. The study of how words arise in children, and the history, as far as it can be deduced, of how words arise in the race, gives another line of approach. A third is the investigation of the relationship actually found between vocabulary and intelligence, especially the individual differences in this respect. And another is to examine the practice of successful teachers and successful teaching methods and see how words and thought are related to one another in good teaching.

Now in teaching there can be no doubt that often for long periods the mistake has been made of supposing that the possession of words implied the understanding of the thought. In such times education has become entirely verbal, memory of rules, definitions, and generalizations, has been mistaken for the power to apply them, and fluency for lucidity and truth. So often has the reform "teach things, not words," been needed in our schools, that it is certain that teachers must ever be on their guard against teaching *mere* words, and that, whether or no thought requires words, words do not always require thought.

Not only in the schools, but in outside life, we find this same danger. Growing up, as we do, into a society speaking our mother tongue and daily using thousands of phrases and catchwords which imply judgments, we are very liable to acquire the phrases and the catchwords without any real consideration of the judgments involved. So we become

INSTINCT, INTELLIGENCE AND CHARACTER

Englishmen or Frenchmen, Turks or Prussians; so we become little Liberals and little Conservatives. And perhaps this is inevitable, and to some extent even advantageous. There is not time for each individual to begin afresh and rejudge all the questions of humanity, any more than there is time for each individual to reinvent all the material appliances which belong to our twentieth-century civilization. Nor could most of us be capable of either the one or the other feat even with our adult intelligence, let alone the impossibility of keeping the mind fallow till childhood and youth were past. But a great measure of elasticity, of readiness to reconsider even the most tightly closed question, should be retained by the scholars of every really great teacher. It is Dr. F. H. Hayward, in his book *Spiritual Bases of Reconstruction*, who demands that the right of entry to schools should be given to every warring sect and creed, whether religious, literary, scientific, or political. The golden mean must lie somewhere between this extreme and that other which appealed so strongly to Stephen Girard, mariner and merchant, and benefactor of the city of Philadelphia, who in his will said, "As there is such a multitude of sects, and such a diversity of opinion amongst them, I desire to keep the tender minds of the orphans, who are to derive advantage from this bequest, free from the excitements which clashing doctrines and sectarian controversy are apt to produce."

But this is a digression. It arose from the consideration that the doctrines, and even the language into which we grow up, limit our freedom of thought, and deceive us as to our ability to think; for which reason the teacher must ever be suspicious of a merely verbal knowledge and must see that the things behind the words are grasped, manipulated, felt, understood. If that is faithfully done, he will find that words are not likely to be lacking. *Verbaque previsam rem non invita sequentur*, as Montaigne quotes. And Florio translates: "When matter we foreknow, words voluntary

THE ASCENT: THE USE OF WORDS

flow." Yet he must not fall into the opposite error of always avoiding abstract and technical terms, and continually talking down to the pupils. To a number of relationships, whether in sciences or in the humanities, their attention will never be drawn unless by hearing the relationship named. Virtues which have no name among a people are apt to die out. Mathematical functions which have no name escape notice. It is bad to have the name without understanding the fact, but difficult to understand or even notice the fact without the name. And so the golden rule is to teach real things and real relationships, but to talk naturally about them, so that vocabulary advances equally with true knowledge, not usurping its place, but not lagging in the rear.

Children do differ enormously in vocabulary, and their vocabulary grows at a rate which is always underestimated by those who have never made an effort to measure it quantitatively. A child has a number of different vocabularies, of which the widest is the number of words which he understands when he hears them. This vocabulary has no definite margin, but shades off through words which are fairly well comprehended to words which are only hazily appreciated, and then only in certain phrases or contexts. A word is not one day unknown and the next day understood, but rather it ripens to maturity in the mind.

Enclosed within this vocabulary is that lesser treasury of words which the child himself actually uses—it is probably a proper aim for the teacher of English to endeavour to make these two realms more nearly coincident in size. And there are other possible delimitations; as the words which the pupil can spell, or will use in a written composition.

Vocabulary has been repeatedly used as a test of intelligence, both size of vocabulary and quality, while indirectly it plays an important part in other tests. Methods of measuring vocabulary are of interest in themselves, as an example of the difficulty attending upon quantitative experi-

INSTINCT, INTELLIGENCE AND CHARACTER

ment in child psychology. With very little children the actual spoken vocabulary can be set down in full, as :

Age eleven months.
Words used recognizably :—

Sthere	= it is there
Thersth	= there it is
Esh	= yes
Dad-dé	= daddy
Mammam	= mammie
My	= my, only in phrase " my mammam "
Boowoo	= bow wow

also several words which we cannot yet interpret with certainty.

With older children this is not possible. But it is interesting and useful to note specimens of their talk from time to time. And it is possible to put down every word used over a given period, perhaps a number of days, as Drever did, in the case of his children, or a single day or a period of a few hours. H., whose vocabulary at 11 months is given above, was thus " reported " continuously for two hours when aged 3 years $1\frac{1}{2}$ months, and used in those two hours 485 different words. Four days later, in another two hours, he used 152 additional different words, making 637 in all (plus two foreign phrases, viz. *pas encore*, and, at the end of a tune which till then had been hummed without words, the fragment—*Reiter, und brak sie ap*). These words fall into parts of speech in the following proportions, Drever's two children of similar age being also shown on page 117.

It is a good exercise for anyone interested in children to make such snapshots of their speech and preserve them. The correlation with developing thought and intelligence will be emphatic. With still older children the manner of measuring vocabulary by sampling is of interest as an example of the modern tendency to standardize and objectify such estimates. It is clearly impossible to test a child's knowledge of all the words in the language or, for that matter, all the words in a given dictionary, which even if

THE ASCENT : THE USE OF WORDS

small may contain twenty or forty thousand. So a sample of the dictionary is taken at random, the easiest way being to take the first, or last, word on every tenth, or hundredth page, according to the size of sample wanted. Suppose 100 words are obtained in this random way and that the child is found to understand 32 of them, we may then assume that as far as we can tell, he will understand about 32 per cent. of the whole dictionary ; and we could test this by trying other random samples of 100.

The best-known such random sample of the language is that of 100 words used by Terman in his revision of the

	H., aged	Drever's Children, aged	
	3 Years 1¼ Months.	4 Years 6¼ Months.	3 Years 7 Months.
Nouns	48·75	59·1	54·5
Proper names . .	5·99	3·5	1·3
Verbs	20·66	16·9	19·6
Adjectives . . .	11·67	11·9	12·4
Pronouns . . .	2·36	1·9	3·4
Adverbs	5·21	3·2	4·7
Prepositions . . .	3·00	1·6	1·9
Conjunctions . . .	0·47	0·9	1·0
Unclassified . . .	1·89	1·0	1·2

Binet tests. On that list, Terman found that a child of ten knew about 30, one of twelve years 40, one of fourteen 50, and an average adult 65, while a selection of more intelligent adults know 75. Just what is here meant by " knowing " the word will be found defined in Terman's book *The Measurement of Intelligence*, but nothing more than fair acquaintance with its general significance was required.

Tests dependent on quality of vocabulary (which is almost certainly associated with extent) include, of course, the time-honoured essay, so difficult to mark consistently ; but also more definite tests, such as asking the difference between *poverty* and *misery*, or for a definition of *charity*, the attempt here being to get at an index of the wealth of abstract ideas possessed, on the assumption that possession of the idea is unlikely without possession of the word. These, and many other tests which depend more or less upon vocabulary, have been found to place children in an order of intelligence closely similar to that based on the considered opinion of teachers well acquainted with them.

It may be retorted that this merely means that we all, and especially teachers, tend to be too much influenced by verbal signs of intelligence and too little impressed by intelligence which finds its outlet in other forms, as in making things. There is undoubted truth in this. But there is evidence that some correlation between vocabulary and intelligence remains even after allowance has been made for this bias. There exist tests which depend only very slightly upon language, such as, for example, the Pintner-Patterson tests, in which children fit together simple jigsaw puzzles, place squares, stars, and triangles into appropriate holes, tap cubes in given sequence, and so on. These tests show a correlation with tests involving vocabulary. In particular, deaf and dumb children, whose vocabulary in early years is extremely limited, do not do so well in these non-language tests as speaking children (though of course there is here, as in all comparisons of classes, tremendous overlapping, and many dumb children rise superior to the average speaking child). It seems to many who have made a study of them that such handicapped children, whatever inner potentialities may be, do actually show a retardation, on the average, in the rate of growth of their intelligence, due to lack of vocabulary and to consequent lack of guidance and assistance in the formation of abstract ideas.

The great advantage of a word over a sign or gesture is its power of dropping away from itself all traces of particular items, and becoming a symbol for a whole class. This can happen to a gesture in a sign language, but not to the

THE ASCENT : THE USE OF WORDS

same extent as it happens to a word. It is easy (I have read somewhere[1]) to imitate by signs making bread, or making hay, or making a hut for Wendy, as children do in their games, but not easy to convey by a sign the idea of just making—making anything—the generalized idea of making. No doubt the sign language would have developed such abstract signs had it been possible for man to progress with only that method of communication. Indeed, some such signs exist among deaf mutes, as the hand placed on the breast with fingers outstretched meaning " I want." But to have developed far in such a direction would have meant employing all the muscles of the hands and arms, at any rate, in communicating with others, so that action of any sort (as fighting or hunting) would have been for the time interrupted ; whereas speech can go on while the body muscles are in action, and in the dark or when out of sight we can convey our thoughts to others within earshot.

This power of a word to drop its particular associations comes gradually in childhood, from hearing the word used in such varying particular circumstances. All the irrelevant concomitants thereby tend to fall away, and the child's attention is directed to something common to all these situations by the fact of hearing the same name given to them. So a common noun like cat comes to mean not any particular animal, but a type of animal which we would have difficulty in defining, but can unerringly recognize. So an abstract word like pity comes to crystallize out with a definite but at first undefined meaning in the child's mind. The proper way to ensure that the generalized, or as we say the conceptual, significance of a word is grasped by a pupil, is to see that he meets it in a large number of different contexts and different circumstances. Any particularized meaning which might have fitted in with one case is gradually corrected, widened, or narrowed, as it is seen not to fit other

[1] I think it is a passage from Tylor, quoted by G. F. Stout in his *Manual of Psychology*, p. 487, which I have here paraphrased.

cases. One feels this happening to oneself with new words, as happened to the psychologist who thought that a "gadget" was part of an aeroplane, since he first heard it used about a flying machine which "had too many gadgets about it": but presently came across the slang word in other connections and realized gradually its meaning as a mechanical device of a pernickety kind often but not always ancillary to a larger machine; as a self-starter, a special backsight, a patent cigar lighter, or a new kind of damper. With children it must happen very frequently. A little boy aged three years and five months heard his parents, discussing accounts, use the word "balance," and interrupted to say "hedgehogs have balances," to which assertion he stoutly adhered, repudiating the suggestion that perhaps he meant quills. "Hedgehogs have balances, those things you weigh clothes with—spring balances. In that story gran'ma told me the hedgehog said, 'I'm very sorry, I've just lost my balance.'" Here was a pretty confusion between three meanings of the word balance: and I feel fairly sure that H.'s first interruption was occasioned by his feeling of something wrong with the word, for often he used a new word wrongly, or rather, in an unusual way, and looked around at us to see how we took it. One sees this tendency in children at work, as it were, from both ends   In the above example H. was assuming that the word, when met with, would always mean the weighing machine. He was associating the one thing with all the words, whatever their context—and, indeed, in a higher stage we come to recognize that there is a common element of balancing two things against one another in all the uses of the word. At the other end is the assumption that one word will do for a large number of things, the trick which children so often show of extending a particular name to cover a wider class, as "daddy" for all grown-up men. H.'s cousin, on a walk with me one day, leaned over a fence against which I was holding him and called "puss puss, puss" to some sheep. H. extended the word "dickies'

THE ASCENT: THE USE OF WORDS

to mean flies and butterflies as well as birds, and at fifteen months he applied it to falling snowflakes. At two years seven months he called the silver-wire network over the rose-bowl a "veil," and a month later, seeing grapes either for the first time or after a long period, he called them "cherries." In both cases it was evident, from his tone and the context, that he recognized the differences perfectly and was using the words as a makeshift. The case is similar to the naming of new objects by savage tribes, as "firestick" for musket, or "birds" for ships with outspread sails. It is indeed the way in which all our class-names have arisen, probably. Children, and people, who are above a certain level of intelligence form classes readily enough, and name them. The assistance given by the educator is not so much needed to stimulate such generalization as to direct it. Growth is as luxuriant in the jungle as in the garden, but the garden is tidier: and the tendency to generalize and classify is as active in a savage or a child as in a scientist, but the scientist's classifications are tidier. And also they are more fundamental. The class of objects which H. formed and called "dickies," including birds, butterflies, and slowly falling snowflakes, is not a very useful class and so has not found general acceptance. Children find their attention directed to those which have found acceptance, by the names which are commonly used. Not otherwise is it with the young chemist learning classes such as the "acids," the "paraffins," etc. Often a flood of light is thrown on some matter by the teacher's apparently casual extension of a class-name to some unusual instance of the class, such as calling a tangent a chord, a straight line a circle, water hydrogen oxide, the monsoons trade winds, comets planets, or man an animal.

In music teaching, the importance of naming is well illustrated by the influence of the Solfa names in tune, and of the patternames introduced with great advantage during the past few years in teaching time. As regards

INSTINCT, INTELLIGENCE AND CHARACTER

Solfa names, many teachers of music urge strongly their importance. The peculiarity, from a psychological point of view, about a Solfa name is that it invests a single note with a background of relationships. If anyone sings to me a single note to the syllable "ah," I hear just a single note; or if I fit it into any set of relationships. it is unlikely to be the same set as that intended by the singer. But if he sings a Solfa name to the note, say *lah*, then its place in a musical scale is fixed, and it has, as sung, certain emotional tendencies which are the result of that position. The name produces in me an attitude or set intended by the singer. In part this attitude is a readiness to go on to other notes, as to go on to *doh* from *te*. For my own part, too, I find that I can often remember a new and still rather unfamiliar melody better by its Solfa names than by any unnamed tone-sequence, as, e.g., remembering that "Rufty Tufty" begins Doh—doh ray me. This one finds in many other spheres of memory also. If one is asked to gaze at a building or other object and then presently, turning one's back, to describe it (as in one lesson of the Army "Eyesight training") one finds it a great assistance—or at least I do —to say to oneself such points as—" the windows have blue curtains, there are two rain-barrels," etc. In part this is because attention is thereby directed to these details: in part it is, I think, because of the facility of recall of words even in a subject with a good visual memory.

The advantage, which has been emphasized in this chapter, arising from the way in which words drop off any particular attributes (such as blackness in a cat) and thereby are enabled to stand as signs for concepts (as *cat* or *charity*, or *although*) is in contradiction to what was said in Chapter X on seeing pictures in words. The contradiction is, however, only superficial. The recommendation there made, to go back to the original pictures in the words, is very much needed, even though words owe their conceptualizing power to the trick of dropping such pictures. In most cases, speakers

THE ASCENT : THE USE OF WORDS

have not originally had allied to their words clear-cut images which have gradually dropped away, but have taken the word too vaguely from current usage. There is a far greater tendency for words to spread their meaning over too wide a field than there is any tendency for them to be restricted to particular instances. Words owe part of their usefulness to the ease with which they become general counters : but this tendency is so strong that a check is needed (and is supplied by visual imagery) to prevent them becoming merely debased coinage.

CHAPTER XIII

MATHEMATICAL AND OTHER SYMBOLS

THE province of thought in which, perhaps beyond all other, symbols have shown their power as instruments and tools of thought is the realm of mathematics. Nowhere else are there such well-worn paths of thought, so often traversed that they can be passed over without any fresh reasoning whatever. When, for example, we solve an equation by some familiar formula or device, we are performing the equivalent of an act of reasoning, but without any expenditure of reasoning on our own part : our available reasoning powers are, as it were, set free from this lower duty to occupy themselves with fresh fields.

This continual use of symbols is at once the power, the difficulty, and the danger of mathematics. The power is illustrated in every piece of mathematical research. The difficulty of mathematics arises at least in part from its divorce from concrete space and time and its transformation into a crowd of symbols. And the danger is ever present that a student may learn to manipulate these symbols entirely without comprehension, so that he not only saves himself the trouble of reasoning now, but has *never* done the reasoning which would have given him the right to use these devices, and without which he is unable to make any substantial advance. The first and most familiar symbols of mathematics are our ordinary numerals 0, 1, 2, 3, and up to 9, together with our most taken-for-granted and yet most wonderful device of place value, whereby a digit placed to the left of another means so many bundles instead of

MATHEMATICAL AND OTHER SYMBOLS

so many units. It took the civilized world many centuries to arrive at this simple conception, and there are to be found in books on the subject accounts of the cumbrous methods of multiplying, dividing and so on with numbers expressed in other forms such as the Roman XXVII for 27. We are ordinarily hardly aware of the extent to which our numerical notation has come to do our arithmetical problems automatically for us. We can place ourselves partly in the unsophisticated position by trying to carry out a calculation in some other notation. Even when the principle remains the same, and a comparatively small change is made such as reducing our numerals to 0, 1, 2, 3, 4 only, and making the effect of a place-change *five times* instead of *ten times*, we feel like fish out of water. Try for example to add, on this understanding, 43 to 12. The answer is 110, which in our present language we call thirty. Yet this notation is probably no harder for us than our usual notation is for little children in school. What has occurred is that certain habits of response to numbers have been firmly formed in us by the arithmetical drills of everyday life ; the pathway through this mental maze has been fixed by habits to which these visual or auditory symbols give the starting cue.

It is exceedingly important that such habits should be quickly, securely, and economically formed in early school days, for which purpose many of our ordinary school drills need overhauling, and the usual random combinations of numbers replacing by combinations designed to distribute practice where it is most needed.[1] But still more important perhaps is it to invite older scholars occasionally to see why some familiar fact should be so, to see $9 \times 7 = 63$, for example, as 70 less 7, or to realize clearly just why we carry out each part of an operation such as multiplying or subtracting or finding the square root. We cannot always wait to understand a procedure before learning and using it, nor can we continuously bear in mind just what it means ;

---

[1] As, e.g., in the Courtis Arithmetical Practice Tests.

INSTINCT, INTELLIGENCE AND CHARACTER

indeed, that is the economy of it all, that we need not. But there is every advantage in doing so now and then. When, for example, I find by the usual process the square root of 29·41 (as I had occasion to do an hour ago, in the absence of slide rules or other devices) I set the work down as follows :

```
     5│29·41(5
      │25
      │ ───
      │ 4·41
```

The number required is evidently a little larger than 5, so I subtract 25 from 29·41, and set 5 down in the answer. I then do the following jugglery. I double the 5 and set it down as 10, and ask myself how many times 10 will go into the remainder 4·41, decide upon ·4, and curiously enough set this ·4 on to the 10 as well as on to the 5, thus :

```
        5│29·41(5·4
         │25
         │ ───
    10·4 │ 4·41
         │ 4·16
         │ ───
         │  ·25
```

I then write down for a new divisor 10·8, got by doubling 5·4, and proceed as far as I require decimals, thus :

```
         5│29·41(5·423
          │25
          │ ───
    10·4  │ 4·41
          │ 4·16
          │ ───
    10·82 │  ·25
          │  ·2164
          │ ───
    10·843│  ·0336
          │  ·032529
          │ ───
          │  ·001071
```

Now this is really a very eccentric procedure and one which has become quite automatic and meaningless. It is exceedingly refreshing to look past the symbols at some concrete representation of the same facts, say a geometrical repre-

MATHEMATICAL AND OTHER SYMBOLS

sentation. I want the length of side of a square cardboard whose area is 29·41 inches.

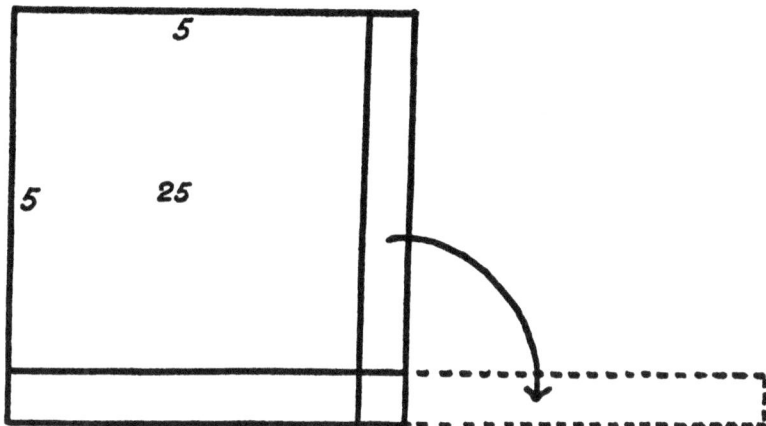

A five-inch square will account for most of it, leaving a strip along two sides as surplus. What I want to know is the width of this strip, to add to my five inches. Suppose I straighten the strip out so that it forms one long, narrow rectangle. What is the area of this rectangle? It is 4·41 square inches.

$$5 | \overline{29 \cdot 41} (5$$
$$25$$
$$\overline{4 \cdot 41} = \text{area of long rectangle.}$$

How long is it? Well, I don't quite know, but it is twice five and a bit more represented by the little corner square, the very same bit more that I want to know, so that is why I double the 5, and why I am going to add a bit to it.

$$5 | \overline{29 \cdot 41} (5$$
$$25$$
$$10 \cdot \overline{4 \cdot 41}$$

Now I have my long rectangle of area 4·41 and length 10 decimal something. I find its width by dividing 10· into

INSTINCT, INTELLIGENCE AND CHARACTER

4·41, and whatever its width is, I have to add it to the 10· I try ·4 and proceed thus :

$$\begin{array}{r|l} 5 & 29\cdot 41(5\cdot 4 \\ & 25 \\ \hline 10\cdot 4 & 4\cdot 41 \\ & 4\cdot 16 \\ \hline & \cdot 25 \end{array}$$

The situation is now like this :

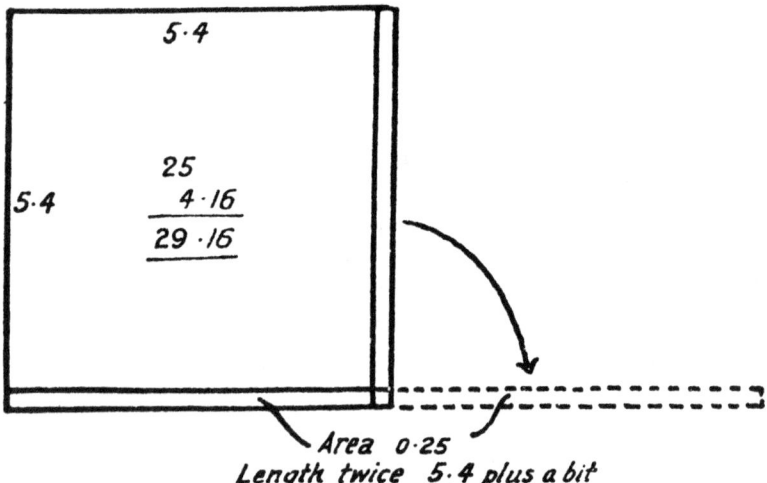

Area 0·25
Length twice 5·4 plus a bit

A narrower strip is left round my square of cardboard, with area ·25 and length a little more than twice 5·4. I proceed just as before, and so on and so on. *The reason I double my answer for each new divisor is pictured in each diagram, it is to get the approximate length of the long strip. The reason I add my new decimal both to my divisor and to my answer is pictured by the little square in the corner.*

In rapid calculation we have not time to see such concrete explanations behind all our operations. In teaching arithmetical operations to children, or mathematical operations to older students, we cannot wait till an operation is *fully*

MATHEMATICAL AND OTHER SYMBOLS

understood before using it; use aids understanding. But no one can be a good mathematician who cannot at any moment see behind the habits of symbolism which have short-circuited separate acts of thought, just what the reasons for those operations are.

An illustration from the integral and differential calculus of infinitesimals may be given. The fundamental proposition of the infinitesimal calculus is that if y is the differential of x then x is the integral of y. In these words, the proposition may convey no meaning to many of my readers. Those who know that it conveys no meaning are all right: but there may be others who have heard, seen, repeated this sentence long enough to have acquired a belief that it conveys a meaning. Many mathematical students are in that self-deceiving position. Especially they remember, or know, that if

$$\frac{dx}{dz} = y$$

then

$$\int y\,dz = x$$

which is just the same fact, set down in mathematical symbols instead of in words.

True, they usually are familiar with the meaning of "the differential of x," or with $\frac{dx}{dz}$, as being the slope of a curve. Less often they are accustomed to think of $\int y\,dz$, "the integral of y," as being the area under a curve. Hardly ever do they see these two ideas sufficiently clearly to realize almost intuitively that the proposition with which we began is obvious. In pictorial terms, that proposition states that "if one curve rises and falls according to the steepness of another, then this other rises and falls according

INSTINCT, INTELLIGENCE AND CHARACTER

to the area under the first." In a diagram (page 131) we have first a curve x (rising and falling in any way). Then we are told that a second curve y is drawn so that it is high where x is steep and low where x is only sloping gently.

> At A x is steep, so y is high.
> At B x is sloping only gently, so y is low.
> At C x is steep again, so y is high.
> At D x is flat, so y is zero.

Now the proposition whose truth we are endeavouring to see, asserts that then, the area under the curve y is represented by the height of the curve x. To take a specific instance, it asserts that the shaded area between A and B in curve y is represented by the height of B above A in curve x. Now that something like this must be true can be seen intuitively. For if curve x had gone on being as *steep* as at A, then B in that curve would have been much *higher*: and curve y would have stayed at *height* A and the shaded area would have been *greater*. More exactly, the height of B above A in curve x depends upon the average slope of x from A to B, and, on the other hand, the shaded area in curve y depends upon the average height of that curve between A and B : and this average height in y represents that average slope in x.[1]

But though there is great need to guard against the meaningless manipulation of symbols in mathematics, just as there is to guard against the parrot-like vocalization of words in ordinary thinking, yet nothing would be farther from the truth than to belittle the importance of mathematical notation. Again and again in the progress of the physical sciences it has occurred that the invention of a suitable notation has enabled, has indeed caused, a leap forward to be made. With a good notation a mediocrity in reasoning may perchance accomplish as much as would

---

[1] Note that if curve x had at any point come downhill, curve y would have gone below the x axis.

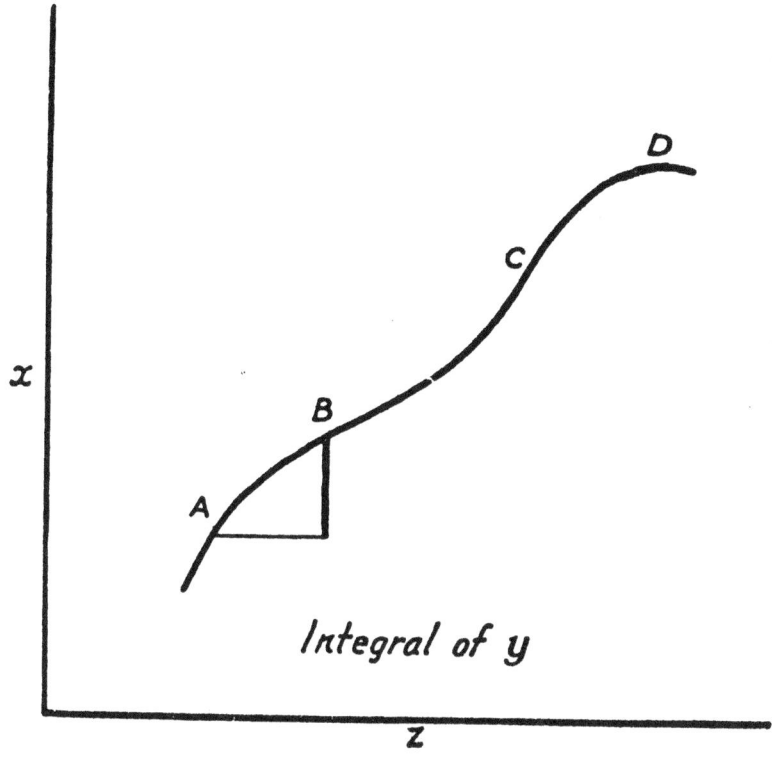

Integral of y

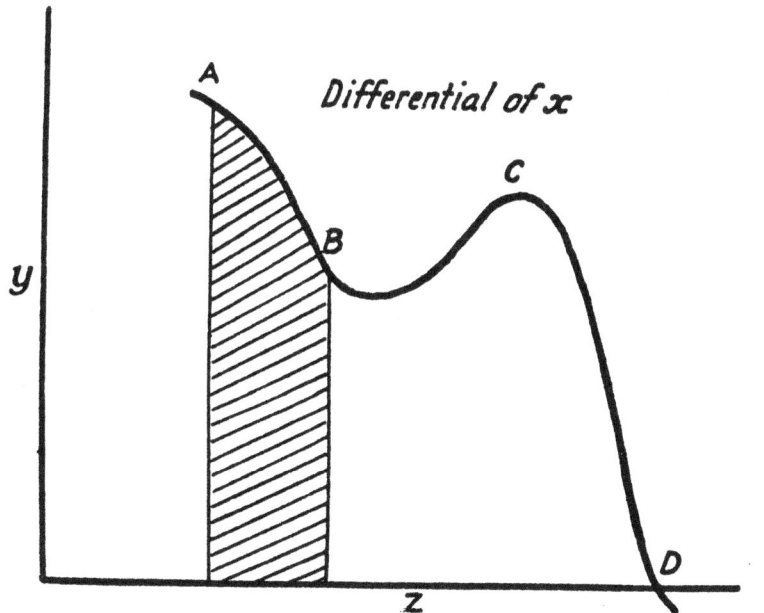

Differential of x

INSTINCT, INTELLIGENCE AND CHARACTER

a genius without it; but genius is needed for the creation of the notation. The help given by the notation comes to pass in two chief ways: by enabling details of situations to be seen at a glance, and by enabling rules of manipulation already familiar in another realm to be transferred to the new province. Good examples of the first point are the chemical notation, e.g. H_2O for water, or $C_nH_{2n+2}O$ for a general class of alcohols; and in mathematics, the second point is illustrated, for example, by the superiority of the notation, in the "Rule of Three," of

$$\frac{3}{4} = \frac{9}{12}$$

over

$$3:4::9:12$$

For by the employment of the former notation we are enabled at once to use all our knowledge about fractions. Instead of learning a new rule, that the "product of the inner numbers equals the product of the outer numbers" ($4 \times 9 = 3 \times 12$), we treat the whole by our former knowledge of simple equations. On a large scale this process is seen all over the realm of mathematical physics. Getting the equations of some new phenomenon into a form where the known mathematics of wave motion in water (say) can be applied, is a familiar task. Just as words represent concepts, represent general ideas divested of irrelevant details, so mathematical symbols represent such general ideas, with the additional advantage that not only are the irrelevant details omitted, but the distinguishing details are indicated in a way not usual in words, except it be in scientific words such as tetramethylbutane. The importance of being able to transfer abilities acquired in one field to do useful service in another, as in these mathematical examples, is very great. It is furthered to some extent also by ordinary words, especially by all the language of relationships. Our word-making, both in the history of language and in every-

MATHEMATICAL AND OTHER SYMBOLS

day slang, shows it. Proverbs show it. Often they are pointed transfers of a relationship from a concrete case to a more abstract case. "The early bird catches the worm." "A stitch in time saves nine."

The whole question of "transfer" in its technical sense is one which has greatly exercised the psychological and educational world. This narrower question is whether exercising one function (as practising Latin composition) will cause, by "transfer," an improvement in another function (such as pleading as a lawyer, or practising as a physician). The discussion of this problem requires a special chapter wherein to follow the somewhat paradoxical results of experiment in this field.

CHAPTER XIV

THE TRANSFER OF TRAINING

THE problem of the transfer of training has three or four different aspects requiring separate consideration. There is first the entanglement with faculty psychology, according to which, if the memory or the reason or the imagination are exercised they are strengthened, and therefore of course can act with greater efficiency in any situation. Closely connected with this is the argument invented by teachers of subjects which have lost with changing conditions of life their once obvious utilitarian value, claiming for them a "disciplinary" effect, improving faculties in the mind. Then there are the views of the laboratory experimenter whose researches show hardly any transfer of training acquired in one field to any other field : of experimenters in schools, who find more transfer though still not much : of teachers and employers, who think they observe a great deal of transfer. And, lastly, there is the paradox that a widely accepted definition of intelligence calls it the power of meeting new situations, of recognizing in novel situations sufficiently familiar points to enable reactions learned elsewhere to be transferred to the new situation.

Faculty psychology, under whose wings those who believe in free transfer of training feel most at home, is almost entirely rejected to-day by competent psychologists, and for two main reasons. In the first place, it separated the mind into watertight compartments labelled "the reason," "the imagination," "memory," "observation," and so on, in a way which seems at variance with the

THE TRANSFER OF TRAINING

obvious unity of the mind, and at variance, less obviously, with the known facts about the brain, which is so closely associated with the mind. And, in the second place, it created entities which were called by the names of these faculties, it almost personified them, and led thus to fallacious arguments such as "Jones remembered the points of that lecture remarkably well, he must have an excellent *memory*—he would be a keen competitor in my job, where I need to remember so many facts about my customers, their names and business connections and so on." Such an argument begs the "transfer" question. And in less crude and less noticeable forms such arguments are being used daily by all of us, often to our later confusion. The school subject which has usually been cited by those who attack "formal training" as a reason for the existence of any portion of the curriculum is Latin. I do not know that the Latin teachers would agree; but according to those who want Latin out of the schools, or dethroned from a place of sovereignty, its teachers claim that through their teaching of that language, and through a study of the classical literature, their pupils gain a mental power which enables them to do almost anything well in after years; do anything well, that is, to an extent proportional to their success in absorbing the Latin teaching of their school period.

I fancy that the Latinists would not put it quite that way, but would lay at least some stress on—not the training of the intelligence, but the amassing of knowledge of human kind and its fundamental passions, and the acquiring of a vocabulary in terms of which to think and speak. Be that as it may, to their triumphant production of many successful and great men who were trained in the classics, their opponents counter with the retort that these men are the result of selection, not of training. They usually come from the already successful class who could send their boys to a Public School. Or if not from this class, they were still more directly selected individually and in their own persons by some Scholarship Examination, and by some discerning headmaster who saw them as clever enough to be put in for such an examination. The Latin course was a stiff one, and those who did well in it almost invariably showed ability in various walks of life later—but not because of the Latin. Rather, because of their own innate intellect, which had enabled them to shine both here and there, both in Latin class and in Parliament. According to this view, indeed, the Latin course is a prolonged intelligence test discovering intelligence of a high order, not making it. And could it have been discovered otherwise and in shorter time (as may perhaps be done some day by " Intelligence Tests "), the time spent on Latin might better have been given to some more directly useful training, closer in its nature to the work to be done in later life.

This argument leaves out of count, of course, the claims of Latin to inclusion for other reasons, such as giving training for leisure rather than for work. It is directed only at the claim that Latin " strengthens the intellect."

But it is time that we turned to experiments designed specifically to test whether training does really transfer. In their earlier forms, some twenty-five years ago, such researches contained numerous experimental errors, but many of these have been corrected, and the form which such an experiment in more recent years has usually taken is somewhat like this.

Two groups of persons (usually school children) are chosen, one of which is presently to be subjected to intensive training in a definite material (say memorizing lists of nonsense syllables—a definitely useless procedure, but one presumably training " the memory," if such an entity exists); while the other, called the " control group," is not to have any such training. Let us suppose that we wish to ascertain whether learning such lists of nonsense syllables will cause an improvement in the power to learn

THE TRANSFER OF TRAINING

useful passages of prose, or to learn historical dates, or what not.

The two groups—the "control group" and the group to be trained—are chosen so as to match each other very carefully. To each member of the one group there corresponds a member of the other group who has the same qualities as far as they are relevant; for example, is of the same or closely similar age, same sex, same race, same school training, same intelligence, same present ability in memorizing prose, and so on. To obtain two such groups a larger number of subjects has to be examined, intelligence tests have to be administered, preliminary memory tests given.

Usually or most accurately, moreover, it is further desirable to have yet other groups, and for this reason. The object is to see how much the groups improve in learning nonsense syllables and in learning prose. For this purpose a piece of prose has to be learned in the preliminary test and another piece in the final test. Now, it is impossible to ensure that these two tests are of exactly equal difficulty: and therefore any change in score may be due to the second test being easier, or harder, than the first one. If, however, the whole experiment as described above is duplicated, and in this duplicate experiment the two tests are given in reverse order, the former preliminary test being here the final test and vice versa, then on the average of the two experiments the errors we have been considering will be cancelled.

To sum up, then, we want four groups of subjects, A, B C, and D, which groups have to be as exactly matched as possible, in the sense that to any member of group A there correspond members of B, C, and D who are at the beginning of the experiment equally able in the things to be tested, and have other qualities as alike as possible. A and B are given certain preliminary tests in memory and certain final tests—C and D are given, for preliminary tests, those used as finals for A and B, and vice versa. A and C are now given intensive practice (for a fortnight, a month, or even a year) in learning nonsense syllables, while B and D are given no such practice, filling in the corresponding time of day with, say, a task in copying drawings. Otherwise the daily round of all four groups should be alike. When at the end of the experiment all the groups are again tested, the following results are those commonly found.

A and C, which have practised learning nonsense syllables, have naturally improved a great deal in this activity. B and D have usually also improved somewhat in this in spite of having had no practice—this is commonly attributed either to " growth " or to the practice effect of the first test itself—but to a very slight extent compared with A and C.

The interesting question, however, is whether the practice in nonsense syllables has " transferred " to learning prose. In the test in prose, all four groups have usually improved, but the improvement of A and C is commonly a little more than the improvement of the control groups B and D. Not a great deal more—it varies from the same to about twice as much. And certainly a great deal less than would have been shown had the time been directly applied to practising prose learning. This last point is particularly well brought out when a still more cunning arrangement of groups is used, as by Dr. W. G. Sleight.[1] It would be a good exercise for a reader to plan an arrangement to test this point.

There cannot be much doubt in the mind of anyone who has studied experiments like that outlined above, that the general picture shown in them is " very little transfer " ; and that to get improvement in a certain function or in certain material it is many times more advisable to give training in that function itself, or that material itself,

[1] See *Brit. Journ of Psychology*, 1911, iv, 386-457.

rather than in anything else with the hope of obtaining transfer. The arguments which could still be brought forward by the believer in transfer are mainly (1) that these experiments are very short, lasting only a few weeks as a rule, and perhaps are not long enough to show results ; (2) that during these weeks the special training of the group undergoing practice is a merely insignificant addition to the training of the whole school day. In practising the memory for nonsense syllables, for example, it cannot be supposed that " the memory " of either the practice group or the control group is lying dormant during the remaining $23\frac{1}{2}$ hours of the day. And (3) that the methods of work, and the incentives to work, are so closely controlled, and everything made so mechanical, that the greatest factor in transfer is rendered nugatory—namely, the recognition of general ways of working successfully.

All these points have something of the truth in them. They may be summed up by saying that the experiments are too artificial to apply to life. In fact, an opponent might make a good debating point by saying : " If you believe that there is no transfer, then you mustn't transfer what you learn in these narrow experiments to anything except to other similar experiments, certainly not to normal school work or to life."

The answer to this is that experiments have been conducted, though as yet in only a few instances, which do actually approximate very closely to natural conditions. The best of these from the point of view of extent and natural background is that conducted by Thorndike in 1922-23 in the United States.[1] The number of children acting as subjects was over eight thousand. They had no idea they were acting as subjects. The work in which they were practised was their actual school work. The function which was tested with a view to detecting transfer, was the power to obtain high marks in portions of the very

[1] See *Journ. of Educ. Psychol.*, January 1924.

INSTINCT, INTELLIGENCE AND CHARACTER

reliable intelligence test known as the I.E.R. (Institute of Educational Research, Teachers' College, Columbia) test. The children were given this test at the beginning and at the end of the school year. Naturally they improved their scores on the second occasion as compared with the first. The question was whether some of the school subjects had improved their " intelligence " more than others, and the answer on the whole was that there was very little difference in this respect, stenography being pretty well as good as any other subject, Latin much the same as cookery, French, or natural history. The general plan of the statistical investigation was to select from the 8,000 children two groups who were taking the same school subjects, except that one group took, say, Latin where the other took, say, cookery. Only one subject was to be different in the two groups. (There were certain permissible departures from this rule which are explained in the article.) Thus differences, if any, between the two groups may be supposed to be caused by the one subject which differs.

The " fallacy of selection " was carefully borne in mind as a possible vitiation, and suitable precautions taken to make reasonably certain that the final results were not caused by this factor. Indeed, it can hardly be appealed to as explaining why cookery students (say) did well in the matter of improvement during the year, for no one will be likely to assert that they are specially selected for intelligence as compared with Latin students. And improvement is, on the whole, positively correlated with initial marks.

In this admirably conducted investigation hardly any loophole is left for the critic who assails the practice period on the score of artificiality or shortness of duration. It was the normal school year with regular ordinary school work. On the other hand, it may perhaps be claimed by opponents that the *test* is still artificial and unlike real life tests : and especially that it was short. If the testing

THE TRANSFER OF TRAINING

could have approximated as closely to real life conditions as the practice did to real school conditions, it may be thought that perhaps the Latin and mathematics training would have emerged. The only way in which one can think readily of this being done is to follow up large numbers of the pupils in life for a few years and see how they do. There would then arise difficulties enough of another sort, the great expense of such an investigation, the difficulty of obtaining quantitative and objective measures of relative " success " in life, the danger of losing track not of an unselected sample of the whole but of special classes, such as those who have greater *wanderlust*, which might well be correlated with intelligence. And then success is not due to intelligence alone.

On the whole, the experimenters must be granted their claim to have shown that transfer is nothing like as easy to detect as it ought to be, were it occurring on as wholesale a scale as once was believed. The belief in transfer among teachers and others, in so far as it survives a study of the experiments, must rationalize itself by supposing that the experiments somehow miss transfer by being too artificial, or by their tests being too short and not measuring quite the right thing.

It is my own belief that the speed factor in tests, while not the reprehensible thing which some lay critics would have us believe, yet does lead to a possible error by minimizing the advantages derived from transfer of training. By the speed factor I mean the fact that tests have to be performed with a time limit at a certain place and on a certain occasion. In some intelligence tests—as in the American army tests—this speed factor distinctly causes a hurried feeling. In these tests only so many minutes are given for each page, or even so many seconds for each question, a device probably desirable in testing for the kind of " on-the-spottitude " (as I have heard it called) needed in warfare, but not perhaps so uniquely essential everywhere. Not all tests have the speed timing in the same degree. In Thorndike's I.E.R. tests the children were *advised* when to turn the page, but allowed to turn back at any point or to go ahead quicker—and the questions were so graded that few children could have done any more even if another half hour had been given.

Yet the fact remains that such tests only measure what can be done in an hour or a half-day of rather pressing work; and it is possible that such is not much influenced by training, and yet that more deliberate work may be influenced. What the person of average ability gets out of a mathematical training, for instance, apart from the actual knowledge, is a habit of mind when confronted with quantitative problems, a belief that an orderly setting down of the problem in a suitable notation will go far towards solving it, a confidence that the right answer can be recognized as such by simple tests when it is obtained, and a familiarity with abstract notions of space and time relationships which is greatly encouraged by the proper association of symbols with geometrical or physical examples. Such habits of mind appear, *a priori*, to be likely enough to transfer to any quantitative problem of life not commonly called mathematical; and to lead to greater power in dealing with such problems; but not immediately to greater speed in dealing with them.

It is true that experiment has an answer ready, and one to be considered with care. It is, that whenever "speed" and "power" of thinking have been measured separately, a fairly large positive correlation has been found between them, they have been found to go, on the whole, together. These experiments have perhaps hardly measured power by sufficiently difficult thinking, but as far as they go they tend in the direction noted. It will be seen that the whole of this transfer dispute is one between wide observation and narrow experiment. Wide observation gets something

THE TRANSFER OF TRAINING

which narrow experiment may miss. But wide observation is open to many more sources of error, fallacies of material, and bias of judgment. And narrow experiment is ever widening. Experiment will have the last word, but its final verdict may not be its present dictum.

Anyhow, certain conclusions seem forced upon the acceptance of the educator. Transfer of training appears, to put it cautiously, to be much less certain and of much narrower spread than once was believed.[1] Subjects of instruction will not therefore be included in the curriculum lightheartedly on the formal " discipline of the mind " argument. Other things being reasonably equal, useful subjects will have the preference. On the other hand, " useful " subjects have a trick of being subjects which anybody can do. Much as it may arouse the antagonism of friends and colleagues, I feel compelled by intellectual honesty to say that almost any girl can learn to cook, or to do school botany, while only few girls can do mathematics or Latin. I think a much stronger case for the inclusion of those latter subjects could be made out on the lines of their efficiency as selective agencies for finding intelligence, than on their training powers. Why not reverse a common argument ? and say, since we must give intelligent tests, let us give tests which are also training the child in something useful in itself. Such an intelligence test is formed by a year's course in mathematics, or Latin ; and the material incidentally learned, though not perhaps so useful as cookery or stenography, is not altogether useless in some circumstances.

Joking apart, it is certain that if any portion of the

[1] According to one writer at least, this has been the salvation of the schools. After remarking on the comparative laxity, in comparison with business practice, which is shown by the schools in matters such as punctuality, regularity of attendance, and so on, he adds : " Let it be fully recognized by the teacher that only the fact that there is little transfer of training between the schoolroom and the office, factory or field, prevents his methods from proving a lifelong handicap to his students in their struggle for a living " (William R. Wilson in *School and Society*, February 9, 1924).

INSTINCT, INTELLIGENCE AND CHARACTER

"discipline" theory is retained by teachers in their working creed—and they retain even more than they admit—they must be up and doing in every aspect of their teaching in order to make transfer more probable or greater in quantity. From experiments of an exact nature such as Sleight's, and from much more numerous and unrecorded experiments of a rough-and-ready sort which teachers are every-day making, it seems very probable that transfer can be greatly aided by methods of teaching. In general, the rule appears to be that any teaching which makes the pupil more *conscious* of how successful results are obtained, is likely to assist transfer.

In memorizing nonsense syllables, it may be an improvement to say them silently: and if so, to realize this and apply it to memorizing a prose passage may create transfer. In playing tennis, improvement may come from keeping one's eye on the ball, and the consciousness of this may cause transfer to playing cricket, in spite of the different stroke. In weighing evidence in history, the actual consciousness of the importance of having all the evidence before one may cause transfer to weighing evidence in business affairs or in a chemical or even a mathematical problem. A conscious effort to make quite certain that one is not looking at a special, instead of a general case, in mathematics may transfer to geography or to biology. A conscious appreciation of the importance of trying a general law on many cases, and especially on limiting cases, may transfer from mathematics to politics, or from the science of languages to the affairs of life. Shortly, if each and every subject is taught as a page or chapter of the universal subject "how to think," and the principles of "how to think" are constantly and consciously appealed to, transfer appears to be much more probable. And what is true on the intellectual side of the mind is, I believe, also true, indeed is still more obviously true, on the side of character and effort. Ideals of tidy records, clean

THE TRANSFER OF TRAINING

apparatus, the power of industry, the importance of experimental honesty, will transfer the more surely, the more they are made conscious.

There are, however, right and wrong ways of getting such ideas consciously grasped by the mind. What is meant above is that they should be understood with conviction, not that they should be reproduced in parrot-like repetition of a verbal form. There comes first an unconscious employment of certain principles or ideals. These gradually become clearer and more definitely outlined. They are recognized by their owner and named, and thereby gain tremendously in effectiveness and in transfer-power. This recognition must, however, await the slow growth of the idea to be recognized. The teacher cannot put the words into the pupil's mouth—or rather, unfortunately, he can do so, but if he does it too early he will give mere words. "Honesty is the best policy"; "Don't jump to conclusions in too big a hurry"; "Test it on a new case"; these are generalizations whose spirit cannot be taught by giving a form of words. Pupils must earn them for themselves.

Really the transfer question, in the way it has been put up to this point in this chapter, is being presented inside out; and a consideration of just what this means may lead to a better understanding of the whole psychological situation. I have just said that it is desirable, in order to get transfer, that certain ways and means of achieving success should become consciously recognized by the pupil. These ways and means are highly abstract matters, such as honesty, or tidiness, or avoiding special cases, or suspending judgment. Now what are the methods of making any pupil conscious of some abstract idea? They are first to present instances in which the abstract idea is embodied, taking care that all the irrelevant concomitants of the idea change and change, until, among the sum total of instances, nothing is common except the idea in question. And secondly, to present many pairs of instances in which all the concomitants remain the same in the two members of the pair, while the idea in question is present in one and absent or in some way greatly changed in the other. For example, in teaching subtraction, cows are subtracted from cows, beads from beads, cups from cups, apples from apples and only finally numbers from numbers. While addition and subtraction are juxtaposed and contrasted.

If these principles are correct, then the way to excite consciousness of, say, the importance of testing a generalization by trying it on a limiting case, will be to present this notion in many varied guises, now in mathematics, now in languages, now in history, in order that it may rise superior to its accidental concomitants and penetrate into the mind. This implies that these ideals of methods cannot be really well taught in any one subject, for they will not become generalized. The mathematician may not learn to be accurate, only to be accurate-in-mathematics. But the chemist-cum-biologist may have a better chance of learning accuracy in itself, having learned it in two different provinces. So it may be, may it not, that transfer from three or four subjects to a fifth, or to life, may be greater than from one even if taught more intensively. Thorndike would be able, on his "theory of common elements," to say that this was due to several school subjects naturally having among them more points of contact with a new subject than any one alone will have. But in part it may be due to the cause I have suggested, rendering methods of work conscious and clear because they are seen against more than one background.

If this has any grain of truth in it, then over-narrowness of curriculum is to be avoided. Not that there is any danger of this in the modern English school, and still less in the American; at least, until the age of sixteen or thereabouts is reached. After that there is danger that the

THE TRANSFER OF TRAINING

pupils, by being shepherded into advanced courses in school, and honours courses in college may over-specialize, a procedure comparatively innocuous to the really clever youth, but very bad for the average person.

Not only is there the danger, in too narrow a curriculum, that ideals of method may not be consciously conceived. There is the supplementary danger that erroneous ideals may be formed and transferred to provinces where they are out of place. A mathematician easily gains the conviction, for example, that all the data of a problem are easily assembled, are perfectly definite, and that the main difficulty is in reasoning out their consequences. Whereas in history or in life, the chief difficulty is just in obtaining all the data and appraising their relative bearing and importance. Or a physicist easily gets the fixed conviction that men must act, under experimental conditions, as predictably as do atoms. Or a historian, since much in this science is open to discussion and differences of opinion, is unable to appreciate the wish for absolute proof which moves in the breast of a chemist, or the fact that absolute proof is ever possible.

There are various theories which explain the facts concerning transfer, especially Thorndike's Theory of Common Elements and Spearman's Theory of Two Factors. But as these theories are more readily discussed as theories of the structure of the intellect, and are highly controversial, we may advantageously postpone them and turn to a matter concerned not with the intellectual side of man's mind so much as with its emotional side and with character.

For after all, the greatest difference between persons who have studied different subjects is not so much in their intellect as in their interests and prejudices. And the effect which studies have on these is perhaps more important than the intellectual spread of ability. As a child grows up he develops ways of looking at the world, and ways of reacting to situations; he grows up into a conservative or

INSTINCT, INTELLIGENCE AND CHARACTER

a radical, a solicitor or a plumber, an atheist or a Wesleyan Methodist, a patriot or a cosmopolitan, and the differences between these are not merely differences in skill or in knowledge or in power of reasoning, not merely differences in the integration of knowledge into science, but also in the integration of the feelings and the emotions into sentiments.

CHAPTER XV

INTERESTS AND PREJUDICES

In the type of psychology which is called Herbartian the "apperception-mass" is an important concept. An apperception-mass is a group of ideas which are related to one another, have links of association which bind the whole together. For example, I have a certain apperception-mass which is centred round the ideas of evolution and natural selection. Within this "mass" are numerous pieces of knowledge of various biological facts, beginning with many from Darwin's *Origin of Species*; various illustrations of the way in which natural selection works (such as the illustration employed in Chapter II of this book); pictures of geological specimens; visions of the slow change of life on this planet through the rolling ages; names and lives of men like Lamarck, Darwin himself, Huxley, Weismann, Wallace. All these ideas and facts are integrated loosely into a whole system which comes, in one or other of its parts, readily into my mind when any new theory is discussed which deals with animal or plant forms.

According to the Herbartian theory of apperception, I shall be interested in a new idea if I possess a strong apperception-mass to which the new idea can be affiliated, and if this apperception-mass, this set of welcoming ideas, is in my mind when the new idea is communicated to me, or if not in consciousness at the moment, at once enters it.

Although this is a very one-sided view of what happens, yet it is an important view, and is worth more careful examination before we contemplate other aspects of the matter. It means, in teaching, that interest in any idea or fact can be obtained if that idea can be seen to fit in with an already organized body of knowledge, to modify and illuminate that body of knowledge and make it hang together better. For example, a boy with a considerable acquaintance with birds' eggs would have, as we say, an active apperception-mass of ideas concerning them. If he were told that seagulls' eggs are very unequal at the two ends so that they will not roll far, but only in a small circle, and thus do not fall off ledges, this new idea would certainly arouse actively a lot of his " birds' egg " apperception-mass, and its acceptance or rejection would depend upon its congruity with what he already knew. And if accepted, the new idea would alter the flavour of many familiar facts about eggs.

I should say as a precaution, and incidentally as another example, that I do not know whether the egg theory is valid or not. When first propounded to me on the Farne Islands by a companion, it fitted in well enough with what little I knew about birds' eggs, and seemed not to be antagonistic to my natural-selection apperception-mass also, since it appeared likely enough that seagulls laying spherical eggs on rocky ledges would leave few offspring.

The famous "Formal Steps," which according to Herbartian doctrine ought to be found in a lesson or teaching unit, were based largely on this idea of apperception. The first task of the teacher, in the *preparation* step, was to recall and refresh that apperception-mass which was likely to welcome and assimilate the new material, which was then presented in the second stage of the lesson, the *presentation*. (The names are English translations of German terms—presumably terms coined by disciples, for the names used by Herbart are distinctly different.) Then opportunity and encouragement and assistance were given, in the third or *association* stage, to the process of bringing the new material into comparison and contrast with all the

INTERESTS AND PREJUDICES

parts of the apperception-mass, and endeavouring to fit it into its place in this particular scheme of things. In this process the new material and the previously existing ideas come, under favourable circumstances, to form a new and wider apperception-mass, the clearing up and defining of which is the task of the fourth step of "generalization." In the final step of "application" the concept thus won is applied to the comprehension of other cases, and receives verification from them.

For instance, it might be the desire of the teacher to lead the pupils to form the generalization that the rapidity with which a pendulum oscillates is inversely proportional to the square root of its length. The problem might arise out of a project to make a pendulum of given speed of oscillation, or out of investigations as to the effects of temperature on clocks by causing expansion and contraction of the pendulum; which facts, and the general knowledge that a pendulum goes more slowly if long, form the apperception-mass called up by the preliminary announcement, remarks, and questions of the teacher. The presentation would consist in requiring measurements of length and time of certain pendula: and the skill of the teacher would in part lie in "requiring" these not by a direct request but by causing a curiosity to know them, by cunningly arranging that they shall be made for some reason or other, or by seizing upon chance happenings and just giving this particular lesson (unpremeditated) when such favourable chances occurred.

The measurements, when assembled, have to be looked over and "guesses" made as to their connection, as to the law governing them, judgment in each case being held in suspense till the guess is tested on other, and if necessary on new measurements. And here a new kind of apperception mass comes into play—or rather it is always in play, but we first notice it here and now—and that is, a general collection of ways and habits of dealing with numerical

INSTINCT, INTELLIGENCE AND CHARACTER

data, and a knowledge that such data generally reveal some law when tried in various ways. Among such ways are making graphic curves, forming simple functions such as products, sines, squares, forming differences between consecutive values, and a host more. By such means a law may ultimately be discovered which gives the connection between the length and time of swing of a pendulum, and enables the one to be predicted from the other.

We must leave for the present [1] the enticing development of how such empirical laws as the above fail to satisfy us and how we only are content when we can deduce the same law from intuitive premises by logical steps: and return to our discussion of the Herbartian doctrine of apperception. The new facts which are introduced in the presentation merge themselves in the apperception-mass, and modify it, as a piece of sugar disappears in a cup of tea, which is itself changed into a drink with a new flavour. The new apperception-mass, being richer and more articulated than the old, will have more points of contact with the unknown, will be more capable of absorbing new data and new ideas. Thus the circle of thought goes on increasing its area, throwing out projections here and there along this or that radius but, in a harmonious education, always from time to time filling in the intervening sectors and making an integrated whole.

The pendulum illustration, though excellent for illustrating the Five Steps, emphasizes mainly a logical aspect of apperception, whereas Herbart was concerned rather with the active power of ideas to seize others even when no such scientific generalization as that of the pendulum law is found. There must no doubt always be a certain logical satisfaction, but the plane of reasoning may be very low. To take examples at various levels, we may cite understanding a new country by comparison and contrast with the home neighbourhood and countries already studied,

[1] See Chapter XXV below.

INTERESTS AND PREJUDICES

comprehending a situation by means of an analogy, as that of the neurone system with a telephone system; being interested in new stamps because one already has a wide knowledge of them; hearing a sonata with greater interest and comprehension after facts about sonatas already known have been recalled, and certain of the themes have been anticipated and played over.

When a man visits a town, he is unlikely to settle there if he is lonely and no one is recognizable as belonging to his set, his profession, his lodge, his church, or his college. But if some of these have been called to the station to meet him, and he is in pleasant fashion introduced and made known to them and they to him, he may remain, settle down, marry into the town, and influence by his presence the particular group which has absorbed him. So it is in teaching, where the art of the teacher consists in part in calling to the front the right ideas to meet the new-comer, and in making suitable introductions.

Now in this Herbartian view of interest, useful as it has been and can still be to the teacher as a guide, there are two main deficiencies. The one is that, in the preparation part of a lesson, it is far more important that a problem attitude should be evoked, that a project to do something should arise, than that certain ideas should be haled into the focus of consciousness.

The other is that the Herbartian view of the growth of interests makes the whole matter far too exclusively an affair of the intellect, instead of being to an even greater extent dependent upon the instincts and the emotions. Herbart and his followers realized and emphasized the way in which cognitive ideas, pieces of knowledge, aspects of a subject, generalizations, are built up into systems which are the working mind, viewed as a logical machine. It was left for a later generation of psychologists to appreciate the fact that there are similar structures on the side of the feelings also, corresponding to apperception-masses on the cognitive side. These are the sentiments, or the complexes [1] of the " new psychology," which, drawing their energy from the instincts, put vital force into the rather marionette-like figures on the Herbartian stage of consciousness.

A sentiment is a kind of structure of the emotions round some object or idea, so that when this object or idea appears in a situation we tend to develop emotions which prevent us from thinking in an entirely unbiassed way and we tend to behave in what may often seem, and be, an irrational manner. In short, a sentiment is a prejudice, if we take the latter word at its face value; or rather, there is no judgment at all except a trumped-up judgment which deceives ourselves more than it deceives others. Sentiments may be very laudable things, and the arguments may be valid with which we support them, and yet not owe their force to that validity.

For example, patriotism is a sentiment. The emotions are organized in a certain way about the idea of our native country, and about persons and symbols which represent it. So we thrill at the sight of our flag in a foreign land, burn with indignation at any insult to our ambassador, feel fear lest the country's prestige should suffer in a world conference, and hatred of all who oppose its ambitions. A sentiment is not itself an emotion, or group of emotions, it is the permanent set or attitude which ensures that emotions of a given sort will arise in situations involving the object of the sentiment. It is an organization of emotions round an object or idea, while the apperception-mass is an organization of ideas and cognitive facts. Without doubt the two should be considered together, for the idea which is the centre of a sentiment is itself part of an apperception-mass, and any other part of that mass may

---

[1] The word complex is used by the more orthodox followers of Freud and Jung, it would appear, to mean only a " repressed " complex. As almost an equivalent of Shand's term " sentiment " it has been widely popularized by Tansley's book *The New Psychology*. There seems also a tendency to use sentiment for the weaker kinds of complex.

INTERESTS AND PREJUDICES

in more or less effective measure act as the cue to release the emotions. Thus, in the patriotism sentiment, any member of a widespread apperception-mass (which includes the flag, the ambassador, facts about my country's foreign policy, and what not) may arouse patriotically directed emotions. In a sentiment of a narrower and more personal kind, such as may form round a favourite pipe, it is more truly a single object which is the focus, and the sentiment is almost wholly an organization of emotions alone. In love for a person of the opposite sex, there is a wide set of cues which may be active; but these are mainly objects and places accidentally associated with the loved one, as a dress, a book, a room, or the like.

When an apperception-mass is called into consciousness as in the Herbartian lesson, the ideas which it is likely to assimilate and accept are by no means those which find logical affinity, which fit nicely into the intellectual structure, or which indicate obvious modifications and simplifications of that intellectual structure. In the case of the pendulum lesson, where no sentiments are likely to be involved, no prejudices toned with feeling likely to be present, the acceptance of the new generalization does mainly depend on its logical congruity with what is already known, though even here the teacher's prestige will be a force to be reckoned with. In the case of many new ideas, however, it is far more the fact that their acceptance depends on the sentiments than on logical suitability. Take for example the ideas of evolution and natural selection referred to in the opening paragraph of this chapter, and consider their reception by the minds of men of the mid-nineteenth century when they were first introduced to widespread notice. Their acceptance or rejection by an individual depended far more upon feelings than upon facts. Only if we extend the apperception-mass to include all the sentimental structure woven into and around it can we follow the Herbartian doctrine. And if we do so, then we have to recognize that the circle of a pupil's interest will grow not only by feeding on ideas but by practising behaviour actuated by feelings.

The preceding paragraphs must be understood as dwelling on the interaction of the feelings and the intellect, not on their separation. Saying that new ideas will be accepted mainly because of congruity with prejudices and sentiments does not mean that the latter are constant and impervious to the influence of ideas. There is constant mutual influence. A biologist is reported to have said of a clergyman who rejected the Darwinian doctrines with vehemence, that if he would only come and take a three years' course in biology, he would change his mind. And doubtless, could his prejudices have been overcome so far as to permit him to take such a course, the influx of new experiences would have considerably modified his prejudices by enlarging his circle of ideas. But could the biologist have taken three years' slumming with the clergyman, possibly he might have changed too.

Certainly sentiments are often formed by processes which cannot be described as consisting in enlarging our ideas. Properly arranged ceremonies of saluting the flag, honouring national observances, and singing national songs can produce patriotism, as Americanization exercises in the United States clearly show. The whole question of this formation of sentiments is one of the greatest importance for education if education is to mean more than the accumulation of knowledge, and more even than the acquirement of skill or the training of intellectual powers. It is based on a proper handling of the instinctive forces of the individual, and it recognizes the instincts as the great sources of energy, the proper direction of which into suitable channels is the main business of character formation.

CHAPTER XVI

REPRESSION AND SUBLIMATION

MAN is descended from the same ancestry as the animals, but he is different from them. He has won in the struggle for mastery on this planet because of the possession of powers which they lack. Viewed from the intellectual side, these powers take the form of the ability to reason, practically lacking in animals even though the psychologist may with interested eye see its germs and beginnings there. And the power of reasoning is based, as we think, largely on a flexibility of response to situations, so that alternatives present themselves and are followed out, not by explicit action, but by imagery or by symbolic internal behaviour mainly in terms of words.

From another point of view, however, man's superiority is in the greater plasticity of his instincts, and the emotional drives associated with them, so that they can be directed away from the bestial gutters in which their untrammelled course would lie, into other channels. And so began in man the conflict of good and evil, for while the primordial path of expression of an instinct cannot be either blameworthy or praiseworthy in a beast of the field which can respond in no other way, in man the channels into which instincts are diverted may be either noble or ignoble. The former choice is what the technical language of the new psychology calls sublimation, as when the sex instinct finds expression for its energy in the ideals of chivalry and knighthood. The latter is perversion, as when the same sex instinct finds an outlet in pornography, or in secret or social vice.

INSTINCT, INTELLIGENCE AND CHARACTER

An analogy which has been much used by exponents of this view is that of water power, the water drainage system of a country. The natural valleys down which the water rushes are the natural instincts, untouched by engineering, by education. In the animal these channels are fixed and hardly changeable. But in man the soil is more suitable for canalizing some of the river courses, diverting others, possibly blocking and damming others. In Thorndike's phrase, education can encourage some instinctive responses, eliminate some, and redirect others. The main contribution of the psychoanalytic schools of Freud and Jung to the psychology of education has been, I think, their discovery of the frequency and magnitude of the dangers of endeavouring to eliminate instincts, and their insistence on the importance of redirection or sublimation.

Merely repressing an instinct is like building a wall across the valley without making any provision for the piled-up waters being somehow drained away. In such a case one of three things may happen. The first is that the wall of repression may from time to time be broken through, and the pent-up energy rush down its old channel in an orgy of primitive passion, like the relapses of the converted drunkard, or the outbursts of the prodigal son of an overstrict home. Such *débâcles*, like the dam-bursts of a real country, do more harm than the unrestrained river would have created. A naïve preventive is to release the flood gates from time to time: a harmless, indeed a beneficial plan in some cases, as when the nerve-strung city dweller runs off to the woods and lives the life of a primitive savage as nearly as he can, calling it camping or hunting or exploring; but in other cases very open to abuse, as were the riots of revelry on days such as accompanied, in the mediæval Church, periods of repression and fasting (the modern Carnivals, Mardi Gras, Fasnacht, Mi-carême). Sowing wild oats is not the best way of preventing the evils of repression.

REPRESSION AND SUBLIMATION

The second thing that can happen to our walled-up valley, our repressed instinct, is that the water behind the wall may seep through in secret places (places unknown or from which we resolutely turn our gaze), and find channels of its own down which it runs to create new problems worse than those for which we built the wall. We prevent emulation in the school, because it so easily breeds envy and conceit, and it finds expression in seeing who can smoke most cigarettes, or know most swear words. We fail to take account of the sex instinct, we wall it off from life, and it leaks out in perversions, or transfers itself to unhealthy friendships and favouritisms.

But thirdly, and perhaps worst, our dam may be a success. The valley below may be quite dry (and sterile), a Pyrrhic victory won at the cost of absorbing the whole energy of the land in preserving and strengthening the dam. The need of restraining that imprisoned force neutralizes whatever else of force the individual possesses, and a tremendous mental conflict is set up, the more disastrous because its existence is denied, or is even unknown to consciousness. This is the analogue of the repressed complex of the Freudians, the source of so much mental trouble. And as a valley may be dammed most easily near its source, so the Freudians find the cause of such repressions mainly in the early years of infancy, and lend by their theories a new importance to Gertrude teaching her children, to the fore-kindergarten and kindergarten years. Repression of instincts in those early years means that we block the natural channel but leave to chance what the result will be. True educative agencies would block no channels, would merely divert slightly the flow of energy. In the hills a little thing may decide whether a spring will send its waters down this or that valley, and a result may be achieved which, if postponed, would have required marvels of engineering.

The Freudian school seeks in the sex-complex most of

the repressions of mental life. And there is, of course, no doubt that it is in questions of sex that the conditions of modern civilization make most demands on redirection of instincts. On the one hand, natural selection will always tend to keep the sex instinct up to a high level of potential, for there must always be a tendency for those in whom it is strongest to leave more numerous progeny, other things being at all equal. And, on the other hand, modern civilization makes marriage an event occurring several or many years after adolescence and leads to post-marital restrictions and small families, while custom throws such a veil over all the questionings of the young concerning their own bodies, where babies come from, and the like, that there is a state of tension throughout society regarding these matters not found in connection with any other instinct. No doubt repression most commonly occurs here, and no doubt, too, sublimation is more difficult. An instinctive pugnacity in a boy can be readily diverted from quarrelsomeness and fighting to boxing, to games and mastery in them, to studies and beating others there, even to setting the teeth and fighting a hard problem in mathematics or Latin translation. The transitions are not unnatural. It is not so easy to know what to do with the sex instinct. There is reason to think any kind of work, physical or mental, games or studies, will carry off some of the energy. Giving such knowledge (through the botanical approach) as makes sex seem natural, and giving reasonable opportunities for meeting children of the other sex even if co-education is not possible, are helpful. Actual sublimation of the sex instinct is believed by many to take place in the provinces of music and art, poetry and the æsthetic side of education generally, and in religious contemplation and practices. Indeed, with adolescent girls, this last can become almost a perversion. With girls, the connection of the sex instincts with maternal sentiments allows of a natural outlet by mothering, playing at house-

REPRESSION AND SUBLIMATION

making, and caring for any tender and fragile things such as chicks or porcelain or embroidery.

According to Freud, the sex instinct is strong even in infancy, and directed towards the parents, especially the parent of opposite sex. Not, of course, the animal sex instinct of puberty, but its emotional core, together with pleasure in bodily contact, kissing and endearment. The development of the individual is for Freud largely the history of how this attachment is directed later to others and ultimately to the sweetheart and mate. Failure to break away from the parental attachment causes, according to this view, much weakness of character. In the process of transference of the affections from parent to mate, the teacher, during childhood, undoubtedly plays a part. Attachment of children for teachers can easily become unhealthily emotional, especially in girls' schools, where a kind of worship of a favourite teacher often clearly draws its strength from the growth of emotions as yet undirected towards the opposite sex.

It is the belief of Freud and his followers that dreams are the expressions of repressed complexes striving to win a way to consciousness, and that they are the guardians of sleep, by giving a certain partial satisfaction and outlet to forces which would otherwise cause an awakening. Freud personifies the repressing force (due to other instincts, or other manifestations of the same instinct) and calls it the Censor. This Censor is less vigilant in sleep, yet not entirely careless of what passes into the dream consciousness; and so the forbidden wishes disguise themselves in symbolic figures (several wishes often compressing themselves into one symbol), which disguised actors form the *manifest content* of the dream, very different in apparent significance from the *latent content*, which would appal the Censor and can only be discovered by the special methods of psychoanalysis.

In one of his early writings (in *l'Année psychologique*)

INSTINCT, INTELLIGENCE AND CHARACTER

C. G. Jung, in part a disciple and in part an opponent of Freud, gives an example of the workings of a repressed complex in the unconscious background behind the mere façade of consciousness, not drawn from a dream but from a chance sung song, apparently chosen at random and without cause—the song sung by Margaret in *Faust*:

> Es war ein König in Thule
> Getreu bis an das Grab.

There was once a king in Thule who was faithful to his true love until death. For as she lay dying she had given him a golden beaker, which he had ever used: and now that his own end was approaching, while he shared among his heirs all that was his of lands and wealth, he took the beaker and repaired to a high pinnacle by the sea, overlooking a whirlpool. And there, having drunk a last draught from it, he cast it into the gulf, where it too drank and sank into the waters as the king sank back to die.

In the Freudian theory no mental event is random and without cause,[1] not even the accident of which song a girl sings as she spins. Margaret, though she would deny it and does, indeed, repress it, is beginning to doubt, below the surface of her conscious thoughts, the fidelity of Faust. The wish that he might prove faithful to her till death cannot find straightforward expression, since that would imply a painful recognition of her doubts. But it actively presses upward, and passes the Censor successfully in what is only a thin disguise; the king in the song being an obvious substitute for Faust, and the "true love" for Margaret herself.

When mental distress and conflict, various bodily tics

---

[1] Freud was, of course, not the first to say this. More than a century before him Hume, in the *Inquiry*, wrote: "Even in our wildest and most wandering reveries, nay, in our very dreams, we shall find, if we reflect, that the imagination ran not altogether at adventures." But Freud followed up the clue.

REPRESSION AND SUBLIMATION

and jerks, or mental phobias, are caused by a repression, it has been found that cure follows if the patient can be assisted to bring the repressed complex into consciousness. It is doing harm, because, though kept out of the intellectual chamber of consciousness where common sense would dispose of it, it is in emotional strength undiminished, and to hold this force down is using up energy. The chief point in outflanking the Censor seems to be to get the patient to practise allowing his mind to follow associations in the freest possible fashion, reporting them to the psychoanalyst: and in order to get starting-points, dreams are used, each item being made the commencement of such trains of free associations. Or in another method, words are said one by one to the patient, who responds with his first associated word, as "white," "snow." When these words touch on complexes, a longer time elapses before the reply comes, or the word is misheard, or an exceedingly far-fetched association is made, or a previous one repeated, etc. In such a way the analyst gets on the track of the trouble and drags it to daylight. Each little forgetfulness of every day, each slip of speech, is similarly asserted to be due to unconscious forces. We forget what is painful; we say by a slip of the tongue what deep in our unconscious we really think, as when a hostess exclaims "Can't you go—must you stay?" Repressed incidents drag down into unconsciousness with them, things which have only slight superficial associations with them, even a punning resemblance being sufficient—as when Freud forgets the name of a character and miscalls him Jocelyn, because his true name Joyeux would suggest his own name Freud and would be painful in the circumstances in question (Joyeux being approximately a French equivalent of Freud).

Perhaps only someone who is engaged in treating mental patients, and knows from experience how helpful as windows to the back of the mind such apparent trifles can be, is competent to judge this hypothesis. Most of us can

INSTINCT, INTELLIGENCE AND CHARACTER

find occurrences in our own lives which seem to fit in with Freud's theories, though remaining doubtful whether they are coincidences such as can be brought in support of any theory, or relevant instances.

For example, the reader may remember that on page 91 I was unable to recall the name of an author. At the time when this actually happened, it struck me that the forgetfulness might be an illustration of Freud's theory, and I wrote down what came into my mind while trying, in vain, to recall the name. My notes with altered names, and one or two consequent alterations in the text, are as follows :

> The first name that occurs to me is Boyes. I have a feeling that this is wrong, but I believe the name is a monosyllable. I cannot write quickly enough to put down the many associations that occur. The Argentine I think of. Did not the man I mean go out to an important post there ? No; was not that the author of another book . . . which I used at about the same time ? Cross ! I believe that is the name—but I am not sure. (Boyes, of course, is the name of the chief assistant of my solicitor from whom I had a letter last week, but that seems irrelevant.) The book was slim and yellowish in colour. I believe the name was Cross. Cross and Blackwell make jam. Boyes seems to keep coming back to me. I feel very confident that the name was Cross. Why can't I remember the initials ? I feel that I would recognize the name better could I get the initials—T. K. Cross is it ? No. Perhaps that came from T. K. R., my old college chum's initials. I must leave it at Cross—or Craggs—no, not Craggs. Cross surely. I feel uncertain.

Six weeks after the above was written down, I chanced to see, in the *New York Times*, the name Craster, and realized at once that it was the name I was trying to recall. I again set down just what came into my mind—paper and pencil were at my elbow :

> Craster at once makes me think of a girl of that name who in 1914 was engaged to someone who was the first of my friends to be killed in the war in September 1914. It seems possible that I have repressed the name because of this painful association. I

REPRESSION AND SUBLIMATION

remember the scene when I heard the news of his death, with that of his chum and fellow-student killed on the same day. I was visiting a school and a teacher and fellow-student of theirs (whose name also at this moment refuses to return—it was P. W.—I have just got it) showed me a newspaper. He too was killed nine months later I do not know why Boyes comes in, unless because of the girl's nickname. . . . T. K. R. was a fellow-officer for a while with P. W., in the same battalion, and with his career another painful memory is connected. Physically he rather resembles the man who was killed in 1914, who was called Blackwood. Is that why I thought of Cross and *Black*well? His chum also, who was killed on the same day, was called Blaylock, a name beginning with the same three letters.

It has been difficult to alter the names without changing the associations, but I have succeeded fairly well, I think, in making them much the same, except that I cannot fit in a fictitious nickname which will suggest Boyes as the original did the corresponding real name.

Now the Freudian theory of this would be, I imagine, that I repressed once upon a time, because of the pain which his death caused me, not only the name of my friend Blackwood, but also names of people who might remind me of him, such as Miss Craster or P. W. And when I wanted Craster, the author, the repression still worked and I could not remember the name. But in its endeavour to escape, the energy of the name Craster, forbidden to come to light in that form, disguised itself as Cross, and Craggs, or brought up the first syllable of the name Blackwood in Cross and Blackwell.[1]

I should add that later again I remembered that Craster had been a tutor at Cross Street College when he wrote the book (the names of Cross in " Cross Street College " and Cross in " Cross and Blackwell's " are not identical in spelling in the real names, but similar in sound).

Wit and humour, too, are in Freud's opinion in part operations of the unconscious mind, as might be antici-

[1] This bringing up of pieces of names is not unlike Freud's case of the names Signorelli Botticelli and Boltrafia (Psychopathologie des Alltagslebens).

INSTINCT, INTELLIGENCE AND CHARACTER

pated from the frequent verbal superficial associations occurring in his analyses. To one reading his writings it seems almost as though the differences between individuals in respect to freedom of imagination, exuberance of fancy, originality of ideas, was not so much due to lack of ability to make these connections as to the action of a Censor in refusing them admission to the stage of consciousness. They are freely made in the unconscious, and if they escape are ingenious or witty or mad; but mostly they are repressed as incongruous. Wit is just such an incongruity with a thread of connection, made in the unconscious but seized on by consciousness. And if this is so there should surely be wit in dreams, as there is certainly madness and poetry. Personally, I know that I often dream puns and jokes. Six months ago, westbound on the Atlantic, and a trifle worried as to what to do with a medicinally minute flask of whisky in my luggage, I dreamt I was making a public speech in which I referred, with great effect, to the United States as " that land of liberty *without licence.*" And in New York, having noted with amusement that each and every taxicab showed a notice " lowest rate," I dreamt I saw a man affixing a detachable S before the former of these two words.

"Variation," says Thorndike in a notable phrase, "is the first requisite for progress in the behaviour of an individual, as it is in the development of the race." The suggestion here made is that this variation, from which the environment by the satisfactions and pains of social taboos selects the adult surviving ideas and habits of thought, is perhaps sometimes too rigidly pruned and weeded out by this Censor of consciousness: that education by taming the wilderness may be turning it not into a garden of delightful surprises but a desert of artificial funeral wreaths, marking the graves of associations which might have been the germs of invention in science or art or poetry. We harden as we grow older. The Censor has

REPRESSION AND SUBLIMATION

more power. And education should not unduly hasten the process.

In another chapter, and indeed in many books on psychology, our brains and nervous systems have been likened to telephone systems. Now the essence of a telephone system is certainty and speed. If I call up Cathedral 3742 I want my friend Smith, and am annoyed with the operator if I don't get him every time. But a mind which made such reliable and predictable connections every time would be a dull and stodgy affair. The analogy breaks down. Business demands the certainty in the telephone system, but it would be ever so much more interesting if, when I called up Cathedral 3742, I might get Lloyd George or Babe Ruth or Howard Carter or Joan of Arc or a fishwife at Cullercoats. Business demands certainty in the mind's responses, and as we grow older it gets it, but at a penalty, the loss of interest and creative force. It is disconcerting in matters of routine if our mind calls up Joan if the situation requires Smith, and we reprove it if it does. But if we train it too well we find it cannot make any suggestions (except Smith) when the situation is a bit new and strange. Thus the Censor, who is mainly awake to the opinions of the particular herd to which we belong, creates sentiments and prejudices in accord with the fashionable ideas of that herd by refusing admission to consciousness of others. And as selection among the individuals of one generation influences the composition of the next generation because these selected individuals become its parents, so selection among the ideas and ideals of childhood influences the adult mind, for these ideas which come to the stage of consciousness intermarry with one another, form alliances and families, and their offspring are the stock in trade of the grown man, while the repressed ideas languish in sterile imprisonment.

Sometimes the fact of belonging to two herds creates two selections which may refuse to intermingle. Psychiatry

INSTINCT, INTELLIGENCE AND CHARACTER

tells us of cases of actual multiple personality, like Sally Beauchamp, or Doris E, where the segregation of conscious ideas may be so complete that the two or more personalities may not have common memories, as Real Doris did not know anything of the life of Sick Doris or Margaret or Sleeping Margaret who were her co-dwellers in the one body. And cases, not of actual multiple personality, but of very different systems of sentiments, may occur and probably do so more frequently than we imagine even among children. The schoolboy who has quite different codes of honour in his relationship with comrades or teacher, is not unlike the business man who is a good father and respectable churchwarden but is capable of very sharp practice at the office. On sex matters very many school children have two ways of thinking, and differ very much when they are among other children or with grown-ups. Their attitude in the latter case may vary between complete repression and giggling innuendo. And in many other ways school and home life may force children to live double lives.

Now it would seem that the lesson to be learned from all this, by teachers, is the desirability of avoiding barriers in the life of childhood, and of taming instincts by employing them, not by either ignoring or combating them. Barriers grow up when discipline is inflicted from without instead of growing from within; when teachers are too aloof and when they shirk discussion; when unnatural separation of sexes occurs (a certain amount of separation at some ages may be natural); when teachers demand standards of behaviour beyond the power of childhood.

* * * *

And above all, inner conflict is certain when we do not early form the habit of appealing always to the intellect and to reason. Reasons do not sway mobs. Reasons, says Nietzsche, make the populace suspicious. But we must

REPRESSION AND SUBLIMATION

work for a day when reason is mightier than now, and aid it in holding sway in ourselves first, then in our pupils and —who knows?—perhaps some day in the world. Wherein the danger is that reason may fall of its own presumption, for it must learn humility, not pride, and must rationally prove, and reasonably accept the proof, that some matters are insoluble. It must consider and envisage matters of the spirit as well as of the material world. But in all it must demand honesty and a ruthless laying bare of the motives which may be active in any behaviour undertaken. In school, then, open-mindedness, the sinking of personal motives (which is achieved by many schools) and equally the sinking of party or sectarian or even patriotic motives (which is achieved by few) is the ideal; free forms of discipline, free debate, freedom of speech, toleration of all things (including even a certain toleration of others' intolerance), the use of emulation only to sublimate it as *esprit de corps*, and the use of *esprit de corps* only to make it sublime as a feeling of the oneness of humanity. And in particular the teacher should be ever on guard against insidious rationalizations, against reasons for certain behaviour which are really trumped up after the behaviour has been actuated by quite other motives, as when we punish a child to reform him or to deter others, but really because we are angry and our self-esteem is hurt.

CHAPTER XVII

INDIVIDUAL DIFFERENCES IN INTELLECT

ONE of the great changes which have come over educational psychology in the last twenty years is that produced by the realization of the tremendous differences which exist between individuals, and of the continuity which yet reigns from one end of the scale to the other. We shall leave to another chapter the question whether these differences are produced by environment and education or are mainly inborn and unchangeable, merely saying here that the present state of our knowledge supports a belief that inborn differences form a very considerable part of the whole.

If a large number of men is assembled and ranked for any quality—such as height, in the familiar army preparation for ceremonial drill, " Tallest on the right, shortest on the left, *size* "—then provided the men are numerous, are all of one race, and are quite unselected, these two facts of wide range and continuity over the range will show themselves.

Of course, if different races are involved, there may well be discontinuity. If some of the men are negroes from Africa, and some are Norwegians, they will fall into two distinct groups for skin colour. And Japanese and Norwegians would fall into two nearly distinct groups for size. But if they are all of one race, then for most qualities there will be continuity.

Again, of course, if they are few in number, there may be discontinuity. If they are sizing for height, there may be a very tall man who is much taller than the next in the

INDIVIDUAL DIFFERENCES IN INTELLECT

row. But if their numbers are increased, more and more will step into the gap, and it will ultimately be filled up by men differing only slightly in height.

And thirdly, if they have been selected consciously or unconsciously according to some criterion, then their ranking according to that or any associated criterion may show discontinuity. For example, if they were a mixed lot of Guardsmen and Artillery drivers, they would probably fall into distinct size-groups. Here the selection is conscious and is set forth on recruiting posters. But it might not in every case be so obvious.

And lastly, it cannot be denied that in some cases actual discontinuity is found, or what is practically discontinuity. There is a continuous range from blonde to brunette, but the red-headed stand apart.

The point of all this is that similar laws have been found to hold for mental qualities, for temperament, good taste, etc., and particularly for intelligence. There is always a danger that the use of class names, such as defective, normal, clever, genius, etc., may lead to the belief that these classes are quite or almost distinct. Thus children were once rather looked upon as falling into a large group of normal children, all very much alike, and two smaller groups, of defectives at one end and, at the other, of geniuses, clearly marked off from the normal.

Now this is not so, as experiment and statistical observation have clearly shown. If men or children are ranked for intelligence they form as unbroken a series of steps from one end of the line to the other as they do in the case of height. There is not a class of defectives at one end and of geniuses at the other at all clearly marked off and separated sharply from the others. There is continuity, there are no gaps which cannot be filled in if we increase our numbers. But there is a difference in the size of the steps between individuals, a law governing the continuity, which can be best shown by the following considerations.

INSTINCT, INTELLIGENCE AND CHARACTER

Let us return to our men who are falling in in order of height, tallest on the right. Let us suppose that we cause men who are identical in height to stand behind one another, so that the front rank is composed of men distinguishable in height from another, while behind each front-rank man stand in file those identical with him. Then what we would find would be that near the middle of the row the files would extend far to the rear, while near the ends of the row the files would be short, at the very end being some who have no one behind them. To make the picture more vivid still, suppose that the men of each file proceed to stand one above the other on their front-rank man's shoulders, as gymnasts do at displays. Then the end men would have to support none or few, while in the centre of the front rank the human ladder would tower to the roof, like this :

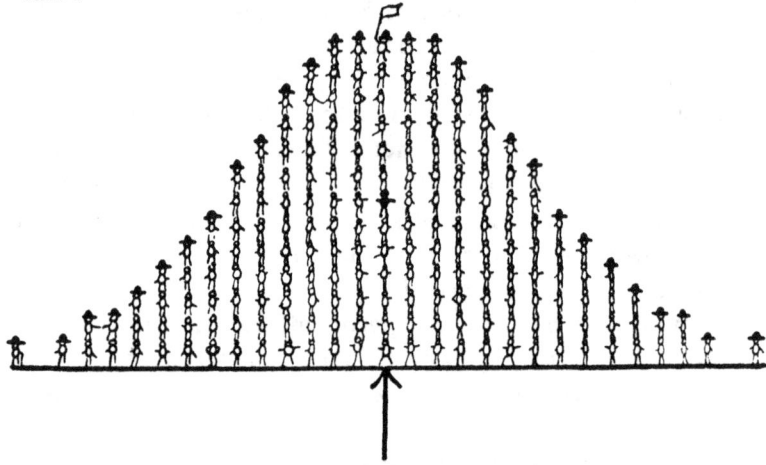

The curve thus visualized is the famous Normal Curve of Probability, associated with the names of Gauss and Laplace, and the thesis of this chapter so far may be said to be that mental qualities also are distributed according to the normal curve, or according to one of the allied skew curves presently to be described.

INDIVIDUAL DIFFERENCES IN INTELLECT

If, for example, the arrangement of the above diagram had been for intelligence instead of size, the curve formed by the line of hats—only the topmost man in each column is wearing a hat—would be of similar shape. In recent years what are known as intelligence tests have been developed, by which a measure of intelligence called the intelligence quotient is obtained, of which it only need be said here that it is high for high intelligence and low for low intelligence, and centres round 100. Thus 140 is very clever and 60 is very unintelligent indeed. When the intelligence quotients of a large number of unselected children are examined they are found to fall into a curve just like the above. Here are 2,710 Northumberland children tested in 1921.

Below 60	61–70	71–80	81–90	91–100
21	83	226	475	644

101–110	111–120	121–130	131–140	Over 140
596	400	189	65	11

Making these into a diagram, we get the following picture exactly like the gymnastic pyramid above:

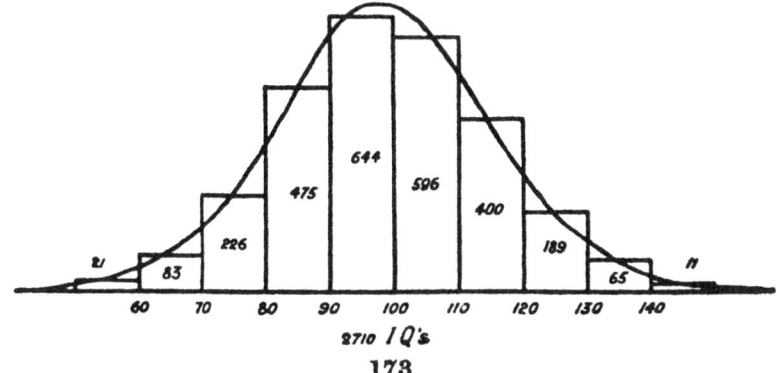

2710 IQ's

INSTINCT, INTELLIGENCE AND CHARACTER

It is in steps only because, for convenience, we have lumped together all the cases into groups of ten points—really the smooth curve drawn through the rectangles should be imagined.

The chief educational problems which an appreciation of the range and continuity of mental differences emphasizes are those connected with classification, with special classes for the defective, with rapid promotion for the child of superior intellect, with lack of homogeneity in classes, with marking examination papers and with borderline cases. One or two considerations bearing on some of these problems can be deduced from facts of which the above is a solitary but typical example.

In the first place, it is clearly a difficult task to separate children, distributed as above, into the sheep and the goats. There is not any chasm separating them. In picking children who are unable to gain anything from an ordinary school, and who ought to be cared for in a special school, there is no question " is, or is not, this child defective ? " There is only the question where to draw the line in a continuously changing variable called intelligence. If one community has one per cent. of its children in such special schools, and another community two per cent., that merely means, as a rule, that the line in question is differently drawn by the two authorities. And it is also clear that in drawing such a line the deciding authority will necessarily be troubled by many borderline cases, and will in all honesty make decisions which another would reverse.

It is also clear that drawing a dividing line is more difficult in or near the middle of the distribution than near the end, for near the middle the individuals are closer together. In the above diagram, for example, all the children represented by the tallest rectangle, 644 in number, have to crowd on a frontage from intelligence quotient 90 to intelligence quotient 100; whereas from 130 to 140 there are only 65 children, who therefore have ten times

INDIVIDUAL DIFFERENCES IN INTELLECT

as much elbow-room. Not only is there plenty of room at the top but the individual differences are greater. It is easier to pick the first and second of a race than to find the middle man. A long steeplechase tails out the fasts and the slows, but leaves a bunch in between of medium runners.

This has a moral for examiners. The most difficult task that can be set an examiner is to divide his examinees into passes and failures in approximately equal numbers without injustice. It is much easier for him to pick the best, or the worst, ten or twenty per cent. But the ease with which he can do these latter tasks, and the efficacy of his examining, depend upon the particular form of distribution which his examination marks give to the candidates. To elucidate this point let us digress to consider another form of distribution, say according to income instead of according to height.

When we imagined our men falling in in order of height, and then men of identical height climbing on one another's shoulders to make the gymnastic pyramid pictured a page or two ago, we obtained a symmetrical figure. If we imagine that the lower men in that figure were standing on a long beam, the beam would balance about the middle point—or rather it would if the men were all the same weight or were made the same by carrying appropriate weights as jockeys do. The figure is symmetrical, is balanced.

But suppose that instead of falling in in order of height the men fell in in order of incomes, and men of identical incomes stood on each other's shoulders. They would make a figure like the one shown on page 176.

Such a distribution is called, in statistics, a skew distribution. If these men were standing on a plank, its point of balance (indicated by the arrow in the figure) would *not* divide the men into two equal groups. More men are below the point of balance than above. The

INSTINCT, INTELLIGENCE AND CHARACTER

fewer above make up by having some of their number farther away, exerting a more considerable leverage.

The point of balance of which we have been speaking is what we commonly know as the *average* or mean. The median man, on the other hand, is the man who has half the crowd to right and half to left of him. In a symmetrical distribution like our first picture he is also the average man. But in our asymmetrical second picture he stands to one

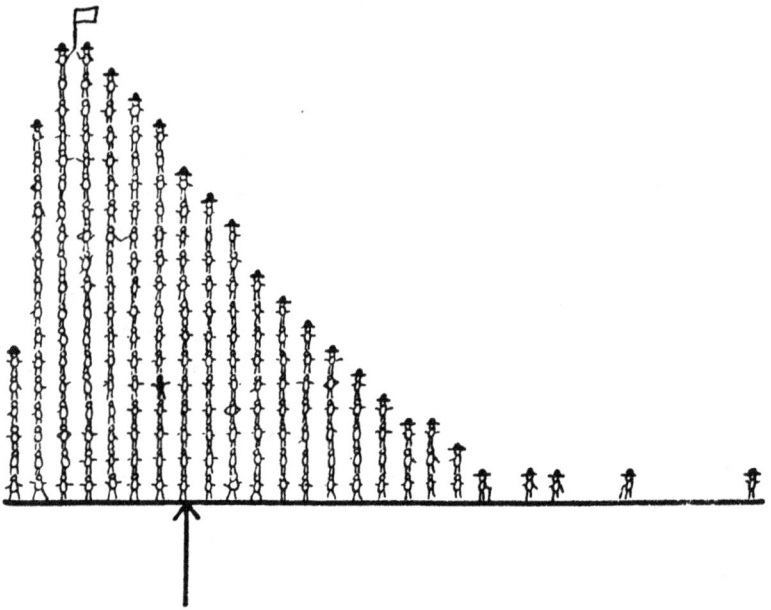

side of the average,[1] and the distance between him and the average is the greater, the greater the skewness of the distribution. For some purposes the median is a better measure than the average. If each man on a jury, for example, agreed to write down the damages he considered proper in the case, then the median would be better than the average. For the average could be made inordinately big by any vindictive juryman who cared to write down

[1] The median man is blackened in each figure.

INDIVIDUAL DIFFERENCES IN INTELLECT

an absurdly high figure, a proceeding without effect on the median.[1] (In passing, since it may occur to some reader that there is no median in a jury of twelve, it may be taken as the point half-way between the two middle values.)

Now the extent to which an examiner's marks show a distribution which is smooth, and skew just to the extent which his particular task requires, is an important matter, and should be borne in mind whenever the number of candidates is large enough to justify statistical treatment —certainly for 300 candidates, and even, with reservations, for only 50.

For example, suppose an examiner finds that his marks (on a percentage scale, say) do not give a curve like either of the above, but show two well-marked peaks, then he is justified in taking thought whether this is due to a real splitting of his candidates into two classes, or to some unconscious idiosyncrasy of his own. If the numbers are large it is almost certainly the latter. For instance, if his marks scale were divided into five classes and they ran like this:

Number of Cases = 810.

Lowest Class.	Next Lowest.	Median Class.	Next Highest.	Highest Class.
77	367	24	239	103

this would be a very bad distribution, almost certainly an unjust distribution. Whereas the following (which was the actual distribution in an examination in English) is more likely to be just and fair:

Number of Cases = 810.

Lowest Class.	Next Lowest.	Median Class.	Next Highest.	Highest Class.
103	239	367	77	24

---

[1] I borrow this, I believe, from Sir Francis Galton.

INSTINCT, INTELLIGENCE AND CHARACTER

If the purpose of the examination is to select a smaller-than-half group of the cleverer students, then the examiner would be justified in making the questions difficult and producing a skew distribution, with the poorer candidates jammed together among the low marks, but the better candidates well spread. Such is the case in the following examination which was to select children for scholarships:

Marks	0–9	10–19	20–29	30–39	40–49
Numbers	2,576	2,605	2,371	2,027	1,674

Marks	50–59	60–69	70–79	80–89	90–100
Numbers	1,137	581	199	49	1

If, on the other hand, the purpose were to select a small group of the least able, the examination should be easy, and the statistics skewed the other way, with a well-spread tail towards the low end.

If for any purpose it is desirable to divide a group up into subgroups of approximately equal size, say three subgroups, a best, a median, and a worst, then it is clear from the above curves and tables that the median group will be much more homogeneous than either of the extreme groups. Even if we make the median group a good deal larger it will still be a more homogeneous group. As an example take the 2,710 children whose intelligence quotients are given on page 173. Let us make the two divisions at 90 and 110. Then the numbers are:

```
Lowest group    805, ranging from   90 to below 60, range over 30
Median group  1,240       ,,        91 to 110, range 20
Highest group   665       ,,        111 to over 140, range over 30 [1]
              -----
              2,710
```

[1] It was, in fact, 63.

INDIVIDUAL DIFFERENCES IN INTELLECT

If these had been a class of 100 children of much the same present level who needed classifying into a slow-moving, a median, and a fast-moving division in a school, it is clear that the median division ought to receive larger numbers, say :

Lowest	.. .. ..	25 children
Median	.. .. ..	50 ,,
Highest	.. .. ..	25 ,,

if comparatively equally homogeneous groups were to be at all approximated to.

It is the facts of great individual differences, and the difficulties of classification resulting therefrom, which have led many to object strongly to the "lock-step" of our usual school curriculum which keeps every member of the class going ahead at the selfsame rate. Even freedom of promotion cannot keep pace with the range and continuity of differences which we now know to exist, which is one of the factors which have caused the introduction of individual methods such as the Dalton[1] Plan, in which each student goes his own gait. He has to cover a minimum assignment of work in the month, but he is freed from having to sit and watch a teacher teaching at the rate of the slowest in the class, and can investigate the meadows on either side of the main route, with advice from teachers and possibly actual assignments of "maximum" work in addition to the "minimum" assignments.

So called after the town of Dalton, U.S.A., though I like to let it remind me of Dalton who first urged the atomic theory in chemistry, for this Dalton Plan proposes to treat children as separate entities, and not in masses.

CHAPTER XVIII

INTELLIGENCE TESTS

INTELLIGENCE tests in their modern form are due mainly to the pioneer work of Binet in Paris, who with his colleague, Simon, published in 1905 the first scale of tests. Twelve years later intelligence testing received its second great impetus from the work of the psychologists who examined with standardized group tests some two million soldiers of the American Army.

Binet's problem was to find a working method of deciding which children in Paris schools should be taken out of the ordinary classes and placed in special classes for defectives. And intelligence testing in its earlier years was mainly aimed at the discovery of lack of intelligence. But it has long outgrown this one-sided development and there now exist tests which can tax the intellect of the cleverest children.

Binet's success in a problem where many had failed was chiefly due to three guiding principles, which, perhaps unconsciously, he seems to have taken as the clue to success. First, he took a medley of different kinds of tests, approaching intelligence from different aspects. Secondly, he made no theoretical assertions about the suitability or otherwise of a given test for this or that age. And thirdly, he employed the mental age scale. Let us consider these in turn.

For a test, Binet chose any simple question the answer to which appeared to be mainly decided by the child's intelligence, and not by any *special* information which some

INTELLIGENCE TESTS

children might possess and others lack. For example, the child may be invited to copy a diamond, to execute a commission, to count backwards from 20 to 1, or to criticize an absurd statement. Some of these depend on knowledge. But the knowledge required is very simple, and such as cannot well be avoided by a child living in any community unless he is unintelligent. Picking up ordinary bits of knowledge from everyday life is, in fact, taken as one criterion of intelligence. By having a medley of questions he ensured that any advantage gained from recent experience with one item would not make much difference in the whole score. Some might have a slight adventitious advantage in one test, others in another, but the average would not be much affected. There was no attempt, it would seem, to test separately any "faculties" of memory, or imagination, or reasoning, the intelligence was just taken as a whole without much worry as to what exactly intelligence means.[1]

In the second place, the order of difficulty of the tests was decided by actual experiment with children, not by any psychologizing *a priori*. Take, for example, the Three Commissions Test. In this, the child is asked to put a bunch of keys on the table, then to bring the examiner a box which is pointed out, then to shut the door. "Now remember," says the examiner, "first the keys, then the box, then the door."[2]

Instead of indulging in guesses as to the age at which a normal or average child would first carry this out without a mistake, the proper plan is to try it on large numbers

---

[1] Binet's own words in describing his procedure are not always consistent. A discussion will be found in Professor Spearman's book *The Nature of Intelligence*, Macmillan 1923, pp. 7 *et seq.* Binet seems to have tried various points of view, and ultimately to have settled down to tests which, as said in the text, are very diverse and unwarped by any attempt to measure separate faculties. Such is the practical result, whatever Binet's theoretical views.

[2] I once had the exhilarating experience of seeing a child correctly place the keys on the table, bring me the box, and then shut the door, *but from the outside*, after which she went off to her class !

of children and find out. In doing so we must take care that we get a random selection of children, not all of one social class or in any other way specialized. In his researches on London children, Mr. Cyril Burt found for the above test the following figures :

Age group centred at ..	3½	4½	5½	6½	7½	8½	9½	10½
Per cent. passing..	26·4	65·3	84·2	96·7	98·4	99·2	99·6	100

Notice here that at a point somewhere between 3½ years and 4½ years, half the children could perform this triple commission correctly, so that if a child of greater age could not do so, he would be below the average. Contrast the figures for another test, that of counting from 20 to 1 backwards. In a similar form they read :

Age group centred at ..	4½	5½	6½	7½	8½	9½	10½	11½	12½	—
Per cent. passing..	0·0	5·7	28	53·6	76	86·1	96	98·3	100	—

From this it will be seen that there is a point somewhere in the 7th year, at which age one child out of two can do this test. If a child can carry out the task of counting

INTELLIGENCE TESTS

from 20 to 1 before this age he is better than the average, in this single test. If he cannot do so till later, he is worse than the average. This age is the age at which the average child, or more strictly the median child, can carry out this particular task. A similar age can be found for each of the proposed tests, and they can be ranged in an order of difficulty, those being deemed more difficult for which a more mature age is necessary. And to each test can be assigned an age, at which 50 per cent.[1] of children can pass it.

In the third place, Binet adopted the mental age scale. This step follows on naturally from the preceding. Having first tested our tests on large numbers of children, we can then—but not till then—proceed to use the tests to test children. An individual child is plied with these questions under exactly the same conditions as those ruling in the work of standardizing. We find which he can pass and in which he fails, and thence are able to state that his performance is equal to that of the average child of x years. This is called his "mental age." If it exceeds his actual age, he is above average intelligence; if it is less, he is below.

We have in this brief statement glossed over one difficulty which early arose. When we test the child we do not, as a rule, find that he can answer all the easier questions up to a certain point after which he can answer no more. On the contrary, what we find is that though he breaks down at a certain question, he can answer two or three of those ranked in our list as more difficult. This is simply because children are not all alike in their talents, and our order of difficulty of the tests is only correct on the average. Under these circumstances the modern practice is to give him credit for all the tests passed. In Terman's revision of the Binet Scale there are six tests per year,

[1] There has been controversy about this percentage, which is cleared up by Cyril Burt on p. 140 of *Mental and Scholastic Tests*, London, 1921.

and a child simply gets two more months of mental age for any test which he passes.[1]

In the early days of testing, the result of the examination was usually expressed by the difference between the mental age and the chronological age. Thus a child was said to be "two years advanced," say, or "fifteen months retarded." But it was soon found that a given retardation was more serious in a young child than in an older child, and that it was rather the ratio of this to the chronological age which mattered. Hence the Intelligence Quotient, or I.Q., introduced by Professor Stern of Hamburg, came to be the recognized way of giving results. This I.Q. is the mental age expressed as a percentage of the actual age, so that if, for example, the child's actual or chronological age is 7 years 3 months, and his mental age is 8 years 2 months, then we have :

$$\begin{aligned}\text{Intelligence Quotient} &= \frac{\text{Mental Age}}{\text{Chronological Age}} \times 100 \\ &= \frac{8 \text{ years } 2 \text{ months}}{7 \text{ years } 3 \text{ months}} \times 100 \\ &= \frac{9{,}800}{87} = 113\end{aligned}$$

Clearly, from the manner of its formation, the average I.Q. is 100, which is the I.Q. of any child whose mental age is the same as his actual age. Quotients are mostly between 80 and 120 ; but about one child in twenty will be above 120, and about one in twenty or so below 80, while some run up to 140, or even 160, and more in rare cases.

There are difficulties in connection with this I.Q. method which become more acute with older children and with adults. They arise from the fact that the mental age as estimated by the usual tests does not go on increasing indefinitely, but slows off and comes to a standstill at some

---

[1] See Terman's book, *The Measurement of Intelligence in Children*, for certain exceptions to this general rule.

age round about sixteen. This fact has led to much controversy, and must be discussed later. But the difficulty in connection with intelligence quotients to which it gives rise can be obviated by giving up the use of the I.Q. and substituting another measure, the Percentile Rank, instead. This is the rank which any individual would have among 100 unselected individuals, the most intelligent of these being ranked 100, and the least intelligent 1, the average man being at number 50. Thus a percentile rank of 83·4 means that the individual so designated is more intelligent than 83·4 per cent. of the whole population, but not so intelligent as the remaining 16·6 per cent. The word population here means those with whom we can reasonably compare him. In the case of a twelve-year-old English boy it would mean all English boys of his age, which in practice we might take to mean boys born in the same month of the same year, perhaps. For adults the "population" is all adults of the same race. An I.Q. of 120 corresponds approximately to a P.R. of 95, an I.Q. of 80 to a P.R. of 5, an I.Q. of 100 to a P.R. of 50. Each method has its advantages and its disadvantages. The I.Q. is best for children up to about fourteen, but thereafter the P.R. is better.[1]

The Binet Tests were individual, and took approximately an hour to give to each child. The desire for Group Tests which during an hour could be administered to a number of children simultaneously had often been expressed, and some progress had been made in their construction, when the demand was intensified suddenly by the decision of the American Army authorities, advised by a committee of psychologists, to submit all recruits to such tests in order to assist in selecting officers, to enable platoons to be equalized in average intelligence, to enable squad training to be done at different speeds by the more or the less

---

[1] Or certain other measures based on the P.R., such as the "sigma" rating.

intelligent, and to eliminate from the Army men unfit by reason of low intelligence. The result was the Army Alpha Test for the majority of recruits, and the Beta Test for the illiterate or foreign-speaking part of the draft. These were to some extent based on material already at hand and partially standardized by Otis, Pintner, and others. Full particulars of the Alpha Test can be obtained in the book by Yerkes and Yoakum.[1] Following the war, this test, and many others largely inspired by it, as well as some more original, were applied to children in secondary schools; and presently forms suitable for elementary schools, and even group tests for infants, began to appear. A very complete list of Group Tests on the American market up to 1923, will be found in Pintner's *Intelligence Testing*;[2] and Ballard's *Group Tests* gives particulars of most of the English forms.

Certain general principles show themselves in a study of tests; and instead of giving random specimens of the questions asked, it may be more desirable to adduce them in illustration. As has already been said, one class of tests measures intelligence by asking questions the answers to which are, it is assumed, sure to have been "picked up" unless there is lack of intelligence. Such tests do actually show a high correlation with other criteria, such as the judgment of experienced teachers who have known the children for a considerable time. In the Binet Tests such a question as "Is it morning or afternoon?" is of this nature. In group tests these information questions may take a form such as "Pearls are found in mines, oysters, palms, wells," the candidate having previously been instructed to underline the correct word. It is difficult to avoid the fear that such tests may be unduly influenced by instruction, and lend themselves to coaching, which would defeat the object of the tester and would waste the testee's time on a particularly bad kind of education.

[1] *Army Mental Tests*, Holt, New York. [2] Holt, 1923.

INTELLIGENCE TESTS

Another group of tests largely identifies intelligence with the possession and right use of vocabulary. The Terman revision of the Binet test has a list of words with which to make a direct trial of vocabulary. Such a Binet test as that asking the child to say as many words as possible in three minutes is certainly connected with vocabulary. The " opposites " test asks for the opposite of words and can be easy (as the opposite of black, or last, or near) or very difficult (as the opposite of stringent, or disdain, or despite). It is particularly in the hard examples that it tests richness and nicety of vocabulary more obviously than intelligence. But experiment finds these two closely correlated, though on the other hand it would seem that country children, for example, might be sadly handicapped and yet be quite intelligent.

This " opposites " test, however, does not merely test for the possession of a piece of acquired knowledge, as the information tests do. It calls for the employment of intelligence at the time, for usually the subject has not previously considered what word stands in the " opposite " relationship to disdain (say), even if he should possess the required word and be accustomed to use it correctly. This requirement of the exercise of intelligence at the moment of taking the test (and not merely previously in acquiring the information or the vocabulary) is also an obvious feature in the " analogies " test first developed by Woodworth and by Burt, and in the completion or missing word test of Ebbinghaus. Both of these call, in addition to vocabulary, for an appreciation of relationships. The former asks for the missing term in such a pair of relationships as

$$\text{fin : fish :: wing : ?}$$

reminding one of the epigram, " Pitt is to Addington as London is to Paddington " ; while the latter asks for the missing words in a paragraph or sentence, as " To . . . . .

friends is always . . . . . the . . . . . it takes," one of the Trabue test sentences. Finally (passing over numerous other forms of test) we come to those which employ the traditional forms of induction and deduction more obviously. The recognition of a general class is required by a test composed of elements such as this: " In this line of five words cross out the word which does not belong there :

> chair, table, sofa, jacket, stool.

And similarly in this, in which the candidate has to find what the first three words have in common, and underline that one of the remaining words which best goes with them :

> Sparrow, eagle, robin (nest, hen, fly, air) [1] (from I.E.R. tests).

Still more obviously in the class of logical forms are questions giving a syllogism and asking if the conclusion is true, or false, or undetermined, as :

> All of the houses on First Street were burned.
> Mr. Smith's house was on Second Street.
> Conclusion : Mr. Smith's house was not burned.[2]

More complicated forms of syllogistic reasoning occur in Mr. Burt's Reasoning Tests, as :

> Where the climate is hot, aloes and rubber will grow : heather and grass will only grow where it is cold. Heather and rubber require plenty of moisture : grass and aloes will grow only in fairly dry regions. Near the river Amazon it is very hot and very damp. Which of the above grows there ?

A test simulating John Stuart Mill's logical methods of Agreement and Difference is the writer's " Hindustani " Test, which was one of those forming the first Northumberland Mental Tests. Its nature will be best understood

---

[1] Both of these can be given with drawings instead of words, to obviate language difficulties : while geometrical figures can also be used. From the above easy examples there is a continuous scale of difficulty up to really hard examples.

[2] Smith College Tests, Northampton, Mass., U.S.A.

INTELLIGENCE TESTS

from the following explanatory introduction given in the Northumberland booklet.[1]

The sentences below are in a foreign language, and their meanings are given in English. In each English sentence a word is underlined, and you have to underline the word which corresponds to it in the foreign sentence. You can do this by comparing the sentences with each other. For example, look at these:
1. Kuchh Malai = *Some* cream.
2. Kuchh Puri Leoge = Will you take some *cake* ?
3. Misri Leoge = *Will you take* sugar ?

By comparing 1 and 2 you see that *kuchh* must mean *some* because it occurs in both sentences. By comparing 2 and 3 you see that *leoge* means *will you take*. Then the only word you do not know in 2 is *puri* which must mean *cake*. Notice that the foreign words are not always in the same order as the English words.

The reader would perhaps like to try a harder example of the same kind of thing; and if so he will find it in the following test, part of one designed to be given to college undergraduates:

Crusoe Test Instructions.

The following sentences are written in the language of Man Friday, and a translation is given of each. The English words are not usually in the same order as the words in the cannibal tongue, but by comparing sentences carefully you can tell which word means which. By this means you can translate the paragraph which comes at the end. Do so, guessing any words which occur in the paragraph and not in the sentences.
1. Prijal o lago ik gamba foobeet foe.
2. Twem ikko trianen pen inkamt.
3. Oran moor famt ikko trianen.
4. Ve inkamt twem enab.
5. Bon papro ikko trian trabamt foobeetem.
6. Twe inkamt vem pen horl.
7. Ve fom papro bon ikko contom.
8. Prijal pasam ikko kinrot brods.
9. Corga fom ikko conto.
10. Ikko trianen mangam ikko contom pr' ikko kinrotenem.
11. Oran prijal o lago foe lega.
12. Ve stapamt venoa carpom rol ikko kinrotenem.

[1] Harrap, Parker Street, Kingsway, London.

INSTINCT, INTELLIGENCE AND CHARACTER

13. Prij famt veve o sakko.
14. Pr' ikko scunom veve brasamt.
15. Antal corga fom bena scuno bon ikko colbom.
16. Ikko trianen rubamt moboo.

  1. To run swiftly is a great satisfaction.
  2. The goats saw me soon.
  3. The goats were very shy.
  4. He saw me first.
  5. The goat found satisfaction in feeding.
  6. I saw him soon after.
  7. He was feeding in the valley.
  8. The rock would fall swiftly.
  9. The valley was green.
  10. The goats like the valley better than the rocks.
  11. To run very swiftly is difficult.
  12. He hurt his foot on the rocks.
  13. They were swift to depart.
  14. They went to the island.
  15. No island in the world was so green.
  16. The goats took fright.

Ikko enab reut twe brasamt als, twe trabamt a trianen famt bon ikko scunom, gova fom ik gamba foobeet pri twem. Don veve famt antal moor e antal prij bin carpom, a vet fom ikko anto lega rel bon ikko colbom o attro pri vevem. Zanzib, twe trabamt a di veve famt rol ikko kinrotenem e inkamt twem bon ikko contonem veve pasam f't-lago bon ik ollola moboo ; dec di veve famt papro bon ikko contonem, e twe fom rol ikko kinrotenem, veve rubamt bena bordom bin twem.

* * * *

The main uses to which intelligence tests have been put are to select children for special instruction in schools for the defective, to assist in selecting children for admission to High Schools and Secondary Schools, and to grade classes into groups capable of undertaking various types of curricula. In schools in which the latter plan is followed, a threefold "multiple track" is a common arrangement. There are three tracks through the school, one suited for children of high I.Q., one for the median group, one for those of low I.Q. In the intelligent group, there are two alternatives open, one being to go ahead at the rapid pace of which these children are quite capable, and finish the

INTELLIGENCE TESTS

school curriculum at an earlier age, thus enabling the children to enter High School or College one or two or even three years earlier than usual. As this may lead to plunging them into the companionship of more mature pupils too suddenly, others prefer to have, for this group, not an accelerated but an enriched programme, so that while traversing the same main route as the normal group, and at the same rate, they find time to deviate into numerous interesting byways of study.

In such classes or groups of bright pupils different methods of teaching are found possible and desirable,[1] for with the cleverer children much more abstract statements of fundamental principles can be given, projects can be planned which involve their application, and independent attempts at solution can be anticipated on the part of the children. This is, in short, the Heuristic method so forcibly urged years ago by Professor Henry E. Armstrong; and the most delightful account of it is in his little book in which he describes the researches which were carried out by a group of children whose curiosity was provoked by the story of the monkey which refused to be drowned. Although the stone tied round its neck was too heavy for it to lift on land, yet at the bottom of the lake it picked the stone up and walked ashore. With the less intelligent children, on the other hand, the matter to be learned has to be broken into smaller units, and these have to be practised separately. Much more drill work is required. For the least intelligent of all a curriculum largely composed of handwork is appropriate.

Intelligence Tests have also been used in lieu of College Entrance Examinations. Columbia College, of Columbia University in New York, has for some years employed the Thorndike Test for this purpose, and has a considerable

---

[1] See, for example, S. A. Courtis reported by Rugg, in *Twenty-Third Year Book* of the American National Society for the Study of Education, 1924, p. 103.

body of data as to the success of the new plan. Reporting on it, Dean Hawkes says : [1]

Just what it measures, I do not know. Whether it is intelligence or not it is hard to say until one defines exactly what one means by intelligence. But I do know that it indicates more definitely and accurately than anything we are familiar with whether the boy will succeed in Columbia College.

And again :

Since the introduction of the Thorndike Test the percentage of men who are forced out on account of poor scholarship has been cut in half, although our scholarship requirements have been lifted during this interval.

[1] *Columbia Alumni News,* 1924, xv, 390.

CHAPTER XIX

ACHIEVEMENT TESTS

THE natural corollary to the intelligence test is the achievement test, a test of what has been achieved in the various school subjects. Binet himself, in his pioneer work, had a scale of school performance as well as a scale of intelligence.

Clearly, we cannot separate achievement from intelligence, even if we may approximate to separating intelligence from achievement. An achievement test must measure the result of intelligence plus application. If opportunity and application have been equal, it will place the candidates in order of intelligence. If opportunity and intelligence are equal, it will place them in order of application, of hard work.

Such tests of schooling are, of course, nothing but the old examinations, but with a difference. The points of difference are that more time is expended on making the questions; that they are " tried out " on very large numbers of children before they are used to test other children; that objective methods of marking are employed which leave nothing to the whim of the examiner; and that the results are expressed in terms which enable a pupil to know his standing, in respect to the performance, among candidates of his own age taken at random from the whole population.

As regards the first of these points, it is not intended, by the upholders of newer methods of testing, to imply that the makers of old-fashioned examinations did not in many cases give much care and thought to the choice of questions. But it remains true that the old-fashioned paper was often, or usually, written in a night or two in the study, and was not tried on any pupils until the actual examination of which it was part; whereas in the modern achievement test the questions are accumulated for months, and are particularly scrutinized to see that they both cover adequately the whole ground to be tested, and are likely to lead to answers which can be definitely and rapidly marked as good, bad or indifferent, without any need of judgment during the marking. During that time they are given to thousands of children and a ruthless rejection is enforced of questions which turn out to be ambiguous, or too easy, or too hard, or which lead to answers difficult to judge. Of the bad points and the possible abuses of achievement tests we shall speak presently; but for this principle of trying questions beforehand there can be nothing but praise, the only conceivable objection being that in the case of important examinations on which a great deal depended, it might be difficult to make the trials with that secrecy which human nature, even the human nature of teachers, makes necessary. All who have set examination papers will agree that in every case some question turns out to be ambiguous *to the children*. Some question turns out to be never or hardly ever answered. Some important branches of the subject can be entirely avoided by whole groups of candidates. In my own experience of setting examination questions for children, I have always found it a very great help, if time permitted, to send the paper to some headmaster friend in another part of the country and have his pupils try it.

During these standardizing trials, too, the marking of the answers can be fixed and tabulated. Usually the answers are required to be short. Sometimes the answer has to be identified, and underlined, among several printed after the question. Often the so-called "True-false" form is used, in which the "questions" consist of a number of

ACHIEVEMENT TESTS

assertions which have to be marked plus (true) or minus (false) by the candidate, in which case, to penalize guessing, the number of wrong answers is deducted from the number of right answers to obtain the score. In another popular form the "missing word" plan is used just as in the Ebbinghaus or Trabue Intelligence Test, except that here definite knowledge as well as general intelligence is needed to fill up the blanks.[1]

These last devices (the Short-answer Plan, the Multiple-choice Plan, the True-false Test, and the Completion Test) can all be used to advantage by the class teacher, or by the college lecturer, in weekly or monthly tests. They permit a tremendous amount of ground to be covered in a half-hour test, and they can be marked by any assistant or even a clerk, who can supply to the teacher or lecturer not only the marks scored by each member of the class, but also the frequency with which each question was correctly answered, a very useful piece of information. They do not permit of padding. Neither, of course—and this is a point some will regret—do they permit of any display of good English composition. But that is probably best tested separately. Its marking needs so much time that it cannot be frequently combined with a wide-range test of subject knowledge.

The principle of the age scale is also used in achievement tests, and a performance or achievement age in each subject can be obtained in the same way as a mental age in intelligence. For example, Mr. Cyril Burt's Reading Tests [2]

---

[1] At the spring meeting in 1924 of the American College Entrance Examination Board, a body which holds examinations admitting to a large number of American colleges, it was resolved to make a practical test of the new type examinations in elementary algebra and in ancient history. For two years a commission of the Board has been directing experiments with the new type examinations in certain schools and colleges. At Bryn Mawr College, for example, it was found that such examinations gave results considerably closer to the school reputation of the pupil than did the regular Entrance Examination in ancient history, and somewhat closer in algebra.

[2] *Mental and Scholastic Tests*, London, 1921, p. 346.

have samples of reading of a difficulty suitable for each age. This suitability is not decided by Mr. Burt's opinion, or anyone's opinion. It is decided by actual trial on thousands of London children. Every child who is tested by that reading scale adds his own small influence to the determination of the norms of performance, as a bet registered by the *pari mutuel* modifies the odds. The piece of reading labelled x years is of such difficulty that 50 per cent. of London children of x years fail in it, 50 per cent. pass, by actual trial. The average child just passes.

In this particular test the paragraphs for reading are suitably printed on cards, and the examiner hands them to the child one by one, beginning with an easy example which he can certainly read, and climbing up the scale of difficulty to where he breaks down. A "reading age" is thus obtained.

A statistical measure which has come into wide use in America of late years is the Achievement or Accomplishment Ratio (in contradistinction to the Intelligence Quotient). We can form a general accomplishment ratio from a combination of tests of different sorts, or we can form a separate accomplishment ratio for each school subject, for instance, for reading. In this last case the Reading Accomplishment Ratio would be obtained by dividing the reading age, not by the chronological age, *but by the mental age*. Thus an Accomplishment Ratio of 100 means that a child's school performance is equal to that of the average child of his own *mental* age. His performance may be considerably beyond the average for his chronological age; but if he is intelligent above the average, this is only what we are entitled to expect from him. Or his performance may be considerably below the average of his chronological age. But if he is handicapped by inborn dullness, he deserves praise if he has made as much of his one talent as can on the average be expected.

ACHIEVEMENT TESTS

To make the A.R. (as it is abbreviated) quite clear, take six hypothetical examples:

Name	I.Q.	Actual Age.	Mental Age.	Performance Age in a Certain Subject.	A.Q.
A	83	10 yrs. 4 mos.	8 yrs. 7 mos.	8 yrs. 7 mos.	100
B	100	,, ,,	10 ,, 4 ,,	10 ,, 4 ,,	100
C	120	,, ,,	12 ,, 5 ,,	12 ,, 5 ,,	100
D	82	,, ,,	8 ,, 6 ,,	9 ,, 1 ,,	107
E	102	,, ,,	10 ,, 6 ,,	10 ,, 8 ,,	102
F	119	,, ,,	12 ,, 4 ,,	11 ,, 5 ,,	93

Here boys A, B and C are of different degrees of intelligence, as is shown by the differences in I.Q. But each of them is doing work as hard as can be expected from him, for in each case the performance age is the same as the mental age and therefore each of these three boys has an A.R. of 100. For their respective handicaps, they are doing equally well.

Boys D, E and F show a different picture, and one more in accordance with what experiment has actually found in schools. D has the lowest I.Q. And his performance too is, absolutely, the poorest. But relatively to his mental age it is a better performance than that of F, and D excels F in A.R. Usually in school experiments, A.R.s have been found more closely grouped round 100 than are I.Q.s, just as here in these six cases. And the high A.R.s have not infrequently gone with the low I.Q.s. This may partly be of mathematical origin, what is known as spurious index correlation. But it may in part mean that the teachers help on the lame dogs, and get them over the stile, whereas the clever boys, on the other hand, though they do good work, could usually do better, and ought to do better in view of their intelligence. Often they should be promoted to a class where more will be required of them.

If a pupil's Performance Ages in all school subjects are set out on a diagram we get a profile of his school performance. Three such profiles are shown on the adjoining figure.[1] In these the mental ages have been found by a Stanford individual Binet Test, and the subject ages and average educational age by the Stanford Achievement Test. The three children are members of a Special Opportunity Class of Public School 165, Manhattan, near Columbia University, and are, within three months, of the same age. The middle profile shows what is often found in ordinary classes where such gifted children are not being given the opportunity to go ahead with school work, for No. 52 has an educational age considerably below his powers. No. 8, on the right, has, however, an educational age practically equal to his mental age, while No. 29 on the left has an educational age exceeding his mental age, a rare phenomenon with cleverer children though common with those below I.Q. 100. The zigzag lines show where each child is strong and where comparatively weak.

For the elementary subjects, profiles such as the above can also be made with the tests given in Burt's *Mental and Scholastic Tests*, or by tests such as Ballard's, in England; while in America a host of tests can be purchased, for example, the Thorndike-McCall Reading Scale (Teachers' College, New York), and Monroe's General Survey Scale in Arithmetic (Public School Publishing Company, Bloomington, Illinois). From these two publishers and from the World Book Company, Yonkers, N.Y., information about a majority of the American tests can be obtained.

The experienced teacher who first hears about these standardized tests is not slow to ask questions about weak points in their use, as he imagines them. First of these is, cannot a teacher coach his pupils in these very questions, so that they will appear to be much better than they really are? Secondly, does not this plan of measuring everybody

[1] From data in an article by Margaret V Cobb and Grace A. Taylor, *Twenty-Third Year Book* of the American National Society for the Study of Education, 1924, pp. 275-89.

ACHIEVEMENT TESTS

Three Educational Profiles

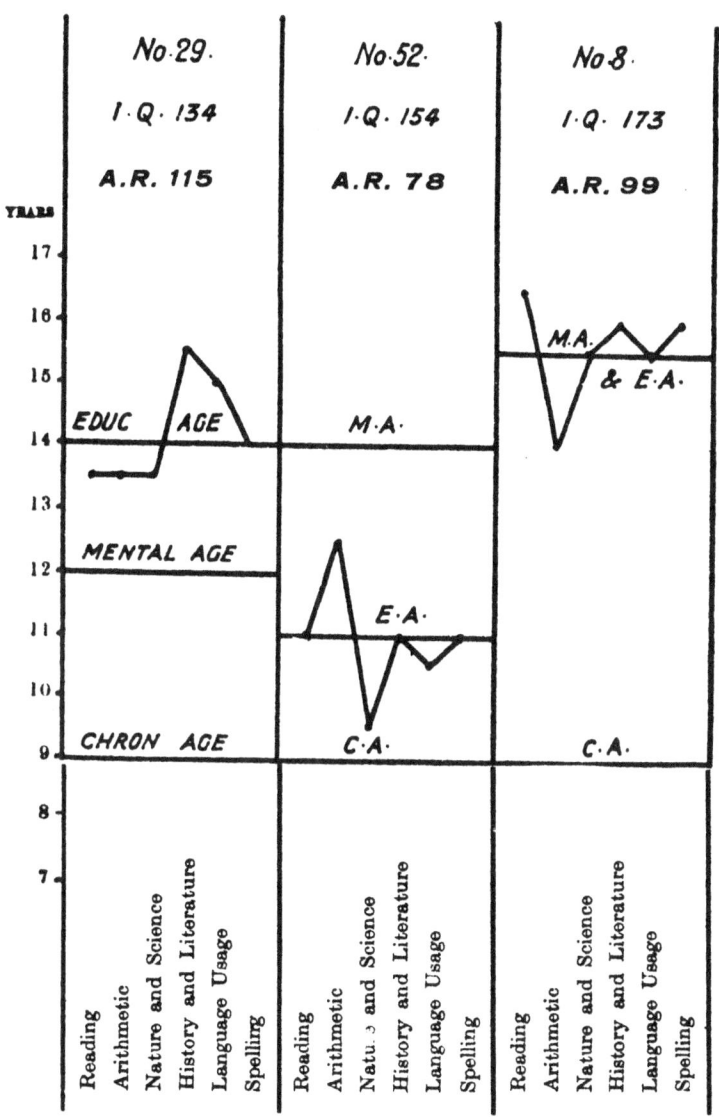

by everybody's average mean giving up ideals of performance, and lead to a steady deterioration in work ? Thirdly, do the tests not encourage mere memory work, are they not far too mechanical ? Fourthly, is not the most important thing about a boy's work imponderable, intangible, only to be appraised by an individual judgment of an experienced teacher, and likely to be quite missed by these patchwork tests ? The parts of the machine may be there, but yet no machine.

To the first question the answer must surely be yes. A child might, for example, learn Burt's or Haggerty's Reading Tests as a medieval hedge clerk learned his neck verse ; and rattle them off on recognizing the first three words, or the general pattern of the printing. In the bad old days (or the good old days) of payment by results in England children did practically learn by heart whole Readers, so that the examining inspector was prone to produce jealously guarded, unknown tests from his pocket. A remedy has been suggested in multiplying alternative forms of the tests. But it seems to me that the only real way to avoid coaching is to hand the tests over to the teacher as a means by which he can satisfy himself as to the standing of his pupils and to accept his verdict. When authorities wish to know in a more formal way how the children in their schools stand compared with other districts, an already published standard test can only be used if it is practically certain to be unknown in the district ; or an *ad hoc* test must be constructed. This latter is comparatively easy if co-operation between authorities can be secured. For let a new set of questions, say in arithmetic, be made as similar in all relevant respects as can be to a standardized test. Let *both* sets then be given to, say, one thousand unselected pupils (whole forms or classes) in some distant district. And let the scores in the new questions be standardized by comparison with the scores obtained in that test which is already well known. This leaves something to accident,

ACHIEVEMENT TESTS

but is a great improvement on any plan which gives quite untried questions. The comparison would not alone be of the home district with that distant district (though that would be incidentally obtained); but through that to the comparison with the wider population on which the norms of the older test were based. The second objection noted above is not, I think, well founded. If a wide enough area is taken for the standardized norms, then I think the natural competitive spirit in man will see to it that there is a steady effort to beat the average; and this will raise the average. In many American schools I have seen charts on the wall showing how the class stood with regard to so-and-so's standard test in such a subject, and have noted the upward climb of the curve to equal and pass the average. In the sublimation of the instinct of emulation, indeed, this rivalry with a neutral set of norms plays an important part.

It is more true, probably, that such tests encourage mere memory work. If I set a general question in class to be answered by an essay, the pupil has the chance of showing a great deal more than his mere knowledge. He can arrange his thoughts clearly or badly, make his points in a telling and emphatic manner or confusedly and unimpressively. And all of this we take into account in giving the essay an α, β, or γ. On the other hand, we must not forget that experiments have shown how variable our judgments of such answers are, and how dependable on the whim of the moment. And although more than memory is required of the candidate, there is sometimes a danger that memory is minimized and that a lot of fine talk hides the absence of knowledge. The best pupils may not like the American achievement test so well, the worst pupils will fear them more for they certainly demand the facts.[1]

[1] " In a large course in English last year, shortly after the new type of examination was introduced, the librarian and the manager of the book store inquired of the professor what had happened to his course. Both reported a quite unprecedented drive on the part of the students to borrow, buy, or steal the required books " (Dean Hawkes, *Columbia Alumni News*, 1924, xv, 391).

INSTINCT, INTELLIGENCE AND CHARACTER

In general, English and American examination questions appear to me to differ in this way, the English questions being less pointed and less likely to lead to similar answers, the American questions more parcelled out into bits, hampering the style of a really good candidate, but finding out more about the other candidates. For example, in a School Certificate Examination in England in 1923, there was asked the question [1]:

What evidences are there to show that the opening of the Panama Canal has appreciably influenced the trade routes of the world ?

In the Regents' Examination of the State of New York in January of 1924 (an examination of somewhat similar standing and performing much the same function) it happened that a question was asked about the same subject, but worded thus :

Write on the Panama Canal touching on (a) location and length, (b) nation controlling it, (c) three cities directly benefited by it, and (d) two commodities that are brought nearer to important markets by this canal, stating from what market and to what market each is shipped.

These questions are by no means identical in intention, but yet there is something common. The second one, however, pins the examinee down much more, is less likely to lead to verbosity, and will be easier to mark. A mature geographer would prefer the former; children, except the best of them, will prefer the latter, and on the whole will, I think, be more justly marked by it.

Each of these questions is good in its way. But sometimes we get questions which are definitely bad, at both extremes; at the one end being the ultra-mechanical (to which weakness the Achievement Test in certain subjects is undoubtedly prone), and at the other the over-ambitious of the kind like that in the story (" Describe the universe and give two examples "). There is here, as everywhere, a golden mean. In their place, however, these new

[1] It was very badly answered.

ACHIEVEMENT TESTS

Achievement Tests are excellent. Especially in the tool subjects of reading and arithmetic they are revolutionary. The law of diminishing returns applies here as everywhere, and some of the very best teachers, there can be no doubt, expend time and energy in attaining an over-perfection of efficiency, when the trial of a few standardized tests would assure them that their classes were already in the top quartile for these subjects, so that attention might better be given to exploring the pleasant fields lying alongside the beaten track of the Three R's. Individual weaknesses can be diagnosed. Poor classes can be confronted with performance results. And rewards can be given for improvement, for beating an average man, not an impossible ideal. I have often wished I knew, for a golf hole, not the " bogey " score, but the norms of actual performance, the median and the quartiles. I might regain self-respect.

CHAPTER XX

GENERAL AND SPECIAL ABILITIES

THERE are two questions concerning intellectual ability which are continually cropping up, and which from different aspects have an interest which is now philosophical, now practical, now scientific, and now even mathematical. In the first place, is the degree of ability of which an individual is capable due mainly to inherited qualities or is it mainly decided by environmental influences ? In the second place, is ability general or specific, can it be guided by schooling and opportunity along any channel, or is its direction as well as its amount settled by inborn fate ? The two are closely connected ; for if the answer to the first is that environment is all important, then the second question is already answered. On the other hand, if ability is mainly inborn, it might yet only be decided by nature whether the individual is to have a lot or a little of it, leaving to nurture the decision whether the given amount shall be invested in this or in that activity.

For their answer, moreover, these questions demand a consideration of all sides of the mind, of the feelings and the will as well as of the cognitive processes, of interest as well as intellect. In theory, the intellectual powers may be general, but yet inherited specific interests may impel their owner to employ them in fixed directions, a result practically indistinguishable from the inheritance of special abilities. The question arises whether interest creates ability or ability interest ; and moreover, we all know men

GENERAL AND SPECIAL ABILITIES

whose abilities and whose interests appear to pull in different directions.

The rise of intelligence tests, and generally of quantitative measuring methods in psychology, has again thrown these questions into sharp relief, and has led to the consideration of new evidence. Early tests, in the late nineties of last century and the first few years of this, mainly endeavoured to measure specific items. Speed of reaction to different kinds of stimuli; discrimination of two points on the skin, of different tones, or of different colours; memory of non-sense syllables, sometimes visual memory only, sometimes auditory or kinæsthetic; these and other functions were measured and, to one looking back at that work from a distance of a quarter of a century, it seems that it was, on the whole, carried through in the belief that the mind was a mosaic of such elements, separately measurable and able to function separately even if they commonly combined in carrying out a complex problem. Whatever the beliefs of the master minds engaged in it, there can at any rate be no doubt that such was the impression likely to be gained by lesser disciples.

With the advent of Binet's work came a new point of view. His tests were a medley of all sorts and kinds. Some of them would have been described as tests of sensorial discrimination, some as depending upon visual imagery, some upon imagination, some upon auditory memory, and so on. But these classifications were immaterial to his purpose. He simply took care that there was a good mixture of different sorts of tests; or else, by not caring at all about it, he obtained the same result by chance. An individual's standing in the Binet tests depends upon his performance in all these different kinds of activities. A Binet score, in short, measures an individual's *average* ability. If we picture two very unlike individuals, with very dissimilar psychological profiles, they may yet have the same average score. Binet and

INSTINCT, INTELLIGENCE AND CHARACTER

his disciples gave up, at any rate for the time being, the attempt to discrimiate special abilities. An intelligence quotient measures an average of the individual's intellectual powers, what M. Claparède calls the "global" intelligence. When we classify children according to age and intelligence quotient we are only putting together children alike in average ability. They may yet have great individual differences, as two countries may have the same average height yet very different distributions of mountain and valley.

At about the same time that M. Binet's work began to attract attention, Professor Spearman had already carried out some of the experiments, and drawn some of the conclusions, which have led him to enunciate his Theory of Two Factors. According to that hypothesis, anyone's ability in any particular form of mental activity is the sum of two factors, one general and common to all mental processes, the other specific and peculiar to that particular activity. Spearman's "g" or general ability is properly so called (if his theory be confirmed) for it is really general to all activities. It is the lowland from which the mountain peaks spring, whereas what is measured by Binet Tests is a hypothetical average height of the mountains. On a psychological profile Binet's average measure, Claparède's global intelligence, is a horizontal line running through the zigzag, with some actual performance points below it, some above. Spearman's general ability is, loosely speaking, the horizontal line below which no performance falls. A third line suggests itself, the line through the topmost peak, the height to which some special talent rises. All three are important educational data. Spearman's concept is of peculiar theoretical importance, but its actual consideration in psychological literature has involved to such an extent the use of mathematical devices from statistics and the theory of probability, and is to so great a degree the subject of controversy (in which the

GENERAL AND SPECIAL ABILITIES

writer has opposed Dr. Spearman) that it would be out of place as material for discussion in a book such as the present. Average or global intelligence is in no danger of being overlooked while intelligence quotients are being so freely discussed in pedagogical literature. There does, however, seem to be a peril in the possibility that our educational machine nowadays may not care about the peaks. To utilize talent of a special kind it may be necessary to let time-tables and syllabuses go by the board, and that is harder nowadays, especially as matriculation approaches, than it was in more primitive educational ages. A colleague of mine once had in his class a youngster who had a talent for drawing so great that my friend absolved him of all necessity of keeping to time-tables or even following any monthly assignments. He could draw when he liked. He is not now a world-famous artist, as the story tempts one to say. But he is a highly successful and artistic designer of well-known posters, and has, I think, justified his freedom.

How does experimental and statistical evidence point in regard to such special talents? The chief fact is one which we learn from correlational investigations, namely, that most correlations between different activities are positive. A correlation coefficient, it will be remembered, is a fraction which expresses the degree of resemblance of two lists of men, say, the one list giving their rank in one ability, the other list giving their rank in another ability. If all ability were quite general, not only in its potentialities at birth; but in its actuality at any moment, then the order of merit of 100 men would be the same for Latin, or for a Binet Test, or for musical discrimination, or for anything else whatsoever. All correlations would be perfect. Now they are not perfect—far from it. But they are almost always positive. They are hardly ever negative.

This means that there is a tendency towards general ability. Not that this admits the existence of a "g" in

INSTINCT, INTELLIGENCE AND CHARACTER

Professor Spearman's sense. It only says in words what the correlation coefficients say in numbers, that if a man is above the average in one line, he is likely to be above the average in another. By no means certain to be. In some subjects not very likely to be. But hardly ever is the betting actually against him.

The popular belief to the contrary can be traced to two sources. In the first place, exceptions are always more noticed by the public than commonplace usual occurrences. And so, any men who are exceptionally good at one thing, and exceptionally bad at another, are remarked, and taken as the type instead of being recognized as exceptions. And in the second place, an easily understood desire for justice in the world makes the mass of the people feel that if Jones excels them so clearly in x, there is probably some other line in which they could individually rise superior to Jones.

One hundred years ago, Sir Walter Scott felt and feared this prejudice:

> The public are, in general (he said) very ready to adopt the opinion, that he who has pleased them in one peculiar mode of composition is, by means of that very talent, rendered incapable of venturing upon other subjects. . . . There is some justice in this opinion, as there always is in such as attain general currency. . . . But much more frequently the same capacity which carries a man to popularity in one department will obtain for him success in another (Introduction to *Ivanhoe*).

Correlations reported between different school subjects, different kinds of mental tests, etc., tend to vary between 0·2 and 0·9, with a frequent occurrence of values round about 0·5. I think, from a considerable experience of the literature of correlation, that this is approximately a correct report of the facts. Now these correlations, even although they are all positive, leave plenty of room for much individual specialization of talent. The best way, perhaps, of convincing the reader of this, is to give some correlational facts *in extenso* in the form of a correlation table. Here is one

GENERAL AND SPECIAL ABILITIES

showing scores of 100 children in an examination in mathematics and in French. It represents a correlation of 0·51, but yet the reader will see that there are many cases of children good at the one and weak at the other subject. The median marks are 45 in mathematics and 60 in French, and of the upper 50 children in mathematics 16 are below the median in French.[1] Of the whole, only 68 per cent.

		Mathematics Marks							
French Marks		0–	10–	20–	30–	40–	50–	60–	70–	80–
	80–				1	2	2	4		
	70–				1	1	4	3	1	1
	60–			2	8	8	8	4		
	50–	1	2	1	4	3	3	4		
	40–			2	5	4	1			
	30–			2	5	4				
	20–	1	1	1	3					
	10–				2	1				

The numbers in the cells of this table are numbers of children. For example, 8 children obtained marks in the forties in Mathematics and in the sixties in French.

are on the same side of the median in both subjects, that is, are strong in both or weak in both.[2]

---
[1] This cannot be checked by the reader because the mathematics median comes in the middle of the group with forty-odd marks.

[2] Of course, in an examination such as this the correlation is dependent not only upon the inherent connection in the child's mind between ability in French and in mathematics, but upon differences in the ability of teachers of these subjects. In the same examination, for these 100 children, the correlation between French and English was 0·35, between English and mathematics was zero. It is tempting but dangerous to

INSTINCT, INTELLIGENCE AND CHARACTER

Indeed, just as among the public there may be an exaggeration of belief in specialization of talent, so there has been, I think, among research workers in psychology and pedagogy, an exaggerated idea of the amount of similarity connoted by correlation coefficients. There has been noticeable during the past year a tendency to emphasize the lack of agreement between lists which a correlation of 0·5 or 0·6 or even 0·8 permits, and minimize the former regard for their resemblance. The general fact seems to be fairly stated by saying, that while it is true that correlation coefficients are positive for the most part, yet they are so far removed from unity that great diversity in talent may yet coexist with them. It is not until a correlation coefficient is well over 0·9 that any predictions based thereon are of much practical value.

Two lines of investigation which bear on the question of average ability being inherited or acquired are (1) inquiries into the mentality of twins and siblings, and (2) researches into the constancy or otherwise, with advancing age, of the intelligence quotient. Twins are notoriously more likely to resemble one another than siblings—brothers and sisters of the same family who are not twins. Again, however, there exists the possibility of explaining this resemblance, as far as mental qualities go, either by saying that the reason is the identity of inheritance, or by claiming that it is due to the exceptional identity of home circumstances. Researches by Galton, Thorndike, and others point to the former factor, inheritance, as being more potent. Thorndike compared twins of different ages, and found that young twins resembled each other mentally just as much as old twins did, whereas if the identity of home circumstances were the cause of the resemblance, then its

draw conclusions from such numbers as to the relationships existing between the inherent abilities, the nature of the teaching, and the skill of examining, in these subjects. It is very desirable that large public examination authorities should employ a statistician to compute and publish correlations of this kind based on their extensive data.

GENERAL AND SPECIAL ABILITIES

effect ought to go on increasing up to the time when they left the home. Galton followed up cases of great mental similarity between twins, and also great dissimilarity, which not infrequently occurs. If home identity were the cause of the similarity, one would expect twins brought up in different homes frequently to show dissimilar mentalities. But in fact, in Galton's data, twins brought up in the one home were as often dissimilar as were those brought up in different homes (having been separated at or near birth). Their similarity or dissimilarity appeared to be independent of the environment.

Mental correlations between twins are of the order of magnitude of 0.7, thus exceeding in size mental correlations between ordinary siblings, which are of the order of magnitude of 0.5. In their turn, however, these latter correlations exceed correlations between pairs of individuals of different parentage, who, indeed, show no correlation if care is taken to make the selection really random, and to avoid certain technical sources of spurious correlation.

Again, we are faced with the question whether this mental correlation of siblings is due to their sharing the same home advantages or disadvantages, or to their inheritance from a common ancestry. Researches are conflicting in their testimony, but when care has been taken to make allowance for various subtle mathematical troubles which tend to camouflage the true facts, they seem to me to speak more decidedly in favour of the importance of heredity than environment. The need for independent repetition of the more important experiments is great. If such repetition were to confirm the following results obtained by Dr. Kate Gordon,[1] the prepotence of heredity would seem to me to be fully established.

Dr. Gordon tested the intelligence of over 200 pairs of siblings, all 400 of whom had lived for ten years and more, not in their separate homes, but in three orphanages in

[1] See Elderton, *Biometrika*, 1923. And see also footnote, p. 217.

INSTINCT, INTELLIGENCE AND CHARACTER

California. Here there is no home environment tending to make brother and sister both better, or both worse, than the average. The common orphanage environment could not make brother and sister resemble each other any more than it made any boy resemble any girl inmate. But the siblings still showed a strong mental similarity in their departure from the average, with a correlation 0·52 practically identical with that found for home-dwelling siblings. If this is not an accident of coincidence, and is confirmed by repetition, and if no mathematical sources of spurious correlation remain undetected, then it would seem that this similarity of siblings is entirely explained either by inheritance, or by the common home environment of very early infancy before transfer to the institution. This latter seems rather unlikely in view of their ten years or more of orphanage life.

We turn now to the question of the constancy of the intelligence quotient. Many psychologists believe in this constancy. That is to say, they believe that a clever child of five will be a clever child of fifteen, a dull child of five a dull child of fifteen. They do not mean, of course, that this is the absolutely unvarying rule. But they do believe that it is much more, very much more, the rule than the exception. For the evidence in favour of this constancy of intelligence quotient the reader should turn especially to Terman's book on *The Measurement of Intelligence in Children*, and to articles which appear frequently in the current psychological literature. Intelligence quotients of children have been measured as much as seven years apart in children's lives, and have been found on the whole to be only slightly changed. The average change reported is about five points of I.Q., sometimes up, sometimes down. I have tested a few children myself over four years, and found practically no change in the Binet I.Q. And by group tests, which give a much less reliable measure, I have tested some eleven hundred children at an interval

GENERAL AND SPECIAL ABILITIES

of one year, and found 84 per cent. of them to have substantially the same I.Q., meaning that they were placed within one category of the former position, a category embracing ten points of I.Q.

Against the doctrine of constancy of I.Q. are voices from various quarters. First of all, in the reports from psychologists themselves, despite the fact that the majority of measured I.Q.s remain fairly steady, there are also instances, in a small but important minority, of cases where there is serious change of I.Q. It can be said of such, however, that they are more rare with careful individual tests than they are with group tests; and they are more rare with carefully trained examiners than when untrained persons do the testing. When such sources of error are removed, and when obvious physical reasons have been eliminated, there are not many discrepant cases left.

In the second place teachers, parents, and members of the public are widely convinced that many children develop late, and do not show their real intelligence during the elementary or lower school years; and that, on the other hand, clever children often wither away mentally, and prove to be no more intelligent, as adults, than their duller school comrades. As Sir Walter Scott said, no doubt there is some truth in any opinion so widely current. But it has to be discounted a little for one or two reasons.

Firstly, the measure of intelligence employed in the school period of these children is usually their success with school work. But the psychologist may assert that had he been given a chance to test these children by modern methods, he might have found out that these apparently precocious children were not really clever but only crammed; and that these apparently poor pupils were not really dull but only uninterested. Martin, in *Tom Brown's Schooldays*, probably did badly in Latin verse, but he probably had a high I.Q.

Then the measure of intelligence in later years is often

success in the world's work, perhaps success in business. Now success in business is by no means ensured by intelligence alone. Zeal, ability to work hard, and even to endure drudgery, a liking for financial rewards, tact in getting on with other men, these and other factors all play their part. In some careers ruthlessness of character may be of great importance, and even a certain disregard for niceties of conscience not a handicap. Especially, persistence and hard work may explain many a slowly developing child without any need to suppose that he has become more intelligent; and lack of those qualities may explain the reverse phenomenon without any actual change in intellect having occurred.

There can be no harm in encouraging average students to hope that hard work may improve their intellectual standing. In effect, it will do so. But there is considerable power for harm, I think, in the exaggerated doctrine preached by some, according to which it would almost appear that the best guarantee of success in life is to be unsuccessful at school. The grain of truth in it is, that bookish success at school, if it is won at the expense of mixing with others, at the expense of exercising powers of leadership in clubs and games, is not worth while. But all-round school success, with a leaning to work rather than to play, is much the best guarantee of later success.

The whole of the question is rather complicated by doubts whether Binet Tests do measure only such part of the intellect as is explicable by heredity. In all discussions about these questions there is considerable danger of arguing in a circle. Here it shows itself in a tendency to say that our tests should only test inherited intelligence, not acquired knowledge, and that such tests can be identified by the fact that they continue to place a group of children in the same order of merit as they grow up. Tests which do not do this are rejected, and then the fact that the surviving tests show constancy of I.Q. is held to prove that intelli-

GENERAL AND SPECIAL ABILITIES

gence is inborn and unimprovable. Now on the whole, I believe that intelligence really is inborn and *comparatively* unalterable, but I feel some danger in the circular nature of the above argument. The fact that some tests can be discovered which show comparative constancy of I.Q. with increasing age is the central fact, and it proves that something intellectual exists which is mainly inherited. But it does not seem to exclude entirely the possibility that other parts or phases of intellect can be changed by schooling, unless we *define* intellect only as that which persists unchanged.

CHAPTER XXI

THE INFLUENCE OF SCHOOLING ON INTELLIGENCE AND THE LIMIT OF ITS GROWTH[1]

Two pieces of work in particular, undoubtedly of first-class experimental character, seem to show very much dependence of intelligence on schooling, or rather dependence of the Binet I.Q. on schooling. The first was a research by Mr. Cyril Burt, in which at great labour he obtained for each child in a whole school the Binet mental age (B), the mental age according to Mr. Burt's own Reasoning Tests (I), the school age (S), and the actual age (A). By complicated, but as I believe perfectly valid mathematical calculations using partial correlation, he then shows that on the average

$$B = \cdot 54\,S + \cdot 33\,I + \cdot 11\,A$$

so that " school attainment is the preponderant contributor to the Binet-Simon tests," and with these tests

a child's mental age is a measure not only of the amount of intelligence with which he is congenitally endowed. not only of the plane of intelligence at which in the course of life and growth he has eventually arrived ; it is also an index, largely if not mainly, of the mass of scholastic information and skill which, in virtue of attendance more or less regular, by dint of instruction more or less effective, he has progressively accumulated in school.

These conclusions are very important, and the experiment ought to be, and doubtless will be, repeated several times. Meanwhile, there are two points which deserve mention in the argument which has followed.

[1] Part of a lecture given in the Graduate School of Education, Harvard University, April 28, 1924.

THE INFLUENCE OF SCHOOLING

In the first place, supposing the above numerical equation were fully confirmed, it might be illuminating to change the emphasis in Mr. Burt's sentences, and say, "*only* to an extent of about one half does performance in the Binet Simon tests depend on schooling." That is a great deal, to have tests half independent of schooling, even if they are not wholly independent as enthusiasts hoped and believed.

Secondly, it has been pointed out that S in Burt's work was not the "length of exposure" to schooling, but the standard attained in the school; and that it might equally be said from his results that inborn intelligence determines school standard as that schooling influences intelligence. The cart and the horse are causally connected, but we cannot tell from the correlation coefficients which is cart and which is horse.[1]

The other piece of research, by Mr. Hugh Gordon, puts to a prolonged trial the assertion made by many test enthusiasts, and not altogether unsupported by definite instances, that almost total absence of schooling leaves the Binet I.Q. uninfluenced. To test this in a systematic way Mr. Gordon turned to two special classes in England, gypsies and canal

---

[1] FOOTNOTE, 1931.—A good deal of water has passed under the bridges since the lecture of which this chapter is a summary was given in 1924. I have discussed the same or allied matters in Chapters VII and VIII of *A Modern Philosophy of Education* (Allen & Unwin, 1929) where, especially on pages 154–6, two repetitions of Burt's, or at least a similar, experiment are described which gave results much more in favour of inborn intelligence than length of schooling as the cause of school success. These researches are described in the 27th Year-book of the American National Society for the Study of Education (Secretary, Guy M. Whipple, Danvers, Mass.) where also a very full bibliography of the present problem is printed, and where also later experiments similar to Dr. Kate Gordon's (see p. 211 of the present book) are set out.

The most fervent exposition of the "nurture" side of the argument (as against inborn "nature") is of course Professor W. C. Bagley's *Determinism in Education* (Baltimore, 1925), which ought to be read in conjunction with Brigham's *Study of American Intelligence*, Princeton Univ. Press, 1923. Logically minded readers who have some training in mathematics might like to read T. L. Kelley's *The Influence of Nurture upon Native Differences* (New York, Macmillan, 1926): but it is very hard reading not lightly to be undertaken.

boatmen, whose children get very much less schooling than the ordinary child. His general plan was to see whether, under such neglect, the I.Q. sinks as the child gets older, and his evidence points to this being indeed the case. True, he did not measure the same children as they grew older, but only older brothers and sisters in the same family. The younger children averaged about 100 I.Q., but this decreased as older children in the family were tested, strongly suggesting that they were handicapped by lack of schooling. The phenomenon was more marked among the canal boat children, who not only go least to school, but mix least with others.

We learn from some references by Dr. Ballard that these same children are being retested by non-language tests,[1] and are giving different results. As they stand at present, the experiments indicate that reasonable schooling is necessary to develop that which is measured by Binet tests. This may mean either that intelligence is developed by schooling, or that Binet tests measure something in addition to intelligence.

But, indeed, it seems incredible that such great lack of schooling should not depress the intelligence. In gardening there is, no doubt, inherent in each seed a maximum limit of size and quality. But no gardener, nobody, but knows that more than good seed is necessary. It is not immaterial whether it be sown upon a rock, or by the wayside, or in good ground; nor must it lack moisture.

As we go out from the city into the rural districts, we often find the average I.Q. of the children, as measured by the usual tests, becoming lower. Is this due to a real decrease in intelligence, or is it due to the fact that the

---

[1] FOOTNOTE, 1931.—The results of this retesting are given in an article by Miss Frances Gaw, *Brit. Journ. Psychol.*, April 1925. Miss Gaw found that the "performance" tests are less influenced by environment and by lack of schooling than is the Binet scale. She states her opinion that "with subjects from so limited an environment as that of the canal-boat children, performance tests furnish a better means of judging intelligence than do the Binet tests."

country children, though intelligent enough, are less ready with verbal responses and are less familiar with the type of material used in the intelligence test? And if the decrease in intelligence is real, is it caused by lack of book-learning, lack of vocabulary, lack of the stimuli to the sharpening of wits which the town child finds; or is it caused by the pull of towns taking away the more imaginative and the mentally more alert?

The results of Mr. Gordon's experiments, showing as they do a considerable influence of schooling on the Binet I.Q., would indicate that part of the difference is due to that factor. Country schools are, in general, less likely to have as many books, or teachers with so much cultural experience, as town schools, though here and there an exceptional man or woman may prefer the peace of the hills to the lectures and library books of the town. Many country schools are small, and intellectual intercourse may thereby be limited. The children live in smaller communities or even in isolated farms, and converse but little compared with their town cousins. All these things may dull the intelligence either fundamentally and really, or apparently and as misjudged by the academic mind.

But there is some reason to think that the selection factor, the draining away of the talent of the countryside to the towns, is even more important; and that the less stimulating life of the farm is the cause of the phenomenon not by actually producing a lower intelligence, as the tests define it, but by repelling the more active minds. Both in Yorkshire and in Northumberland experimental tests have shown, not conclusively but at least suggestively, that at a still greater distance from the town and out of the immediate range of their attraction, a change in the opposite direction sets in, and the average I.Q. rises again, though not to the level of the suburbs populated by the successful members of the city.

In 1916-17 Miss M. E. Bickersteth tested individually

INSTINCT, INTELLIGENCE AND CHARACTER

a large number of children in the Yorkshire Dales, and found some surprising instances of remote talent.

> Some of the schools (she tells us) [1] were only reached after a walk of many miles over the fells, and ... at these schools, far from any village, and attended by children living in lonely farms on the moors, sometimes three or four miles from the school, the performance at the tests was almost invariably above the average for the Dales as a whole. In these remoter Dales 84 per cent. of the children were above the average for the Dales as a whole in the Reasoning Test, and 74 per cent. in the Memory Test, while very marked ability was not infrequently shown in the case of individual children.

In 1921 and 1922 the present writer devised, and standardized by preliminary experiments, group tests which were administered to large numbers of children in the schools of Northumberland, about 3,000 in the former and 14,000 in the latter year. The primary object of these tests was to discover children worthy of free secondary education among those elementary schools which had not sent in any candidates for the orthodox examination in English and mathematics on which such free scholarships were usually awarded. For it was feared that the lack of candidates from these schools might at least in part be due to a feeling that in such an examination their pupils could not successfully compete with the more favourably situated town children. The distribution of intelligence suggested by the 1921 tests was that the highest ability was found close to the cities and far away from the cities, as though the intermediate areas had been drained by selection.

In 1922, when larger numbers were available, this phenomenon was, though less well marked, still I think apparent. Northumberland is divisible into an urban area along the River Tyne, bordered by a densely populated coalfield, beyond which lies the large and sparsely populated hill region of the Cheviots. In the urban region the

[1] *Brit. Journ. of Psychology*, ix, 23.

THE INFLUENCE OF SCHOOLING

proportion of children with I.Q.s over 130 was 1 in 96, rising in one very favoured suburb to 1 in 30. Outside this urban region, up to the 250-foot contour line, the proportion fell to 1 in 231, to rise again in the hills to 1 in 95. The possible errors of these experiments are such that one dare not feel certain about the conclusions. But they seem to point in the direction indicated.[1] A factor to be borne in mind is that the population of these hills is not descended from a peasantry but from the very active reivers and raiders of the marches, who pitted their wits against the equally alert Scots across the Border.

* * * *

A question which has aroused even more controversy than the preceding, and one which is fundamentally connected with it, is that of the limit of the growth of intelligence. Probably no one, who, before the advent of tests, had been asked to what age he thought intelligence continued to develop, would have replied with any age less than twenty-one; and I judge that most would have given a much higher age. One of the surprises of tests has been the discovery that average performance in them, which has been increasing steadily from year to year up to about 11, begins to slow down and reaches an upper limit at or about 16 years. The exact age is disputed, whether 14, 15 or 16, but workers with tests agree on the general fact.

The first answer of a plain man to such a statement is, so much the worse for the tests. But the phenomenon needs more careful description. It is seen most clearly in group tests in which a point-score is given. For example, in the Otis Advanced Tests the maximum score is 230, and the average score obtained by different age groups is as shown on page 222.

[1] See Thomson, *Brit. Journ. of Psychology*, 1922, xii, 201; and Duff and Thomson, in that *Journal*, 1923, xiv, 192.

INSTINCT, INTELLIGENCE AND CHARACTER

After the age of 18 there is no increase in the average score, and not much after 17.

Now one possible flaw in this is that it may be due to the speed factor. The Otis Advanced Test is timed page by page and, we may think, perhaps 130 is not the limit set by intelligence but by speed. Some individuals, however, obtain a very high score, over 200, so that there is evidently no physical impossibility in exceeding 130. What one would like to know, nevertheless, is how the above numbers would have run had as much time been given as the candidates wished for.[1] My own experience with college students leads me to believe that in their case all but a very small number would get scores of 200 and more

Age	10	11	12	13	14	15	16	17
Score	55	68	80	90	100	110	120	127

Age	18	19	20	21	22	23	24	—
Score	130	130	130	130	130	130	130	—

if given more time, and many would get perfect scores. Now English college students probably approximate to the level, intellectually, of the upper 10 per cent. of the population, so that one cannot make any general conclusion from them. But it is at least possible that giving plenty of time would not only raise the above curve bodily, but displace its turning-point towards a higher age.

Another possible criticism of the 16-year limit of intelligence is that perhaps there is something in the tests which creates it, in this way. The commonest form of test is one which uses material which, it is supposed, is the common property of everyone, the possession of which does not

[1] See Ruch, *Journ. of Educ. Psychol.*, 1924, ix, 39.

THE INFLUENCE OF SCHOOLING

depend upon schooling, or only upon such schooling as inevitably comes to every child. Now towards the age of 14 it becomes increasingly difficult to make questions which are confined to such material and are hard enough to extend the cleverer children. They could do more difficult thinking, perhaps, but examples of such are always placed in some province of reasoning where particular knowledge is also necessary, such as mathematics, economics, or engineering. Perhaps the curve turns at 16 just because it is impossible to make tests which both are hard enough to extend the older cleverer subjects and also are confined to common knowledge for their materials.

There is, however, another type of test which gets over the difficulty of community of knowledge in another way, namely, by giving a lesson, as it were, on the subject and then testing. Such, for example, is the cipher test in the Terman-Binet series, where a standardized lesson is given on the cipher, and then the pupil is examined as to his ability to use it. Such, too, is the Hindustani Test,[1] in which a method of identifying the words is taught, and then a test which can be worked in the same way is applied.

It seems possible that tests of this sort might push the " limiting " age up past 16. In the case of the Hindustani Test the average marks obtained by elementary school children in Northumberland who were neither retarded nor accelerated in school were as follows :

Age	$10\frac{1}{2}$	$11\frac{1}{2}$	$12\frac{1}{2}$	$13\frac{1}{2}$
Marks, per cent.	16	27	39	54

These marks show no signs of reaching a limit at 14 (as the American Army Tests did) nor even at 16. The slight curvature of the graph is against the idea of any limit being even near at hand. There is, perhaps, some possible

[1] See page 188.

fallacy in the circumstance that only children in their normal school class were taken. But there were at the time in Northumberland as many accelerated as retarded children. It is true also that the 3,000 children tested at the time included a large proportion who were put forward by their headmasters as candidates for scholarships. But they were mainly accelerated in school, and as such are not included in these norms. In any case, this is a perfectly well defined set of children, those who go through school with one grade or standard per year; and in their case at least it seems certain that what is measured by the Hindustani Test does not cease improving at 14 years, and improbable that it ceases at 16, from the shape of the curve.

The other and more orthodox point of view (for a psychologist) is well illustrated by curves which can be drawn from the figures in Mr. Burt's book [1] on page 133. There the percentage of children who can pass each test is given for each year of age. In the easier tests this percentage reaches 100 at an early age. With tests lower down the list this point is later. The curves of increasing percentage for the hardest tests are more and more gentle in slope. Many of them, at the highest age (14) which Mr. Burt's table shows, have by no means reached the 100 per cent. point; but a little consideration of their shapes convinces one that it is improbable that they ever will, and that it is not at all unlikely that they turn and run parallel with the base line at some age such as 16.

We do not know. If I confess myself as by no means convinced that the limit of growth of intelligence occurs as early as sixteen years, I must confess also that the evidence on the whole points that way. We need many individual studies to learn whether the age of cessation is different in different individuals or the same closely for all. And if it is different, whether a high or low I.Q. at 10 years goes with prolonged growth. Most prediction to-day is based

[1] *Mental and Scholastic Tests*, London, 1921.

THE INFLUENCE OF SCHOOLING

on the belief that the intelligent child of 10 will go on developing *at least* as long as the dull child, and most research tends to confirm this. I think that if tests could be devised and standardized which would give a fair chance to the superior intellects to show their powers of abstract thinking, they would be found to go on developing for years after sixteen. Excepting for the speed limit, there is nothing in any intelligence test which cannot be done by such adults; and they could do far more difficult thinking than is there represented. And I do not believe they could do it at 16. It is impossible to make tests which are difficult enough to strain superior adult intelligence (as distinguished from judgment) and yet are confined to everyday situations common to educated and uneducated alike, if we except questions of a catchy or puzzle nature. If we could make such, or could measure in some other way, I think we would find intelligence growing far past 16 in the case of the superior. And they would cause the average also to continue with an upward tendency, if a slight one, past that age.

* * * *

It will be seen that there is here a connection between the two parts of this chapter. My belief is that intelligence of a superior sort can, after about 16, no longer find in *commonly* grasped situations opportunity to show itself (though good judgment may); but that only in the more abstract situations attained through education, including self-education, can this occur. It is impossible, even in tests before 16, to keep out those which require some schooling. After 16, there are none, except tests requiring schooling, which are capable of measuring the more intelligent. It may not be a mere coincidence that the age given for the cessation of growth of intellect is approximately that at which schooling commonly ceases. However, here as everywhere, we must bow to experiment, though while awaiting experiment's decision we may be content with experience. Experiment finds it impossible to demonstrate a growth of intelligence (in the average man) after sixteen. Experience must not refuse to note this interesting fact, and may not pooh-pooh it. We have to remember that doubt which creeps in when we decide against an argument which we dislike. We may have decided against it *because* we dislike its conclusions. And assuredly none of us likes to think that he is no more intelligent now than when he was sixteen.

CHAPTER XXII

DIFFERENCES IN WILL AND TEMPERAMENT

MORE important for the happiness of the individual than differences in intellect are differences in disposition, which also no doubt have their inherited foundations, but are, it would seem, more open to education and more influenced by environment. But whereas intelligence is measured, as it were, up and down a single scale, in speaking of temperament or of disposition we commonly use several variables. The traditional classification of temperaments, and it is still pretty well as good as any other, is into the sanguine, the melancholic, the phlegmatic and the choleric.[1] The sanguine is fickle, changeable, mercurial. The phlegmatic is difficult to move, unenthusiastic, takes things as they come; is placid and solid. The melancholic is emotional enough, but of a sentimental poetic mood, inclined to mysticism, and to depression. The choleric is single of purpose, headstrong, bigoted, the stuff that reformers and die-hards are both made of. Micawber was sanguine, Columbus was choleric, Don Quixote melancholic; but no great or interesting person was ever phlegmatic. At most, he put on the appearance of it.

When we cast round in our minds to place heroes of history and of fiction, and persons whom we know, into their appropriate category in these four temperaments, the

[1] These four traditional types are named in conformity with an ancient medicinal theory, curiously like the hormone theory of to-day, that our temperaments are the result of the preponderance in us of one or other of four humours—blood, bile, black bile, and phlegm; of which blood gave the sanguine, bile the choleric, the black bile the melancholic or atrabilious, and phlegm the phlegmatic.

INSTINCT, INTELLIGENCE AND CHARACTER

most striking fact we notice is that they refuse to fit in. Always they have some tincture of other types. Always they fail to supply some aspect of the type to which otherwise they seem most to approximate. Indeed, people are not divided into any such clearly defined classes, nor are boys and girls in school. They deviate more or less in radiating directions, from one general average individual. And yet it is convenient to make the attempt to classify, provided we do it with caution; and useful to have a stock of names to identify the classes. The best way to treat the fickle, sanguine, mercurial, butterfly-minded child in school is to scheme to engage him or her, together with a group of steadier comrades, in some interesting project which will last for some time. The choleric has to be given his head, but other things than those to which he naturally attends have to be linked on to his rather narrow interests so as to appear indispensable to his main object. Such a boy has energy, and will do his mathematics if he believes it will help him to go to sea, if that happens to be his aim. The melancholic, the artistic, should above all not be ridiculed for his probable lack of interest in games and the common life; but can be linked with a mixed team of temperaments to do a combined job, such as getting out a school play, where his usually wide reading and his good taste can be utilized and he can be saved from becoming too self-centred. The phlegmatic boy will take no harm. If he is too easy-going he needs the spur, and he is not necessarily stupid because he is unresponsive. Some interest will be the strongest, and should be sought out and cultivated.

Very many other temperamental classifications have been made through the ages. As the above is one of the oldest, so one of the newest is the division into extrovert and introvert, and into stable-minded and unstable-minded. Tansley gives one of the best expositions of this product of the New Psychology; and in his book references will

DIFFERENCES IN WILL AND TEMPERAMENT

be found to Jung (who mainly created the introvert-extrovert distinction) and to Trotter (whose book on *Instincts of the Herd* gave us the classification stable- and unstable-minded). The extrovert looks outward for the outlets of his energy. He is a man of action. The introvert creates his world within, and is a thinker, perchance a mere dreamer ; but if he does turn again to action, his powers of thought make that action often of far-reaching importance.

The stable-minded man has fixed opinions, generally consistent with those of the " herd " to which he belongs. He does not readily change them, or conceive them as open to question. The unstable-minded is more changeable, being sensitive to experience : a trimmer and opportunist, his enemies would say, were he a politician. The four combinations give us as types the stable-minded extrovert, the typical man of action, guiding his life by principles which he has accepted from his caste and will never change ; the unstable-minded extrovert, setting his sails to catch every wind of public opinion or of changing opportunity ; the stable-minded introvert, the thinker along traditional lines ; and the unstable-minded introvert, inconstant even with himself. Education cannot want to create any one of these uninviting types. Rather it will wish to encourage true flexibility (rather than instability) which will modify principles when that is really shown to be necessary, but not lightly. Education will desire a combination, or an alternation, of introversion and extroversion, rather than one or the other exclusively. The great trouble about all classifications is the danger of making divisions where none exist. This particular classification strongly suggests that men of action cannot think ; that men of thought cannot act ; that men of principles cannot abate one iota of them ; and that men who learn by experience are unprincipled. Each is called these things by his enemies. The truth is that any man is more or less each of these four, it is only

INSTINCT, INTELLIGENCE AND CHARACTER

a question of balance; and further, any man is the one thing at one time, and another at another, is of the one type in one province (say religion) and of the other type in another province (say his profession).

Many classifications have been made which are as much classifications of the intellect as of the temperaments; as, indeed, in fact those already considered have been. Such, for example, is that made by Ostwald into the romantic and the classical types.[1] It is given by Ostwald as a classification of intellect; but it seems to me to be a classification mainly of temperament. All the cases quoted by Ostwald are men of genius. There is no suggestion that the one type is more intelligent than the other. Rather the one is sanguine and impulsive, the other steady and long burning. As Rignano says, "in the determination of the different characteristics of the logical faculty which above all one would call intellectual, the affective nature of the individual has yet a very great importance."[2]

Ostwald had been asked by a young Japanese student, who was inspired thereto by his government, "how one could know in youth those who were destined to be great scientific discoverers"; the inquiry being directed to Ostwald because he had had great fortune in discovering such men as young students and assisting in their development. Thinking it over, Ostwald came to the conclusion that the essential criterion was that the young student should demand more work and wider work than was laid down for him in the regular courses in which he was engaged.

He was impelled, however, by this request to probe deeper into the matter, and he did this by what would now in America be called the "case method"; that is to say, he took what appeared to him to be typical specimens of the type of man in question, and studied them in detail, in what he calls a biological manner. From these studies,

[1] *Grosse Männer.*   [2] *The Psychology of Reasoning*, p. 289.

DIFFERENCES IN WILL AND TEMPERAMENT

several of which form chapters of his book, he draws a number of conclusions which he emphasizes from time to time and then puts together at the end in special chapters.

In the first place, he distinguishes sharply between the two types for which he coins the names *romantic* and *classical*. The man of romantic type is especially differentiated by the extraordinarily rapid character of his thought, the varied nature of his researches, his precocity, his usually early decay, and his tendency to dilettantism which in all but the greatest leads to much second-rate work. Such was Humphry Davy, and such was Liebig.

The classical type, on the other hand, is distinguished by a slower form of thought, a slower development in his life history, and a devotion to one particular problem, the solution of which is often obtained intuitively early in the history of the research, the remainder of the individual's powers being occupied with the scientific justification and proof of the position then taken up. Ostwald's first and most typical example is (and the choice will seem strange to English eyes) Robert Máyer, the physician who first calculated the specific energy of heat and whose priority to real scientific claims in this matter were, especially at first, strongly opposed in favour of Joule, whose work was admittedly more definite and exact. Gauss, also quoted by Ostwald, would seem to us to be a happier example of the classical type; Faraday, whose life is given very fully, to be rather a doubtful case; while the clearest example which occurs to one is that of Darwin, with Huxley as his correlative *Romantiker*.

The *Romantiker*, according to Ostwald, has a much greater personal influence, a greater power of inspiring either students or audiences.

The man of classical type does not publish his results in the way he has arrived at them, but in a classical and often deductive form, whereas the real approach was by induction and intuition. The crying example is Euclid, whose deductive method in his publication tempted the whole world for centuries to follow this most unnatural method of study and discovery.

Ostwald is strongly of opinion that a great mass of genius is submerged by the unfavourable environment of its early years, either by reason of physical harm, perhaps even jeopardizing survival, or by the crippling effect on the mind. Faraday he cites as almost the only case of a really first-class scientist coming from the very lowest stratum, the majority coming from the middle classes.[1]

In the vocational guidance of individuals, in addition to tests of intelligence and skill, estimates of temperament and disposition are coming to play a larger part. Schneider, quoted by Hollingworth, gives a number of pairs of adjectives descriptive of dispositions, which are useful in considering children; including settled or roving, indoor or outdoor, directive or dependent, creative or imitative, adaptable

---

[1] Ostwald concludes by giving, among others, the following criteria of extraordinary scientific ability between ten and sixteen years of age.

(1) Precocity, or early maturing.
(2) The boy strives after something more than the school, since the mental activities of the latter do not suffice for him.
(3) Therefore, there are often conflicts with the school authorities, which become sharper with advancing years. The reports of teachers are, therefore, to be taken with caution. They usually assert that the scholar was formerly excellent but that he has deteriorated owing to attending to hobbies and other interests.
(4) The boy produces work of great intensity in some one-sided province, that is to say, in subjects and matters oriented about some special tendency.
(5) Definite traces of creative activity, i.e. inventive or independent work, such as collections, compositions, physical or chemical experiments.
(6) He is frequently able to inspire his fellows of like age to similar activities, in which he acts as leader.
(7) He succeeds in all manner of ways in obtaining books with which to satisfy his thirst for knowledge.
(8) The chance and possibility of working freely in his chosen province appears to him the highest possible happiness, and he especially prefers it to any other path leading to gain or distinction.
(9) His companions of like age bear towards him feelings of mixed ridicule and respect. Which of these two is the greater depends much on his disposition, and probably upon the kind of home he comes from.

DIFFERENCES IN WILL AND TEMPERAMENT

or self-centred, deliberate or impulsive, concentrated or diffuse, rapid or slow, dynamic or static. Finally, in recent years attempts have been made to measure will and temperament by short tests, as intelligence is measured. This side of human personality would seem *a priori* to be even more difficult to estimate in an hour than is the intellect. On the other hand, the attempt is very often made to do so in interviews, as when candidates for scholarships, or for posts in a business, are sized up by the interviewer according to their general manner of answering questions : and the tests may be looked upon as standardized interviews. The best known and one of the first, if not the very first, is the Downey Will-Temperament Test. In it suggestion seems to play a not inconsiderable part ; and, indeed, self-confidence and resistance to suggestion is an important part of character. For example, early in the test period (in the group form of the test) ten words are read from an oblong white card by the examiner, twice over. Later, after several other tests have been carried out, the subject is asked to mark sixteen statements (which have reference to the words read, to the examiner's position while reading them, etc.) as true or false, and to underline doubly the response if it is made with conviction and certainty. The scoring here depends on the number of replies thus made confidently and marked as certain. Now the sixteen statements (statements such as : " The first word was book " ; " The shortest word was ice " ; " In my right hand I held a pencil ") are, as a matter of fact, all true. But, as a test of compliance, the pupil is next told that eight were true and eight false, and invited to reconsider his verdicts ; the scoring here depending on the extent to which he resists this suggestion.

This kind of test may seem rather unfair. But whatever it may be as a test of the individual subject, it is instructive as showing to what an extent suggestion, when made by a person occupying a position of prestige, can succeed in obtaining responses clean against the facts. For though we recognize the *suggestio falsi* when it concerns a neutral matter like the shape of a card, do we always do so when it concerns the form of an opinion, political, religious, or æsthetic ? In this realm of testing suggestibility Binet was again an early pioneer, and one of his experiments is very instructive to the teacher. A card was shown to each of a large number of children who were afterwards questioned as to the objects attached to the card. These included a button, a postage stamp, a small picture of a crowd outside some gates, etc. Before being questioned, the children were divided into three groups. To one group the questions were put in a perfectly straightforward non-suggestive way, as " How was the button fastened to the card ? " [Even this suggests that it *was* fastened.] To a second group a more suggestive form was used, viz. : " The button was sewn on to the card by thread, was it not ? " The third group was asked, " What was the colour of the thread by which the button was fastened to the card ? "

Now the button was in fact glued on, and there was no thread there. The three sections of the class responded as might be expected, the last group being almost unanimous in accepting the suggestion that thread was used. The first lesson for the teacher is to beware lest his questions are worded so as to suggest too strongly one particular answer. The teacher is not entirely forbidden, as is the advocate in a court of law, to ask suggestive questions. But he should know clearly that he is asking them and for what purpose, and on the whole he should avoid them, lest he deceive himself as to his pupil's ability.

But a still more important lesson to learn, one dealing not merely with teaching technique, but with fundamental principles, is that we may, all unconsciously, be assuming in our teaching that the button is sewn on, and be busying ourselves only with the colour of possibly non-existent thread. In matters of æsthetic taste, of religion, or of politics we are peculiarly liable to word all our teachings and

DIFFERENCES IN WILL AND TEMPERAMENT

all our questions in such a way, and to be unable to put, either to our pupils or to ourselves, the direct question. In these matters, indeed, it takes a genius or a man of remarkable character to do so.

*　　　*　　　*　　　*

We have seen, in Chapter XVI, how important the years of early infancy are, in the opinion of the Freudians, for the formation of character, in view of the repressions and sublimations of instincts which may then take place. Another school of psychologists, led by John B. Watson, sees the importance of these early years for other reasons, and attributes to chance actions of the environment in that period many deep-seated emotional reactions which profoundly modify the subsequent character. According to these workers, the original emotional reaction patterns are few, consisting probably only of fear, rage, and love : and the complexity of emotion and impulse in the adult is accounted for mainly by the " conditioning " of the simple reactions, that is their attachment by coincidence to some stimuli other than the natural and inborn stimulus. They suggest that " the early home life of the child furnishes a laboratory situation for establishing conditioned emotional responses."

For example, fear reactions can be called out in the baby by sharp noises and by the sudden removal of support : and Watson and his co-workers doubt whether any other situation can produce fear, except by accidental association with one of these. Albert B., at nine months, had never been seen in a state of fear or rage, and practically never cried. He responded without fear, and mainly by " manipulation," i.e. playing with the object, to a live white rat, a rabbit, a dog, a monkey, masks with and without hair, cotton-wool, burning newspapers, etc. Then, however, arrangements were made to produce a loud sound (by striking a hammer on a suspended steel bar) at the moment when his hand just touched the white rat in reaching for it (at eleven months). Seven such joint stimulations, given two on one day and five more a week later, were sufficient to cause the baby to show pronounced fear reactions at the sight of the white rat. This fear also was shown when the rabbit, a dog, a sealskin coat, were shown, though he had previously played freely with these. This persisted for many weeks, with two or three " freshenings " by giving the sound with the rat, or with the dog : and once the latter provided an unexpected bark which had the same effect. The experimenters conclude that such " conditioned " emotional responses " persist, although with a certain loss in the intensity of the reaction, for a longer period than one month " and state that their view is that they " persist and modify personality throughout life." Had Albert, who was of an extremely phlegmatic type, been emotionally unstable, they believe that the results would have been much more marked.

Both the Watsonians and the Freudians then attribute to the action of the environment a great deal of the formation of personality. In the Freudian theory, it is repression, mainly of the sex instinct, which is responsible. In Watson's it is association of fear (or rage or love) with situations other than the natural stimuli which plays the major part. In both, the home life of the first two years is all important. But both admit the influence of heredity ("Albert was extremely phlegmatic "). It is the form which hereditary forces take which is determined by the home, not the strength. There can be no doubt as to the substantial truth of this, even if we take leave to doubt whether it would have been as easy to associate the fear reaction with (say) the child's playing blocks, though one of the experimenters familiar with these trials has assured me of his conviction that this also could be done. All nurses and mothers act on the assumption that fear and love can be thus associated, and their failures as well as their successes show it. Differ-

DIFFERENCES IN WILL AND TEMPERAMENT

ences, if not of temperament, at least of forms of reaction, may then be products of education as much as of inheritance, and if, as is hoped, positive constructive results can be obtained as definite as the undesirable reactions, we may yet have a definite technique for influencing character in infancy. At present we have only the belief that the tree grows as the twig is bent, and the general conviction that a placid, regular, lovable existence is best for baby's character, without repressions due to adult anger or secrecy, and without fears caused by tales or threats.

CHAPTER XXIII

PYGMALION OR PROCRUSTES?

SINCE William James did so, no psychologist has dared to write a chapter on the influence of habit in character formation. All one can do is to tell the reader to take down from the shelf that "best sermon ever preached," and read it again. But a secondary and very practical question may perhaps be discussed. To what extent do habits *enforced by authority* improve character? Are such habits, enjoined by rule and regulation, merely a Procrustean bed to which character cannot be fitted except by amputation and rackings which kill the spirit? Or was Sadoleto right when he said:

> True, habit impressed by careful government from without is not real virtue, but only the semblance and image of virtue; yet, as legend and story tell of Pygmalion's statue of a woman, by the kindness of heaven, it comes about in the course of time that this image takes on the spirit and life of true virtue.[1]

The truth is that either of these things may happen. One school creates a living independent character, another produces only unwilling obedience to the letter of the law. There must be some difference in the nature of the authority which produces such different results. Two things are largely responsible for the deadening, antagonizing effect which authority sometimes produces. The one is having too many rules: the other is their arbitrary nature.

It is a great mistake in school, or class, or community, to make any rules which can be done without. For whoever

[1] Campagnac and Forbes' translation of *De Pueris recte Instituendis*.

makes a law creates a crime. Without china one cannot break crockery. Some laws, of course, need no making, they only need setting down exactly. Such are some of the ten commandments—perhaps all of them. But some other rules are very obviously man-made, teacher-made.

Any law creates a crime. An *arbitrary* law creates criminals. "If there was a special law enacted against red-haired men," said Hugh Miller in his essay on *The Crime Making Laws*, "red-haired men would in a short time become exceedingly dangerous characters." They would become a race of outlaws, their hands against all men. And since one might as well be hanged for a sheep as a lamb, they would probably commit numerous real crimes, and acquire a reputation which would be cited whenever anyone proposed to ameliorate the "red-hair laws." Now many school regulations are about as absurd as these, being directed against innate childish impulses hardly more preventable than red hair : and they have a similar effect. Before making a rule, therefore, the teacher should consider whether it is humanly possible for the healthy boy to keep it. He cannot, for example, sit still for hours. He cannot, as a young boy, keep from talking to others without unnatural repression. He cannot always remember to close the gate into the garden.

In another way, too, a rule may create criminals, when insufficient steps are taken to enforce it, to detect infringement, and to inflict punishment. For then the temptation to break the rule is too great, and a habit of breaking rules is being inculcated. Any authority making a rule which may be broken without much danger of discovery is faced with a dilemma. Either the law will be broken right and left, or a punishment must be inflicted on those who *are* caught sufficiently severe to outweigh the unpunished offences : and that would be too severe a punishment to receive the endorsement of public opinion.

It is this endorsement of public opinion which is the

essential requisite. For then the law will certainly be policed, since the majority will be policemen, not to report to authority or to tell tales, but to punish by public displeasure. And this endorsement of public opinion, or of school opinion, can only be obtained if the government grows from within, instead of being enforced from without. Hence the feeling that systems of self-government are psychologically sound. They have been tried in many forms, some moderate, some extreme. The dominie who tries the more extreme forms is liable to be dismissed as at least unnecessary. Wiser is he who remembers that children walk before they run and guides their steps. Government by fellow-comrades has for half a century or more been the rule in the great English Public Schools, though there the prefects are chosen by a " tyrant," the head. Self-government on an elective basis has been tried in " Little Commonwealths," and in " School Councils," and the like. All are efforts to enlist public opinion on the side of the laws when made, as well as means of training pupils to fulfil the duties of citizens.

Authority has, however, ways of moulding character other than the making of rules. Very potent weapons are the school assembly, traditional ceremonies, and the presentation of models to be imitated, of heroes to be worshipped. In the school assembly the members of the school feel themselves to be one body. When gathered together *en masse* children and adults alike are more open to suggestion, which seems to infect the less enthusiastic by contagion from the more easily influenced. The singing together of school songs, giving American college yells or just plain British hurrahs, answering in turn to a roll-call, tossing a pancake on Shrove Tuesday, or meeting a famous " old boy " at the school gates, all these things help enormously in creating *esprit de corps*. They can be used just as well to inculcate narrow-minded class ideals as broad. Indeed, they probably have been used more often for the

PYGMALION OR PROCRUSTES ?

former than for the latter purpose. They are not only in that case regrettable because the end is less desirable, but also because they are more liable to lead to that defect of character resulting in " going to the dogs." For a man must be an officer *and* a gentleman. If he is only a gentleman because he is an officer—if his keeping to the right path of conduct is *only* motivated by the wish for the approval of a narrow class of comrades, and is defined by an unbreakable code of convention which is accepted without fundamental understanding—then should that code be broken, that approval lost, no anchor remains. Whereas, if in addition there is a wider sense of right and wrong there is no escape from self-condemnation, nor need to give up self-respect even if one be ostracized.

The path to that higher type of character, however, probably lies through the lower. The unselfish motives began no doubt when co-operation came into play in the evolutionary process, in addition to competition. Sometimes the importance of competition in Darwinian and allied theories makes one forget the equal importance of co-operation. In any multicellular animal, co-operation has largely taken the place of competition as between the cells of the body. The right hand does not compete in cut-throat fashion with the left. And then in the family, the tribe, the nation, co-operation finds further scope. It is, no doubt, co-operation in order that the body corporate may compete the more successfully with others. But still, co-operation it is, calling for unselfish sacrifice in place of selfish striving. So the road to unselfishness seems to be through the herd instinct, *esprit de corps*, team games. The only danger is stopping too short. Everyone stops somewhere. The great distinguishing feature of Christianity was the height to which it rose in this respect, far beyond the level of paganism.

And though the ascent seems to have been from the instincts which centre round the ego, up to those which find

INSTINCT, INTELLIGENCE AND CHARACTER

their function in the herd, yet strangely enough the energy seems to come finally from the former. For it is in a self-respect which does not permit of selfishness that the best character appears to find its strength.

*   *   *   *

One of the greatest dangers of failure in character training arises from the assumption that teaching ideas will lead to actions. Ideas, of course, have an influence on actions; but when they come into conflict with habit impressed by past activity, or with sentiments based on instincts and emotions, they lose the battle. The saying that there is no impression without expression is true in the intellectual sphere, but doubly true in the moral. For teaching moral ideas without causing them to emerge at once into action is not merely failing to produce that action; it is encouraging a habit of dwelling on moral ideas without acting on them. These are the good resolutions which pave the road to Hell.

Character training means, therefore, behaviour training, and the methods of controlling behaviour here are the same as the methods of controlling behaviour of the cognitive and manipulative kind. Situations must be planned which are likely to lead to the occurrence of the desired behaviour. When it occurs it should be "rewarded." When its opposite occurs it should be "punished." But not all punishments and rewards are equally efficacious, equally desirable, or equally free from unwanted by-products.

Under "rewards," of course, we include not only actual tangible prizes, as money or books, not only visible privileges such as extra holiday or permission to have tea in one's study, but also more subtle matters, as the approval, felt or expressed, of teacher, comrades, or one's inner self. And a similar list may be made of punishments. It is because of this that the legal view of punishment, which Bentham clarified, is so inapplicable in education. Legally, a punishment is clearly inefficacious if it does not outweigh the

PYGMALION OR PROCRUSTES?

benefit gained by the crime. When this benefit and that punishment can be exactly measured, then such a principle is workable. Were the fine for stealing five pounds only four pounds and nothing else, the merry game of pilfering five-pound notes would go on faster and more furiously. But in school, and in large measure in the courts also, the punishment is less easily sized up, and the art of the trainer of boys lies partly in making the same punishment have greater effect, the same crime appear to bring less pleasure. Nevertheless, it is true that to "punish" too lightly is encouraging "crime"; yet as lightly as possible is best.

The more important point about rewards and punishments is that they should be as inevitable as possible. They need not be of great magnitude, but they must be certain. It was in part this which Herbert Spencer emphasized in his book *Education*, when he urged that punishments should be "natural": for Nature's punishments are, he said, certain. Fire *always* burns. The only trouble about this is that it is not true. Certainly fire always burns, but a draught does not always give me a cold, nor mince pie indigestion. No doubt other circumstances explain these inconsistencies, but to the onlooker many of Mother Nature's rewards and punishments appear just as erratic as those of the weakest of human mothers. However, it is still true that certainty is desirable. The other factor in Nature's punishment which Spencer stressed was that of fitting the crime. And he urged that this should be so in the nursery and schoolroom too, that the punishment for leaving toys about should be the natural one of losing them (nurse having cleared them away), or the punishment for lateness in coming to school be the natural one of getting away late at the close. There is much truth in this, for such punishments tend to sidetrack any resentment against a person. They are in some measure felt to be only natural.

In this discussion of rewards and punishments there is not intended to be any suggestion that school discipline is only to be obtained by prizes and canings. On the contrary, the terms are merely used to cover all marks of approbation and all signs of disapproval. Whether we will or no, we do " reward " and " punish." " The mother neglects her children when they are quiet, and plays with them when they cry," says Thorndike; " consequently there are many crying babies. The child is refused a favour when he asks once, but if he teases a score of times it is finally granted; consequently there are many teasing boys."

One of the most potent rewards, one of the most satisfying situations which exists for human adult or child, is the realization that one can do what one's fellows can do. Imitation in the automatic narrow sense may be of rare occurrence in man, as some aver. But in a wider sense, as the habitual result of finding satisfaction in being like others, it is one of the commonest of human qualities. Children naughty at home become quiet, obedient, and cheerful at school, because it pleases them to be like others. A child who has found no pleasure in trying to read finds a pleasure in trying to do what his comrades can do. Clearly this kind of imitation easily shades off into emulation and competition. But it is desirable that its main strength should not go down this channel. There is another way in which the instinct can develop. Instead of the child's impulse to be like his comrades growing into a wish to excel them, it may grow, if properly directed, into a wish to be like other and more ideal characters. Out of imitation may grow emulation, but also hero-worship. Very early the baby wants to play at doing what father and mother do. For some years this occupation employs much of the child's leisure time. The imitation becomes more fundamental and less superficial. Knowledge of the details and the meaning of the parents' occupation grows, and the imitation grows *pari passu*. It extends to comprise imitation of many other adults, the milkman, the policeman, the blacksmith. The manipulative instinct joins forces and helps to develop

PYGMALION OR PROCRUSTES ?

the imitation of the other occupations, leads to making a sawmill, or a derrick, or a fire engine. The love of adventure leads the imitation into paths peopled by soldiers and sailors, cowboys and Indians, Vikings and Cavaliers. Heroes are chosen and abandoned. Everything depends on just which heroes come to have a prolonged influence. For the imitation will extend to matters other than those which are the primary source of attraction, and it is in this way that a shifting of the focus of imitation sets in which may lead either upward or downward. The boy imitates, is attracted by " Single-Shot Sam " because of his thrilling adventures, his bravery, his personal prowess. But he also imitates his bad language, his disdain of the law, his cruelty. Luckily, there are heroes of fiction in boys' stories who are more desirable characters, though it is, apparently, hard to keep them equally interesting. But several writers of a generation ago did so with success ; and, on a very high plane of literature, Kipling does so now, and others with him. Boys' characters are more moulded by what they read, I believe, than is commonly realized.

It comes all to this, that the hammer of Procrustes is the rule or law arbitrarily enforced, and grudgingly obeyed ; while the chisel of Pygmalion is the tone set by the school as a community, the unwritten law enshrined in custom and tradition. As ever, direct suggestion is likely to fail, suggestion believed to come from within likely to succeed.

Not without a bearing on character training is the question, to what extent education is a preparation for the future, to what extent it is for the present. One type of schooling looks upon childhood as *entirely* a period of preparation for manhood. Sometimes it is preparation for the cultured leisure, sometimes for the business or vocation, sometimes just for the snobbishness, of later life. In its noblest form it is preparation for the trials and moral struggles of this world, into which the pupil at adolescence is to be thrown. Many of these are right and proper aims of education. But

INSTINCT, INTELLIGENCE AND CHARACTER

if they loom too large they tend to make school gloomy and distasteful, and divorced from the proper interests of childhood. At the other extreme is that education which says to the children, "Eat, drink, and be merry, for tomorrow you grow up," that education which lays itself out to give the children just what they are interested in now, and knows no drudgery, no monotony.

With little children, life must be lived in the present. Things which are in themselves immediately interesting alone hold their attention. But as they grow older, there must be training in forethought. They have to learn to do things which at the moment are in themselves distasteful in order that some goal may be attained. And so more and more the subjects attacked are, as the first novelty wears off, means to some end. But when habits of regular work and study have carried on the machine over the next stretch of the road, the reward comes in a quickening of interest in the study for its own sake. In this sense, too, it may come about that the image takes on spirit and life, and the student becomes wedded to studies which were undertaken merely to pass an examination.

CHAPTER XXIV

BACK TO THE LEARNING PROCESS

THE BEST METHODS OF MEMORIZING AND OF ACQUIRING SKILL.

IF we wish to memorize anything (as a poem, a formula, a list of dates, an argument), or if we wish our pupils to do so, the most important points are to see that it is understood, that a need for it is felt, that it is attended to intently, that it is attended to as a whole as well as in parts, that several senses are brought to bear on it so as to reinforce one another, that the time devoted to the necessary repetition is scientifically distributed, that the repetition does not lapse into passive repetition but involves active recall, and that the material when learnt is not only integrated within itself, but is linked up with the other knowledge possessed by the mind.

The influence of the understanding on the memory can be shown very readily by attempting to learn by heart a set of nonsense syllables, and comparing the difficulty of doing so with the comparative ease with which an equal number of syllables, forming a paragraph of connected prose can be learnt. There are, of course, some matters which have to be learned by heart which are quite arbitrary, and are not, in any ordinary sense, understandable, such as the fact that the port light of a ship is red, or that "address" has only one "d" in the French language, or that in measuring angles, the positive direction is counter-clockwise. Such things, however, are either unimportant, or, if they play an important part in our lives, we grow into their usage by frequent repetition without conscious memorizing. They are the cases when, at need, a mnemonic may be excusable, as when a landsman remembers that the *port* light is *port* wine coloured, or when we say " Thirty days hath September, April, June, and November."

Whenever possible, however, pupils should be discouraged from memorizing by means of such tricks, or by means of sheer repetition, and encouraged to remember by understanding. Having children understand and be interested is of far greater importance psychologically than any of the other facts about economical learning which experiment has given us. For example, it is better that they should rather slowly reconstruct a required formula than that they should learn it so as to reproduce it quickly by heart. This is one of the ways in which examinations encourage bad teaching; for it pays a teacher to make his pupils learn formulæ by heart, whereas it would be far better for their mental development if they relied entirely on understanding them. True, by making them memorize, teachers can get some pupils through an examination who would never pass on the other method. But they never should pass, they ought to be doing something else.

It should not on the other hand be assumed that a formula, or any piece of mental apparatus, should necessarily be completely understood before it is used. Use leads to understanding, if there is from time to time a conscious effort to understand, and use will lead to memorizing. It is only conscious learning of stuff which is unappreciated that is reprehensible. Examples should be worked from first principles rather than from rules.

Understanding will go a long way even with historical dates. At least it prevents a child from dating Sir Walter Raleigh before the voyage of Columbus. Sheer memorizing of dates can be done before the age of eleven: but the experiments of Sturt and Oakden have shown that the development of an understanding time-sense is not to be expected much

BACK TO THE LEARNING PROCESS

before that age, so that a mere date to a boy of mental age nine is almost nothing.

Material will not be learned by heart unless there is a felt need for its memorizing—at least, not easily. This is the interest doctrine in another form. A boy will rapidly learn a formula if it enables him to do something he wants to do, such as make a propeller for his model aeroplane, or tune his radio set. He will learn poetry more willingly if he wants to take part in the fifth-form play than if he is merely required to learn it as a task. It is hard for a teacher to discover real needs which will, in a boy, lead to a demand for all the mathematics, or for the classical languages, or any of the school subjects. But by using the pupil's manipulative instincts he can get a lot of mathematics and science out of needs connected with motor bicycles and similar toys; and from the dramatic and adventure instincts a good deal of literature and language.

In learning by heart, ten minutes' really close attention is worth an hour's slack repetition. As, in physical exercises, one can often see pupils languidly going through the motions, and others putting force and snap into them, so here in memorizing. Close attention is facilitated by putting on its outward bodily signs, the unwavering direction of the eyes, the characteristic muscular strain in the bodily attitude. But these things do not guarantee it. They may, indeed, become themselves the object of attention, as may often be seen in a class sitting in military stiffness. They may lead to just gazing at the material to be learned, whereas an attitude of inward questioning is wanted. Actual questioning of the class by the teacher, actual self-questioning by the student, helps. Various aspects of the things studied have to be sought for. In a poem, the alliteration in this line, the visual picture called up by that phrase, the frequency of long vowels in a certain verse, all help, if noted consciously, to assist recall.

The experimental work on memorizing which is best

known, and has been most often repeated with consistent results, is probably that which contrasts the " whole " method of learning with the " part " method. By the " whole " method of learning a poem, is meant the plan of saying the whole poem through and through, over and over again, whereas in the more usual " part " method it is learned a verse at a time or a few lines at a time : even one line at a time perhaps, with little children. Experiment has almost invariably shown the former method to be from 10 to 30 per cent. better than the latter. The poem is learned more quickly and is retained more completely.

Obviously, there must be a limit to the length of the poem thus to be learnt as a whole. If the principle were being applied to school work, the poem would presumably be such as could be learned by the " whole " method in a reasonable time, say half a term.

But there are difficulties in the way. In the experiments which have demonstrated the superiority of the " whole " method, the subjects have taken special pains to work as hard when using the one plan as when using the other. When this is so, then the superiority of the " whole " method can show itself : a superiority which lies in the fact that no unnecessary associations are practised (such as occur, in the " part " method, between the last word of a verse and the first word of the same verse, when it is said over and over).

But with children the case is different. By the " part " method they know at what rate they are making progress, and gain confidence. The teacher, too, can test a pupil to see how many lines he knows, but cannot easily test him to see how far he has advanced in the " whole " method. And so the learner is apt to lose heart. He cannot believe that presently the whole poem will rise above the threshold of his memory, somewhat as the one-horse shay disappeared all at once. So all one can assert is, that *provided confidence and a sense of progress can be sustained*, it is better to

BACK TO THE LEARNING PROCESS

learn as large portions of a poem as possible and avoid snippets.

There is one special case of learning where the "whole" method is quite inapplicable, that is in cases where the material does not really constitute a whole, a unit, but is essentially a collection of separate associations. Thus in the seven times multiplation table the final aim is not to know it in serial order, though that order may be convenient for building it up and for understanding it, but to know 7 × 6 (say) when standing along by itself, plucked out of that order. While, therefore, the serial order will be used in the stage when the whole table is being built up by the repeated addition of seven, presently what is wanted is practice in random order, not in serial order, to avoid the weakness of having to say the whole table through up to that point in order to remember 7 × 6. To assist in this, a useful device is to print the items of the table on separate cards, which can then be shuffled like playing cards before being shown, one by one, to the pupil who is required to give the answer to each item, as 7 × 3, 7 × 8, etc. If a pupil or a class shows special weakness in one item, say in 7 × 6, then it is easy to add a duplicate or triplicate of that card to the pack and thus obtain additional practice in the weak association.[1]

For most individuals, it is an aid to memorizing if several senses are used. Then the one may come to the assistance of the other when recall is attempted, as when we write a word to see what it looks like, when we are not sure of the spelling. A little child, taught its letters by the Montessori plan, where they are formed of sandpaper and are traced over by the finger, will sometimes be unable to recognize a letter by sight alone, but will do so if it is traced. Students who find it difficult to recall the substance of a lecture find it

---

[1] One of the things which struck me in the schools of New York City was the greater amount of drill work, in which such "flash cards" play a constant part.

helpful to say some of the lecturer's sentences to themselves, or to see in the mind's eye headings and chief points, as the lecture progresses. Largely, no doubt, this is because of the direction of attention thus introduced, but partly because not everything is left to hearing. And just as a good teacher puts headings and unfamiliar words on the blackboard, so the student, teaching himself, writes these down and looks them carefully over.

The distribution of time in learning is definitely of great importance. Suppose that only one hour can be devoted to learning securely a poem, and suppose that it can be just repeated without error after fifteen minutes' practice. There remain 45 minutes in which to deepen the impression by further repetition, so that the poem will be known not barely but confidently. In such a case it is the poorest economy to use the remaining time at once. Far better is it to postpone further practice till next day, and to use the time in short practices on successive days, stopping on each occasion shortly after the poem has been brought up to the point where it can just be said. The main reason for the superiority of this over the solid hour is that one gains a knowledge each day of which parts of the poem are most liable to be forgotten, and directs special attention to these weak spots, not so much by separate repetition as by closer scrutiny.

It is desirable, when repeating a poem in order to memorize it, to try as soon as possible to look away from the book. The active effort to recall the lines is more effective than merely repeating them passively. In the same way, when next day certain parts cannot at first be recalled, it is inadvisable to fly at once to the book. A little patience often leads to the restoration of the missing words or phrases, and they are then much more firmly fixed than would have been the case had they been taken again from the text. It is astonishing how a verse of which at first only fragments can be remembered will come to mind in the course of an hour, if it is reverted to again and again in the intervals of some other work. Probably one of the reasons why some students learn so much better than do others, is that they utilize odd moments in the day to recall pieces of knowledge, and each such recall serves as several repetitions. When a piece of knowledge acquired in a certain classroom and in a given subject is only recalled under exactly the same circumstances, it cannot be said to be available for use. Whereas if it is required or revived against other backgrounds it gains an independent strength, another reason for the correlation of studies and the avoidance of bulkheads between subjects.

People sometimes acquire the unfortunate habit of believing that they have bad memories, a belief which is usually unjustified. It is true that our brain substance probably does differ from one individual to another in that quality which corresponds to memory. There are probably these vital and inherited differences in memory just as there are differences in the durability of paths through different forests. A path made through one forest will last for years, through another it will be overgrown again in a week. Through one kind of vegetation paths are made only with immense difficulty, through another with the greatest ease. But the condition of the path system of a forest, though it depends somewhat on these differences, depends far more on the interest which men have in traversing it, and the frequency with which they do so. In the same way a man's memory in a given province will depend far more upon interest and frequent recall than upon the quality of inherited memory. A boy knows his favourite cricket team's performances by heart because he is interested in them and is always running over them. Powerful instincts of competition, possession, and pride in personal prowess cause the interest. If equally powerful interests could be enlisted in the subjects of classics or chemistry, he would remember the oxides of nitrogen or the tenses of *sequor* just as well as he remembers sporting records. It is probably curiosity and wonder which are at the root of most success in studies, and so again we come back to the instincts. "The most vital factor is curiosity," says Dewey in *How We Think*. "Desire and curiosity are the two eyes through which he sees the world in the most enchanted colours," says R. L. S. in *El Dorado*. And so a teacher's task in " making children learn " is largely the job of arousing their curiosity in the lesson and obtaining keen attention.

* * * *

Acquiring skill and dexterity is very like memorizing in some respects. Indeed, for the Behaviourists, even thinking is only a language habit. Many of the ways in which memorizing can be facilitated are also applicable to skill. The best distribution of practice has been studied in learning to typewrite, to juggle with balls, etc., and has been found to follow the principles laid down above. The felt need, careful attention, and active effort are as important here as there. The " whole " method has, however, been, questioned in this province by one experimenter [1] who caused his subjects to trace by touch alone miniature mazes of grooves, with many blind alleys. The mazes could be learned in parts, and though the " whole " method was superior to a " part " method in which no attempt was made to put the parts together till each had been learned separately, yet a modified " part " method was still more superior, in which first *a* was learned, then *ab*, then *abc*, and so on.

Two new points attract attention in a survey of the literature of acquiring skill. One is the existence of *plateaux* on curves of learning, the other the much greater permanence of skill over knowledge. Once a man has learned to swim, to skate, to cycle, he possesses the art for life. He may feel a trifle clumsy for a few minutes when he has not skated for ten years, but there is no question of beginning to learn

[1] Pechstein, *Journ. of Educ. Psychol.*, 1917, viii, 303.

BACK TO THE LEARNING PROCESS

again. Very little practice brings him quickly to his former skill, and beyond. Most probably this is because the neurone connections involved are on a comparatively low level, and not so far removed from instincts and reflexes as are those concerned in recalling a poem or a series of facts or an argument. Indeed, some of them, as those involved in swimming, were perchance once innate.

Though less likely, it is, however, possible that the greater permanence of skill is due to the greater amount of overlearning. In a poem, a new verse is a new verse, and can be learned without deepening the memory of the earlier verses. A new part of a skilled action, however, usually demands for its practice or for its very existence that earlier and simpler movements be repeated and thereby made more certain. I cannot practise tossing three balls in the air without practising tossing up one ball. I cannot learn to rattle off -*tion* or -*able* on the typewriter without practising striking *t* or *a*, or without practising moving the spacer or the line changer. And so certain fundamental motions get a tremendous amount of practice beyond their immediate needs, and may form the scaffolding which persists so obstinately in the face of neglect.

" Plateaux " are flat places in the curve of improvement, periods during which little or no advance is made, though practice be continued with unflagging perseverance; after which there is again improvement, as though paths in the brain were gradually perfected, and then suddenly thrown open : as though canals were being dug, into which after much weary spade work the water rushes and communication is established.

In part such plateaux may be due to the nature of the task, which requires in the first place certain simple acts which are learned rapidly, but then have to be practised a considerable time before the next stage of combining them into complex acts can be attacked. Thus in reading telegraphic dots and dashes, the separate letters have to be mastered, then syllables and words come to be recognized as wholes, then phrases and sentences. There would thus be three curves of improvement, separated by plateaux, during which reorganization without advance went on.

Instead, or in addition, it may be that plateaux are due to boredom, and then a sudden fresh access of energy and interest, due to a holiday, or a new aim, or a threat of dismissal, or realization that someone else is improving. All these things may occur unconsciously. When plateaux occur with pupils or with ourselves we should not be unduly disappointed nor give up heart. The teacher should try to call attention to the new problem, if the case is anything like the passing from words to phrases in telegraphy. A special effort should be made after a while to get the new rise in the curve to begin.

Finally, we should realize that many of us, and many of our pupils, are living contentedly on such plateaux, mere shelves in the upward sloping hill of progress, under the impression that we have reached the peak of our powers. It may not be worth while, but in almost any of our activities any one of us probably could, if he wished and gave thought and effort to it, lift himself on to a new upward curve and reach a higher level of skill. We have to choose, for time and energy would not permit each of us to be expert in everything. But in what we choose we could probably improve further and possibly attain a new permanent level from which we would not slip back.

CHAPTER XXV

THE WINGS OF THOUGHT

IN discussing the ascent in the animal scale from instinct to intelligence we have distinguished several levels which can be seen exemplified in different animals as their respective normal modes of reaction, or can be seen, each of them, in man, in his responses to various situations. There is first the automaton, unable to make any response except that which is fatally called out by the situation, as when " the mole-cricket, which is in the habit of escaping pursuit by burrowing in the earth, makes violent motions with the forelegs, even if it be placed upon a plate of glass into which it could not possibly burrow." [1]

Slightly above this level is the animal which, although it always makes response a to a given situation, will then proceed to make response b and c if a fails. Its inner " attitude " changes with failure, though we do not know whether this attitude is a consciousness or not. Its responses, however, are always in a definite order a, b, c, d. Considerably higher comes the animal whose responses to any situation which is at all novel are much less predictable; the animal which, to escape from captivity or to reach food, will try, one after the other, a very large number of responses in what appears to be almost a random order, from which the reward of success selects one which, when the situation recurs, will be prepotent, and will occur sooner than otherwise, and ultimately will be the habitual response. So far these responses have all been actual pieces

[1] *The Evolution Theory*, August Weismann. Trs. J. A. Thomson, 1904.

of explicit behaviour. But hereabouts certain substitutes for overt muscular behaviour begin to show themselves. Actions are imagined instead of being actually carried out. These substitutes are (probably) first images which not only stand for the actual objects and the actual actions, but look and feel like them, albeit less vividly. Later, pieces and fragments of these images come to stand as symbols for the actual behaviour, and last of all come pure symbols, such as are most words, which do not in any way resemble the objects but *mean* them.

In man, who has the power of using this last weapon in the armoury of response, one nevertheless sees all the other stages occurring. To more brilliant light he "responds," quite unconsciously, by a contraction of the pupil of the eye. To an unexpected loud noise, as a pistol shot, he responds not quite so inevitably and certainly, though usually, with a start. To a situation such as a difficult puzzle he responds by a number of almost random actions and manipulations. To some situations he responds largely by images, as, when climbing a mountain, he hesitates before tackling a difficult bit. Finally, he often responds, in addition, by thought in terms of inner speech, as when he sits meditating on some problem of policy of a more abstract kind, say on how he should vote in an election. To some extent these stages are passed through with advancing years. "We grown people can tell ourselves a story, give and take strokes until the bucklers ring, ride far and fast, marry, fall, and die ; all the while sitting quietly by the fire or lying prone in bed. This is exactly what a child cannot do, or does not do, at least, when he can find anything else. He works all with lay figures and stage properties," says Stevenson. And largely it is true that the more abstract substitutes come later.

With the growth of symbolic response there comes the possibility of responding to very abstract elements in a situation, the power of seeing the qualities and properties of objects, and discussing them apart from the things, the power of formulating general laws by observation of many situations, and of applying these general laws to other situations to assist in deciding upon the proper response. The stage of reasoning proper has then been reached. For the teacher, two things about reasoning seem to me of prime importance. The first is that the traditional division of reasoning into inductive and deductive reasoning is dangerous in the classroom, because real thought must necessarily use both intermingled. We can no more think inductively, or think deductively, than a bird can fly with one wing, or a man breathe only by inhaling. The second is that the ordinary processes of reasoning, either inductive or deductive, are comparatively easy matters to grasp, and are commonly used correctly by all but the least intelligent. It is rather the degree of abstraction and complexity in what is reasoned about which makes reasoning more or less difficult, and the care with which its results are tried and verified which makes it accurate. "The inductive method has been practised ever since the beginning of the world by every human being," says Macaulay writing on Bacon. "It is constantly practised by the most ignorant clown, by the most thoughtless schoolboy, by the very child at the breast." The teacher's task is not so much to get his pupil to make inductions, it is rather to get them to do so, in Macaulay's words, "with patience, attention, sagacity and judgment": and also to lead them to apply their powers to more abstract matters than they would commonly choose as subjects for their exercise. This is again a matter of interest: and given an interest in the subject, children are not likely to make errors in deductive reasoning either, though fallacies here are more common.

It is in the teaching of science that the alternation of induction and deduction is best seen. All thinking involves the examination of data, the recognition of a problem to be solved, the tentative formation of a hypothesis, its application to the already known data to see if it is consistent with present facts, and its employment to predict new facts which are then searched for and, if found, held to be very strong evidence of the correctness of the hypothesis. I believe this outline to be true of all thought, both deductive and inductive, but it is more obviously applicable to what is commonly called induction, so let us begin with that side of teaching. In Chapter XV a lesson on the common pendulum was introduced as an illustration. Let us now trace the details of such a lesson, considered as an exercise in thinking. The problem, which we may suppose had arisen in connection with inaccuracy in the school clock, is to find how the rate of oscillation of a pendulum depends upon its length. Simple experiments show that it is constant for constant length (with small oscillations) and that the rate increases, the pendulum swings more quickly, as it is made shorter. The obvious next step is to measure the length and the time of swing and put them down in black and white for a number of cases. When this has been done older pupils of college standing might find the square root connection, or those of higher intelligence might find it, with no more help. But with younger pupils the course of events has to be stage-managed by the teacher if the class is to have any chance of success. The proper time at which to introduce any problem to a class is when their habits of methodical thinking and experiment have reached such a development that not too much " stage-managing " is needed. In the present case a little change in the form of the problem at a certain moment makes all the difference. Suppose we start with a yard-long pendulum and see how often it swings through the position of rest in one minute, and say that it is found to do so 58 times. Then the next question may be worded in two ways, either

(a) How many times would a 2-yard pendulum swing in a minute ? or
(b) How long would a 2-yard pendulum take to swing 58 times ?

THE WINGS OF THOUGHT

The second form is much easier from the point of view of ascertaining the law, especially if the instruction is added: "Express your result in minutes and decimals of a minute." Suppose, however, this last advice is not given. The tabulation of the work done is as follows:

Length of Pendulum.	Time to Swing 58 Times.
1 yard	1 minute
2 yards	?

How long will the 2-yard pendulum take? The proper scientific attitude is to hold judgment in suspense. But it is equally a proper scientific attitude to try to form a working hypothesis. "I wonder if twice as long in yards will mean twice as long in minutes" is a germ of a hypothesis. Already a tentative generalization has been made (during what would ordinarily be called the "presentation"), and we really proceed to an application or trial of it when we time our 2-yard pendulum over 58 swings. It takes 1 minute 25 seconds! So our hypothesis was false. However, let us go on to try a 3-yard pendulum:

Length of Pendulum.	Time to Swing 58 Times.
1 yard	1 minute
2 yards	1 minute 25 seconds
3 yards	?

Commonly when I have asked a class at this stage how long they think the 3-yard pendulum will take, someone has suggested 1 minute 50 seconds, a number based on a generalization that for each yard added to the pendulum 25 seconds will be added to the time. Let us try. It takes 1 minute 44 seconds! So this theory is also wrong, it would seem. A state of mind rather like that of a pupil of Socrates after a course of his famous questions is apt to ensue. But in many pupils there is distinctly present a realization of the fact that time is not increasing at the same speed as the length. A guess for 4 yards which I have frequently had presented to me is 1 minute 57 seconds. This is based on the idea that since the steps in time are getting shorter

INSTINCT, INTELLIGENCE AND CHARACTER

their decrease may be constant. 25 seconds was the first step, 19 seconds the next step (6 less) : so this will be 13 seconds.

Length of Pendulum.	Time to Swing 58 Times.
1 yard	1 minute
2 yards	1 minute 25 seconds
3 yards	1 minute 44 seconds
4 yards	?

On trial the time is found to be not far from that predicted, and possibly three or four trials will be needed to make certain that a discrepancy exists. It takes almost exactly 2 minutes.[1]

Now note that instead of going through the formal steps of preparation, presentation, association, generalization, and verification once each,[2] we have already generalized three times and verified the fact that our generalization was wrong each time. All the while the "presentation" has gone on, the accumulation of data. ("Presentation" suggests too strongly that the pupil is a recipient, instead of participator.) Instead of going through five regular steps, 1, 2, 3, 4, 5, to the solution of one question, we rather ascend a winding staircase in which the steps 3, 4, and 5 keep recurring on higher and higher planes :

$$1, 2, 3, 4, (5)$$
$$3, 4, (5)$$
$$3, 4, (5)$$

the (5) representing the fifth step resulting in disappointment. How many times had Archimedes gone round that circle before he ultimately could cry Eureka ?

I have only occasionally got the actual solution of the pendulum problem from unaided pupils. But I have got

---

[1] NOTE.—A 4-yard pendulum is too long to get into most classrooms, and even if a thread can be got round a hook on the ceiling, a very heavy bob is needed to keep it going long enough. Yards are better to talk about; but I have used a 2-foot measuring rule often as unit. Feet are too short for demonstration.

[2] See page 151ff.

THE WINGS OF THOUGHT

it from pupils to whom I suggested putting the times into minutes and decimals

    1 yard 1 minute
    2 yards 1·42 minute
    3 yards 1·73 minute
    4 yards 2 minutes

and who then recognized the square roots. Now in each application of a tentative hypothesis to a new length of pendulum we have an example of deductive thought, inasmuch as a general law is applied to a specific case. In crudely syllogistic form the reasoning runs, " the time is the square root of the length, the length is 5 yards, therefore the time will be $\sqrt{5}$ minutes." Or more formally, " all pendula obey this law, this is a pendulum, therefore it will obey this law." But this is a very primitive form of deduction, and induction has undoubtedly played the major part in the lesson. A law obtained in this way, by repeated guesses which are verified by trial, is called an empirical law, and does not satisfy the mind in the same way in which a law deduced from first principles satisfies it. Deductive thinking seems, therefore, at first sight to rise above the trial and error procedure which we have followed up from its lowest stage to the level of scientific induction. But we shall make the attempt presently to show that in deductive thought also there is a large element of groping, feeling along now this and now that path, and that the difference is not so striking as might at first appear.

An empirical law is unsatisfying because of some inner wish to know " why," and because of the fear that, in the absence of a rational foundation, the law may be found to be only an approximation. Sometimes empirical laws will carry one as far as experiment will at the time reach, and yet break down when further testing is possible. For example, in the above pendulum lesson, I have had the hypothesis put forward that the second order differences are being halved each time, as shown on page 264. The pre-

INSTINCT, INTELLIGENCE AND CHARACTER

diction for 5 yards based on this would be that the next second order difference would be 1½ seconds, the next *increase* therefore 14½ seconds, and the next *time* therefore 134½ seconds, which would agree with any measurements the class could make. Yet further experiment would show the incompleteness of the law suggested.

We have the wish, therefore, to "prove" the formula, as we say, after we have arrived at it : that is, to show by deductive thinking, of a higher level than the mere application of a general law to an obvious instance, that the formula is already contained in those simple intuitive generalizations to which we give our assent without question, such as that things equal to the same thing are equal to one another. This proof, in the case of the pendulum law, contains, how-

Length.	Time for 58 Swings.	Increase.	Second Order Difference.
1 yard	60 seconds		
2 yards	85 seconds	25 seconds	
3 yards	104 seconds	19 seconds	$(25-19) = 6$ seconds
4 yards	120 seconds	16 seconds	$(19-16) = 3$ seconds

ever, too much mathematical reasoning to be suitable for illustration here.

In similar fashion, when a class has learned by many trials that the three angles of a triangle equal two right angles, they can presently be led to see that this must be so from simpler facts, for instance, from the two facts (1) that if we walk right round a triangle we must have turned through four right angles, and (2) that at each corner an external and internal angle total two right angles, making six right angles in all. Those four right angles subtracted from these six leave the two right angles inside.

In realms other than the mathematical it is not always easy to see the way in which a deduction of a general law from first principles can follow its discovery by an inductive leap.

THE WINGS OF THOUGHT

But in intelligent pupils there is always a satisfaction in making a deduction which is at any rate plausible even if not certain, a rationalization, in fact. Indeed, it is doubtful whether a true inductive leap is ever made without some feeling in the thinker's mind of a " reason " for the generalization, a reason deduced from principles, not formed by induction from data. Even the theologian who called attention to the beneficence of Providence in placing large rivers near so many towns was giving a reason for his observation. And it would be difficult for any observer to conclude from a number of examples that great towns often are situated at the junctions of rivers without an inkling of the mundane reason.

Yet some generalizations remain on the empirical level. I am aware that p – f – b – p often pass over into one another in that order as we go from a Latin word to its English equivalent, and that similar series are formed by t – th – d – t and c – h – g – c. If I were teaching that law, I would cause the pupils to collect instances which show it well, as

pater	father
frater	brother
cornu	horn
pellis	a fell or skin
tres	three
duo	two
pedem	foot
dentem	tooth

and many more. But I do not know whether this law of Grimm has ever been deduced from more intuitive or more widely accepted laws of phonetics, so I must rest content with the induction. Yet, whenever I can do so, I want to arrive at the deductive proof. For example, I had occasion once to perform a long statistical calculation which frequently involved squaring numbers of the form $6\frac{1}{2}$, $3\frac{1}{2}$, $8\frac{1}{2}$, etc.; and it dawned upon me after a while that the square of such a number is rapidly obtained by multiplying the whole number by the number next above it and adding a quarter unit; the square of 6½ being thus 6 × 7 and a quarter, or 42¼. As soon as I realized this I had to stop work for a minute to think out (deductively) the truth of this law, which I had discovered inductively, by imaging a 6½ square which I turned into a 6 × 7 oblong, with a little square—the ¼—to spare. An empirical law is a provocation to the pupil to find the "reason" and should be used as such by the teacher. Newton's great law of gravity, an induction inasmuch as it is evolved from a mass of data, is as much deductive as inductive in its psychological nature, for the facts are complex, and the possibility of seeing that each case is an instance of the law depends upon ability to carry out a considerable flight of deductive, mathematical thinking. Darwin's law of the origin of species was an induction, but most of his book is concerned with working out, deductively, the way in which it explains case after case.

Wrong thinking in the classroom is not infrequently due to making the work too exclusively inductive or too exclusively deductive. A teacher causes a class to perform an experiment whereby they learn that iodine in contact with starch produces a blue stain. She then gives them leaves from which the green chlorophyll has been removed by alcohol, and invites them to test them with iodine. The leaves turn blue, and without any further encouragement, the pupils agree that this proves the presence of starch. As an introduction to a homily on the crime of jumping too hastily to conclusions this would be all right. But young teachers have been known to agree with the children and say, "Yes, this proves the presence of starch in the leaf." The fact that the conclusion is correct makes the bad reasoning all the more insidious. Apparently a syllogism is present in such a teacher's mind after this fashion :

> Starch turns iodine blue.
> This leaf turns iodine blue.
> Therefore this leaf contains starch.

THE WINGS OF THOUGHT

Now this fallacious deduction is so because an induction is lacking, a set of experiments which would entitle us to change the first sentence into :

Only starch turns iodine blue.

For instance, alcohol (in which the leaves have been recently steeped) might also turn iodine blue, or sugar might do so, or common salt. One might maliciously suggest a parallel experiment of stabbing a pig with a knife. The knife turns red. Evidently a good test for pigs. An animal in a poke, being then produced and stabbed, is shown to be a pig by the redness of the knife, though further investigation might let a cat out of the bag.

If inductive and deductive thought interpenetrate as closely as is being suggested, and if it is agreed that inductive thought at least, as exemplified by the pendulum lesson, is largely a matter of trial and error, it may be worth investigation whether even deductive thought is not of the same nature. Take for instance any detective story. Does not the endeavour to deduce the explanation of the crime, and find the criminal, take the form of trials ? Is it the new butler, or the mysterious stranger, or the bankrupt brother, who killed Mr. Smith ? The reader may reply that it is only the clumsy policeman who thinks thus, whereas Sherlock Holmes " deduces " the answer to the riddle. But is the process really different in his case, or is it that the rejection of these trial solutions is more rapid and certain ?

Here is a reasoning problem used as a test by Mr. Burt. Is it not also solved by rejecting, after trial, the hours which do not fit the data ?

John said : "I heard my clock strike yesterday, ten minutes before the first gun was fired. I did not count the strokes, but I am sure it struck more than once, and I think it struck an odd number." John was out all the morning, and his clock stopped at five minutes before five the same afternoon. When do you think the first gun was fired ?

INSTINCT, INTELLIGENCE AND CHARACTER

Or take a "rider" (a "deduction," an "original") in geometry. If it is just too hard for you to solve easily, do you not find yourself trying now this path and now that ? Or if it is so easy that you do it in a flash, try it on a less accomplished mathematician, and find that he makes false starts. Is it not probable that the only difference in your own thinking was that these false starts were more promptly, almost instantaneously, rejected ? That the reader may not lack a geometrical problem, here is one : A B C D is a parallelogram, E is the middle point of A D, and C E meets B D in F. Prove that the area of the triangle B C F is one-third of the area of the parallelogram.

It is these false starts, of which thinking so largely consists, which give to any piece of written work the character of being thoughtful. It is the careful trial and rapid rejection of the alternatives which impresses the reader, who values the work the more highly, the more abbreviated these false starts are, provided their rejection is conclusive. Thinking over an essay which we are reading consists mainly in trying the paths which the writer has declared to be blind alleys, and in endeavouring to discover others.

As a practical corollary to this point of view we can conclude that it is very desirable to encourage children to make trials even should they prove to be false starts. The answers to deductive problems of any sort are not usually found as a mechanical result of logical procedure. They are selected from a number of possibilities which occur to one, selected because they fulfil the logical requirements. In algebra, it is true, there are rules guaranteed to give the solution of equations of given sorts : but the employment of these rules is not thinking, though the choice of the proper rule may be. And how often does one find a student unable to solve a certain equation because it is of a new form. when a little trial would easily find the answer and probably suggest a rule for new examples ?

It is bad teaching, therefore, to discourage any ways of

THE WINGS OF THOUGHT

solving a problem which a child is willing to try. If persisted in, it results in inability to attack any problem for which a rule is not known. The pupil should, however, be taught to put the trial to the test, and reject it for other means if it proves unsatisfactory. A common reason for failure is persistence in a certain unfruitful method of attack and reluctance to try new points of view.

There are ways of eliminating errors which are of general use and which are worth encouragement. One such special form of trial is that which pushes right on to the end of the problem disregarding minor mistakes, disregarding quantitative inconsistencies, disregarding lack of knowledge as to just how a certain step can be performed, but assuming that it and the other steps have in fact been carried out and the goal attained, after which the steps are retraced and the difficulties attacked in reverse order. The "hypothetical construction" in geometry is of this class. By pushing on to the complete solution, even though gaps remain in the chain of reasoning, a view of the whole is obtained which enables the gaps to be filled.

The process is particularly clearly seen in quantitative details. Suppose, for instance, that I am desired to draw the figure known as the Walls of Troy. Even an adult, attempting to do this, is liable to leave insufficient room for some part of the figure. Either in the imagination, or actually with pencil on paper, he pushes on to the complete figure, and then, going back over it, he scales it and then redraws it correctly. He reduces his trials to one, and even that may be only an image. A similar process occurs when the child is asked to subtract 7 from 12, and says, "Seven and *what* are twelve—seven and five are twelve." The use of an x, or any symbol, which can be manipulated as though it were the thing it stands for, is similar in nature. A half-way step is to carry out the manipulation with some standard quantity, as when we are asked how much money will amount to 676 dollars in 5 years at 4 per cent. per annum compound interest, and we find first what 100 dollars would amount to in that time.

There is nothing in all this, except the degree of abstractness of the material, which differs from a practical workman's behaviour in face of a concrete problem. The first boat which Robinson Crusoe constructed was a failure, just because he did not imagine it completed and picture to himself how he was going to get it into the water. You remember that, after spending many, many days in laboriously hollowing out a huge tree which he had felled, he found that he could not move it. He made actual attempts to do so with the aid of rollers, and other attempts to dig a canal to bring the water to the piragua, but gave them up. That was thinking of a primitive sort. More refined thinking operates with images and words instead of with rollers and a heavy canoe, that is all. The naval architect, designing a new ship, makes his trials with sketches and formulæ before he makes them in the trial tank, or ultimately with the finished boat.

A considerable part of our education consists in learning to recognize something general in a situation, and to reject in consequence a number of possibilities which are known to lead only to failure. That " something general " is then usually given a name. It need not be anything very difficult of recognition, it may only be recognizing that a triangle remains a triangle even if it is now long, now short, now scalene, now equilateral. With these concepts we learn to operate as we did with pieces of actual behaviour, and later with images; and with their aid many deductive problems are solved because they are seen to come under a higher concept. Children and students cannot be given these concepts; they have to win them for themselves, but the teacher can plan situations where they are likely to be seen, and can consistently give his encouragement to their formation.

In the inductive portions of a lesson, the great need is

THE WINGS OF THOUGHT

to encourage freedom of hypothesis making, accompanied by honest trial and rejection. The line between wild guessing on the part of the pupils, and legitimate hypothesis, is hard to draw, but so it is also in real scientific work.

> I should not be surprised (said A. S. Eddington after proposing a hypothesis concerning the internal constitution of the stars), if it is whispered that this address has at times verged on being a little bit speculative; perhaps some outspoken friend may bluntly say that it has been highly speculative from beginning to end. I wonder what is the touchstone by which we may test the legitimate development of scientific theory and reject the idly speculative. We all know of theories which the scientific mind instinctively rejects as fruitless guesses; but it is difficult to specify their exact defect, or to supply a rule which will show us when we ourselves do err. It is often supposed that to speculate and to make hypotheses is the same thing; but more often they are opposed. It is when we let our thoughts stray outside venerable, but sometimes insecure, hypotheses, that we are said to speculate. Hypothesis limits speculation. Moreover, distrust of speculation often covers loose thinking; wild ideas take anchorage in our minds, and influence our outlook; whilst it is considered too speculative to submit them to the scientific scrutiny which would reject them.
>
> If we are not content with the dull accumulation of experimental facts, if we make any deductions or generalizations, if we seek for any theory to guide us, some degree of speculation cannot be avoided. Some will prefer to take the interpretation which seems to be most immediately indicated, and at once adopt that as a working hypothesis; others will rather seek to explore and classify the widest possibilities which are not definitely inconsistent with the facts. Either choice has its dangers; the first may be too narrow a view and lead progress into a *cul-de-sac*; the second may be so broad that it is useless as a guide, and diverges indefinitely from experimental knowledge. When this last case happens, it must be concluded that the knowledge is not yet ripe for theoretical treatment, and speculation is premature. The time when speculative theory and observational research may profitably go hand-in-hand is when the possibilities, or at any rate the probabilities, can *be narrowed down by experiment, and the theory can indicate the tests by which the remaining wrong paths may be blocked up one by one.*

And in a passage later in the same address, Eddington urges us to be bold in making hypotheses, as both Icarus and Dædalus were bold in venturing to use wings: but then to soar like Icarus right up to the sun, to put our hypotheses to the hardest tests, to strain them " to the breaking point till the weak points gape," and not fly safely like Dædalus through the middle air, and by excess of caution fail to bring their hidden weakness to light.

The differences between aviators are largely temperamental, and so, too, the differences between makers of hypotheses are not entirely intellectual in origin. One man will be willing immediately to change his hypothesis as soon as contradictory instances are met, another will attempt far-fetched interpretation in order to smooth over the difficulty, another is unwilling to make any change in his pet theory, and shuts his eyes to the facts which do not fit in, and yet another is emotionally upset, and gives up the problem as a bad job. These types are well shown in an interesting experiment made by Mr. Zing Yang Kuo, in which English-speaking students were asked to memorize 88 Chinese characters, although, unknown to them, it was not really their memory which was being tested, but their powers of inductive inference. For through groups of the Chinese characters there ran certain radicals, such as a roughly oblong character meaning *mouth* (not unlike part of the Red Dragon symbol on a Mah Jong tile), just as a general law can run through a number of special instances. Some of these characters containing the oblong *mouth* symbol might have other ideas in common, as *to bark, to hoot, singing*, which all include the idea of sound. But other instances showed that this was not the meaning of the oblong symbol, such as *to bite, drinking*, or *saliva*. The behaviour of his subjects towards these " negative instances," as shown by their answers after the conclusion of the test, and by the type of mistake they made, led Kuo to formulate the above types of reaction to instances disagreeing with a theory. And we can, I think, see these types in everyday life. [1]

[1] *Journ. Exp. Psychol.* 1923, VI, 247-93.

CHAPTER XXVI

REVIEW

THE general idea which I have taken as my beacon in writing the previous chapters has been the way in which man's mind has grown out of the animal mind. And in following this course I have, from time to time, gone about on two different tacks, not always heading directly towards the beacon, but always, I hope, nearing it; some chapters have dealt mainly with intelligence, and others mainly with character.

Out of instinctive behaviour which at first is blind and automatic, grows the beginning of reason, as the reactions grow less inevitable, as the animal comes to have a repertory of responses which it tries over and over in solving a problem. Its "thinking" at this stage is active, actual behaviour. Evolution creates out of this animal, in turn, an animal which replaces some of the behaviour by substitutes which save time. Even our sense organs which act at a distance serve this purpose, so that we need not run our heads against a stone wall, it is sufficient to see it. But imagery, born of such senses, in particular of the distant senses of sight and hearing, comes in as a more obvious substitute, and we stop when we see the stone wall merely in the mind's eye. Finally, symbols, unlike the actual behaviour, come to replace it still more subtly. Words, particularly, whose meanings have to be acquired and passed on by each generation, play an extraordinarily important part in reasoning, and bring with them the dangers of parrot learning as well as the powers of abstract thought. Especially has the attempt been made to see how far the idea of trial and error can carry us, trial and error at first among acts, then among images, then among symbols. The alternatives which are presented for selection become increasingly more abstract, increasingly more plastic and indefinite. It seems possible that the only physiological concomitant is increasing complexity in the neurone patterns which accompany the reasoning. The educational implications of this way of looking at intelligence are first, that we should in our teaching recognize the trial and error aspect of creative thought, and secondly, that we should provide for increasing abstraction in the materials. We should provide opportunities for problems to arise, and treat them as the children of our pupils' brains, not as inflictions or set tasks. We should encourage the widest variation in the solutions offered, the hypotheses formed, but should insist on ruthless rejection after trial. We should have our pupils push their theories to the limit, to discover their breaking points. We should praise intellectual honesty which tries and finds out, and we should condemn intellectual laziness which theorizes and does not verify. We should see that the apparatus of abstraction is supplied to the pupil as fast as he feels the need for it—vocabulary, mathematical symbols, moral fables, parables and instances—and no faster. Throughout, we should ask whether our thinking hangs together, is consistent, and whether its predictions are verifiable. We should avoid formulæ and cut-and-dried methods and go back to first principles. Above all, we should encourage thinking, theory-making, and have the selection made by trial, not by authoritative repression.

The same plasticity of response which, in the task of finding means, leads to intelligence, leads in the choosing of ends, to character. Between muscular responses to a situation, and intellectual responses to a situation, the difference is one of abstraction, and the latter is made possible by the possibility of the former. In not dissimilar fashion, the fact that in man emotional drives and sources of energy can readily be tapped by numbers of diverse situations, and not merely by certain narrow stimuli, gives rise to the possibility of

REVIEW

directing the impulses along noble or vicious channels. For the simple situations which are the desired goal of animal action, such as obtaining food, or possession of a mate, or regaining contact with the herd or pack, are substituted lofty ideals or ugly passions. Both in intellect and in character, education means redirecting behaviour along new channels. In both, education means learning to look ahead. In both, the mistake of repressing instead of redirecting is one which leads to failure or even to disgrace. In character formation, it has to be recognized that good habits grow out of instincts, and that the latter have to be accepted and remodelled. In intellectual education, it has to be recognized that abstract thinking grows out of actual action, and is a substitute for it : so that to divorce thinking from acting, to make "book-learning" different from doing things, to repress activity of muscular behaviour instead of sublimating it into thought, is as harmful to reasoning as blind repression of impulse is detrimental to character. There can be logic-tight bulkheads between thought and action as injurious as those between religion and everyday life.

Another leading idea which has emerged is the necessity for a very real integration of school life into one whole of diverse yet interconnected subjects of study. For otherwise, I do not see any way out of the " formal training " paradox. If the training we give our pupils is only going to improve them in that subject alone, and not transfer except in minute amounts to life situations, then logically we ought to give up teaching most of the subjects found in school and practice vocational training only. But if, in a study of various subjects, each under different aspects, and with different material, there are used general methods of reasoning, verifying, controlling, testing, then from them all, the student may get by abstraction the lesson of *how to think*, which may transfer from the whole though not from any one. The specialist at 16 would be in danger of merely learning his subject, while the pupil getting a wider education was learning to think—provided this second pupil was not only being made a specialist in each of six subjects. It is with many misgivings that some of us see the increasing departmentalism of schools, and the growing wish on the part of teachers to teach one subject exclusively. I know well the answer, that the subjects are becoming so advanced that teachers must specialize, and cannot become expert in special methods unless they stick to their lasts. But I am not altogether convinced, and fear that only cobbling may result : and, on the principle that if you want really honest criticisms, you should send the Sporting Editor to the play, and the Dramatic Critic to the match, I would like the English teacher to teach a little chemistry and the chemistry teacher to teach a little English. And having thus made many enemies (for I know what they will say, and perhaps they are right), I will remember, too late, that least said is soonest mended.

Perhaps all of the rest is summed up in the general notion that play has been the great maker of mankind. Fixed inherited instincts got a long way, but they could never, I imagine, have given us speech. Speech, and the innumerable muscular dexterities of which man is capable, came because man inherits random tendencies to make noises, and enjoy playing at the game of doing so, and random tendencies to manipulate things this way, that way, and any way. We call the period childhood. It is helpless first because it has so few really definite responses, but for the same reason, it is potential of everything. And in nature the random activities which ensue are called play, and from them the environment selects the fittest : a Darwinism of responses rather than of responders. Play is therefore the natural form of education, and school must use it, passing over gradually to earnest as the years go by.

And as they go by, school will watch anxiously, to strike, as James says, when the iron is hot, to use each impulse as it comes up. And this, whether the theory of the transitori-

REVIEW

ness of instincts is correct or no. If they are transitory, so much the more important. But in any case, it were foolish to have the newest impulse against one instead of acting with it.

These, then, appear to be the main ideas urged : the continuity of action and thought, the importance of originality, and the danger of authority in intellectual things, the need of subjecting theory to trial, and of seeing general methods in several subjects, the importance of re-directing instincts and avoiding mere repression, the value of play methods, and methods seizing upon the instinct of the moment with younger children. Throughout, education should look more and more ahead, both in cultivating intelligence and in creating character. For the latter can be created, while intelligence, it would seem, is much more a matter of heredity. In it, individual differences seem more inborn than in character : and the task of the school is rather that of discovering than of making talent, the task of finding the shape of the pegs, not whittling them to fit the square or the round holes. Intellectual *guidance* and character *training*.

> Each member of a free community (said the late Lord Bryce in a Yale address) must be capable of citizenship. Capacity involves three qualities—Intelligence, Self-control, Conscience. . . . Of the three requisities, the two former are the more frequent and are the more easy to produce by proper training.

Contrary to his opinion, however, seems the verdict of psychology, as regards intelligence. Self-control and even conscience seem much more modifiable by the influence of education than is intelligence, even though the latter may not be entirely unchangeable. A certain type of character can almost be guaranteed by a school if it has its pupils long enough, but not a level of intelligence. It seems to be the function of the teacher to form character and find out about intelligence. In so far as he can influence the latter, he will do it through the former.

INDEX

Achievement Tests, 193
Acquired characteristics, 24 ff, 38
Adrenin, 71
Aphasia, 106 ff
Apperception, 149 ff
Archimedes, 262
Armstrong, Henry E., 191
Army analogy, 49, 50, 53, 54
Army Tests, 141, 180, 186, 223
Axolotl, 75, 77
Axone, 49

Baden Powell, 76
Ballard, 186, 218
Behaviourists, 254
Belloc, Hilaire, 83
Benson, 82, 93
Bentham, 242
Bickersteth, 219 ff
Binet, 117, 180 ff, 193, 198, 205, 206, 207, 212, 214, 216 ff, 223, 234
Boy Scouts, 12, 73, 76, 77
Brain Localization, 101 ff
Broca, 107
Bryce, Lord, 277
Bryn Mawr, 195
Burt, 182, 187, 188, 195, 196, 198, 200, 216 ff, 224, 267

Calculus, 129 ff
Campagnac, 238
Canal boat children, 217 ff
Censor, 161 ff
Cerebral hemispheres, 52, 101
Chain instincts, 35
Chicken, 42, 45, 74
Claparède, 206
Classical type, 230 ff
Cobb, Margaret V., 198
Columbia University, 191, 198, 201
Completion Tests, 195
Conceptual, 119

Conditioned reactions, 235
Control group, 136
Co-operation, 241
Correlation, 20, 207 ff
Courtis, 125, 191
Crusoe Test, 189
Cube Test, 88
Current, nerve, 51
Curwen, Mrs., 100

Dalton Plan, 179
Darwin, 19 ff, 149, 156, 231, 241, 266, 276
Deaf and dumb, 118
Deductive reasoning, 259
Defectives, 174
Dendrites, 50
Dewey, 254
Dog, 85 ff, 103
Dominant factors, 23
Downey, 233
Dreams, 161
Drever, 116
Duff, 221

Ebbinghaus, 187, 195
Eddington, 271
Effect, Law of (*see* Satisfaction)
Ego, 27 ff
Elderton, 211
Emotion, 28
Environment, 24, 31, 34 ff
Epeira, 14
Examinations, 175 ff, 202
Extrovert, 228 ff

Fabre, 14
Faculties, 134 ff, 181
Faraday, 94
Faust, 162
Fear, 236
Fissures of brain, 102

Five Formal Steps, 150
Forbes, 238
Frequency, Law of, 59, 64
Freud, 77, 154, 158 ff, 235, 236
Friday, 189
Frog, 75

Galton, 93, 111, 177, 210, 211
Gangs, 72
General Ability, 204 ff
Girard, Stephen, 114
Glands, 69
Gordon, Hugh, 217
Gordon, Kate, 211
Grimm, 265
Groos, Karl, 34
Gypsies, 217 ff

Habit, 16 ff, 238 ff
Haggerty, 200
Hawkes, 192, 201
Hayward, F. H., 114
Head, Henry, 103 ff
Herbart, 149 ff
Herd, 27 ff, 167, 229, 242
Heredity, 19 ff, 210 ff
Hero-worship, 244
Heuristic Method, 191
Hill, D. S., 95
Hindustani Test, 188, 223
Hogben, 75
Hollingworth, 232
Hormones, 70
Hume, 162
Hunter, W. S., 85
Huxley, Julian, 75, 76

I. E. R. Tests, 87, 140, 142
Imagery, 79–100
  in memorizing, 94
  in music, 97
  in reading, 91
  in science, 93
  in translating, 92
  in words, 90
Imitation, 28, 244 ff
Individual differences, 170 ff
Inductive reasoning, 259 ff
Infancy, 32
Instincts, 13 ff, 35 ff, 52
Intelligence, *passim, esp.* 113, 180

Intelligence quotient, 173, 184
  constancy of, 212 ff
  influence of schooling on, 216
  limit of growth of, 221 ff
  of rural children, 218 ff
Interest, 149 ff
Introvert, 228 ff

James, 27, 35, 74, 238, 276
Jennings, 39
Jung, 154, 158, 162, 229

Kammerer, 25
Keith, Sir Arthur, 48
Kelvin, 93
Kinæsthetic imagery, 83, 95
Kipling, 76, 245
Kuo, 272

Latin, 135, 140
Learning, 39 ff, 247 ff
Left-handed, 104
Lobes of brain, 102

Macaulay, 259
McCall, 198
McDougall, 28
Mathematics, 115, 124 ff, 142
Maze, 38, 57 ff
Mean, 176
Median, 176
Memorizing, 247 ff
Mendel, 21 ff
Mental age, 183
Metcalfe, Cranstoun, 84
Miller, Hugh, 239
Mnemonics, 248
Monkey, 82, 85, 103, 191
Monroe, 198
Montaigne, 114
Montessori, 251
Moore, 92
Morgan, Lloyd, 16
Müller, Max, 111
Multiple Choice Tests, 195
  Personality, 168
  Response, 41
  Track Schools, 190
Music, 97, 121, 160
Mutations, 24

Nervous System, 48 ff

INDEX

Neurone, 49 *et passim*
Newton, 266
Normal Curve, 172
Northumberland, 105, 173, 219 ff
Notation, 130
Numerals, 124

Oakley, 248
Opposites, 187
Ostwald, 230 ff
Otis, 186, 221

Patterson, 118
Pawlow, 25
Pechstein, 254
Pendulum Example, 151, 260 ff
Percentile Rank, 185
Percept, 105
Peterson, 61, 63
Picnic fire analogy, 81
Pintner, 118, 186
Plateaux, 254 ff
Play, 32 ff
Porcupine, 86
Postal system analogy, 48, 69
Practice, Law of, 43 ff
Procrustes, 238 ff
Profiles, Educational, 199
Psychoanalysis, 162
Punishments, 242 ff
Puzzles, 45
Pygmalion, 238 ff

Quotient, Intelligence 184
    Achievement, 196 ff

Raccoons, 82, 85
Rat, 57 ff, 85 ff, 236
Rationalization, 169
Readiness, Law of, 65
Reasoning Tests, Burt's, 188, 216 ff, 267
Recapitulation Theory, 74 ff
Recency, Law of, 59, 64
Recessive factors, 23
Reflex, 13, 50, 52
Regents' Examination, 202
Regression, 21, 216
Repression, 157 ff
Rewards, 242 ff
Rignano, 230
Ritchie, 92

Romantic type, 230 ff
Ruch, 222
Ruger, 45
Rugg, 191
Rules in school, 238 ff
Rural intelligence, 218 ff

Sackett, L. W., 86
Sadoleto, 238
Satisfaction, 43 ff, 57, 65 ff *et passim*
Schneider, 232
Self-government, 240
Sentiments, 148, 154
Sex, 27 ff, 77, 157, 159 ff, 168
Shand, 154
Sheep, 104
Siblings, 210 ff
Skew distribution, 175 ff
Skill, 247, 254 ff
Sleight, W. G., 138, 144
Socrates, 261
Spearman, 147, 181, 206
Special Abilities, 204
Specialization, 146, 210
Speech, 34, 111 ff
Speed factor, 141 ff, 222
Spencer, 243
Square root, 126
Stable-minded, 228 ff
Stanford Achievement Test, 198
Stentor, 39 ff
Stern, 184
Stevenson, R. L., 254, 258
Stewart, Sir James, 107
Stout, G. F., 119
Sturt, 248
Sublimation, 157 ff
Suggestion, 233 ff
Symbols, 89, 124 ff, 142
Synapse, 50

Tansley, 27 ff, 154, 228
Tarkington, Booth, 30
Taylor, Grace A., 198
Telephone or telegraph analogy 49 ff, 67, 167
Temperament, 227 ff
Tennyson, 94
Terman, 117, 183, 184, 187, 19 212, 223
Thomson, Sir J. J., 93

Thorndike, 17, 27ff, 42, 65, 66, 68, 77, 80, 139, 142, 146, 147, 158, 166, 191, 192, 198, 210, 244
Trabue, 188, 195
Transfer of training, 132, 134ff
Transitoriness of Instincts, 74
Trial and Error, 43ff, 79ff, *et passim*
Trotter, 229
True-false Tests, 194
Twins, 210ff
Tylor, 119

Unstable-minded, 228ff

Variation, 21, 31
Vocabulary, 113, 115ff, 187

Ward, James, 81
Warden, 63
Washburn, 87
Waterworks analogy, 71
Watson, 235ff
Weismann, 149, 257
Wells, H. G., 112
Wernicke, 108
Whole v. part method, 250
Will, 227ff
Wilson, W. R., 143
Woodworth, 187

Yerkes, R. M., 85
Yerkes and Yoakum, 186
Yorkshire, 219

For Product Safety Concerns and Information please contact our EU
representative GPSR@taylorandfrancis.com
Taylor & Francis Verlag GmbH, Kaufingerstraße 24, 80331 München, Germany

www.ingramcontent.com/pod-product-compliance
Lightning Source LLC
Chambersburg PA
CBHW061436300426
44114CB00014B/1710